THE
FIRST
FREEDOM

THE
FIRST
FREEDOM

The Tumultuous History of Free Speech in America

NAT HENTOFF

 DELACORTE PRESS/NEW YORK

FOR WILLIAM O. DOUGLAS
AND I. F. STONE

Published by
Delacorte Press
1 Dag Hammarskjold Plaza
New York, N.Y. 10017

Photographs on pages 1, 151, and 239 courtesy UPI.
Drawing on page 55 courtesy The Granger Collection.
Drawing on page 77 from the *Industrial Worker*, October 1, 1910.
Drawing on page 121 courtesy N.Y. Public Library Picture Collection.
Photograph on page 185 courtesy Wide World Photos.

Manufactured in the United States of America

First printing

LIBRARY OF CONGRESS CATALOGING IN PUBLICATION DATA

Hentoff, Nat
 The first freedom.

 Bibliography: p.
 Includes index.
  1. Liberty of speech—United States—History
 [1. Liberty of speech—History]   I. Title.
KF4772.Z9H46   342'.73'085   78-72860
ISBN: 0-440-03850-2

ACKNOWLEDGMENTS

For my abiding concern with the First Amendment, I am particularly indebted to those officials at Northeastern University in Boston who tried to censor the writings of the staff when I was editor of the *Northeastern News* in the early 1940s. Most of us finally resigned in protest, and I never lost my sense of rage at those who would suppress speech, especially mine. Those administrators truly helped inspire this book.

I owe much to many who, through the years, have illuminated First Amendment history and law for me. Among them: Professor Thomas Emerson, who has set extraordinarily high standards for First Amendment scholarship, analysis, and passion both at Yale Law School and far, far beyond.

Being on the board of directors of the New York Civil Liberties Union has been an invaluable aid to my continuing education in civil liberties—due to such rigorous instructors as Aryeh Neier, Ira Glasser, Burt Neuborne, Alan Levine, Kenneth Norwick, and Paul Chevigny. I have also learned a great deal from First Amendment

v

ACKNOWLEDGMENTS

lawyer-paladins Floyd Abrams and Victor Kovner, as well as from Sidney Zion, a journalist-lawyer whom James Madison would have welcomed as a hearty ally in pressing for the strongest possible Bill of Rights.

My appreciation too to the Student Press Law Center in Washington, and especially to those students throughout the country who have contacted me while engaged in their battles to keep the First Amendment exuberantly alive. My best hope for this book is that it will help forward many such battles, among students and all other citizens under the Constitution.

NAT HENTOFF

Amendment I (1791)

Congress shall make no law respecting an establishment of religion, or prohibiting the free exercise thereof, or abridging the freedom of speech, or of the press; or the right of the people peaceably to assemble, and to petition the Government for a redress of grievances.

Contents

CONTENTS

PART VII
The Outer Limits of Protected Speech—
and Beyond

I begin this account of the foundation of all our liberties with the young, for if they do not have reason to believe that the First Amendment is of real, palpable, personal value to them, its future will be in some peril.

Students/Teachers/Librarians: Free-speaking "Persons" under the Constitution

Mary Beth Tinker, having been declared a "person" under the Constitution—with First Amendment rights—celebrates with her younger brother, Paul. (An older brother, John, had joined Mary Beth in the Supreme Court action.) They are wearing the black armbands that made Mary Beth Tinker a figure in constitutional history. (UPI photo)

I

It can hardly be argued that either students or teachers
shed their constitutional rights to freedom of expression
at the schoolhouse gate.

On the morning of December 16, 1965, thirteen-year-
old Mary Beth Tinker arrived at her junior high school
in Des Moines, Iowa. She was wearing a black armband.
So was a friend, sixteen-year-old Christopher Eckhardt.
And so too, the very next day, was Mary Beth's fifteen-
year-old brother, John.

They and their parents had planned what one of the
students called a silent "witness of the armbands" from
December 16 to January 1. The parents at their jobs and
the teen-agers at school wanted to express their deep
opposition to the war in Vietnam. Instead of giving anti-
war speeches, or marching, they were engaging in symbolic speech. By wearing the black armbands they were
both mourning the killings in Vietnam and also urging
that they stop.

The principals of the Des Moines public schools had
somehow learned of the silent protest, and two days
before Mary Beth Tinker and Christopher Eckhardt appeared at school with their armbands the principals had
met to decide how to deal with these nonviolent wit-

3

nesses against war. It was agreed that any student wearing an armband would be told to remove it. If the student refused, he or she would be suspended and could return to school only when the armband had been left at home permanently.

The principals believed they were being entirely reasonable in barring the black armbands. They saw through the small band of black cloth. Silent or not, this was going to be a demonstration; and as one of them said at their meeting, "The schools are no place for demonstrations." Said another principal, "If the students don't like the way our elected officials are handling things, they should deliver their message through the ballot box and not in the halls of our public schools." That is, let them hold their messages until they are old enough to vote.

On December 16, Mary Beth Tinker and Christopher Eckhardt refused to remove their armbands. They were suspended. John Tinker went through the same process the next morning. The three did not return to school until after New Year's Day, when by their own previous decision the period of protesting by armbands was over.

Although the school principals considered the incident closed, the three students brought suit in federal court to establish their First Amendment right to wear the black armbands. At first, the students lost. The Federal District Court ruled that since this kind of symbolic expression *might* disturb school discipline, school officials could reasonably and constitutionally compel the students to leave the armbands at home. The next higher court, the United States Court of Appeals for the Eighth Circuit, was divided equally (4–4); and so the lower court's decision stood.

There was only one more place to go. On February

24, 1969, to the joy of the Tinkers and Christopher Eckhardt, the United States Supreme Court, by a vote of 7 to 2, decided in their favor. The decision, *Tinker v. Des Moines Independent School District*, is a Magna Carta for all students in this nation. Previous High Court decisions, to be sure, had dealt in various ways with students' rights and liberties, but in the Tinker case the Supreme Court for the first time directly spelled out the free speech rights of students. As the *Harvard Law Review* put it, "The Court adopted the view that the process of education in a democracy must be democratic."

Speaking for the majority of the Court, Justice Abe Fortas wrote, "It can hardly be argued that either students or teachers shed their constitutional rights to freedom of speech or expression at the schoolhouse gate."

What of the opinion of the Federal District Court that since the Des Moines principals were afraid that disturbances might break out because of the offending armbands, it was reasonable of them to ban this symbolic speech? Fortas answered that in a democracy a vague fear of disturbance "is not enough to overcome the right to freedom of expression. Any departure from absolute regimentation may cause trouble. Any variation from the majority's opinion may inspire fear. Any word spoken, in class, in the lunchroom or on the campus, that deviates from the views of another person, may start an argument or cause a disturbance. But our Constitution says we must take this risk . . . and our history says that it is this sort of hazardous freedom—this kind of openness—that is the basis of our national strength and of the independence and vigor of Americans who grow up and live in this . . . often disputatious society."

5

In the resounding key section of the *Tinker* decision, the Court declared: "*In our system, state-operated schools may not be enclaves of totalitarianism. School officials do not possess absolute authority over their students. Students in school as well as out of school are 'persons' under our Constitution.* They are possessed of fundamental rights which the State must respect, just as they themselves must respect their obligations to the State. In our system, students may not be regarded as closed-circuit recipients of only that which the State wishes to communicate. They may not be confined to the expression of those sentiments that are officially approved. In the absence of a specific showing of constitutionally valid reasons to regulate their speech, students are entitled to freedom of expression of their views" (emphasis added).

What *could* be a constitutionally valid reason to regulate students' speech? If, said Mr. Justice Fortas, a student exercises his or her free speech rights in a way that "materially disrupts classwork or involves substantial disorder or invasion of the rights of others," then the speech, symbolic or vocal, is not protected.

Mary Beth Tinker, John Tinker, and Christopher Eckhardt had caused no disruption or disorder. All they did, Justice Fortas pointed out, was wear on their sleeves "a band of black cloth, not more than two inches wide. They wore it to exhibit their disapproval of the Vietnam hostilities and their advocacy of a truce, to make their views known, and by their example, to induce others to adopt them. They neither interrupted school activities nor sought to intrude in the school affairs or the lives of others. They caused discussion outside of the classrooms, but no interference with work and no disorder. In the circumstances, our Constitution does not permit officials of the State to deny their form of expression."

As soon as it was delivered, the Supreme Court's decision in *Tinker v. Des Moines Independent School District* became the law of the land. This did not mean, however, that throughout the country students' First Amendment rights were instantly and automatically recognized by school authorities. It often takes considerable time for even a landmark High Court decision to be widely known, understood, and implemented. Except for a relatively few large newspapers, there is not much coherent, let alone comprehensive, reporting on Supreme Court rulings. Television, from which the majority of people get their news, is quite cursory in its coverage of the Court's decisions.

Accordingly, some school officials, for a time, did not even know about the *Tinker* decision, and therefore it had no effect on their schools. To this day, for that matter, there are probably principals and school board members who could not pass a simple test on what *Tinker* means. Other school officials who knew of the landmark ruling felt no pressure to bring the First Amendment into school life because their students had not heard of the decision in or out of school. To this day, a spot quiz on *Tinker* in any classroom in the country would result in all too many pieces of blank paper.

In the years since the *Tinker* decision, however, certain principals have moved to reexamine school regulations in order to make certain that students are being assured their constitutional rights. Others have been forced to comply with the Constitution when challenged in the courts by students and parents who have become very much aware of their rights.

7

Six months after the *Tinker* ruling, for example, Melanie Johnstone wore a black armband to her high school in northern Maine. She was told that, as punishment, her grades would be lowered. But when Melanie's father, who knew about the *Tinker* decision, threatened to take the school administrators to court, her grades remained as they were.

Once the Supreme Court has handed down a decision, the work of the citizenry—including students—may have only begun. Where there is official resistance, often hidden, to a particular ruling, any concerned citizen can become a working constitutionalist by fighting that resistance, often with the free legal help of the American Civil Liberties Union or one of its affiliates throughout the country. Otherwise, even a Supreme Court decision will not get off the paper on which it's written.

A few years after the *Tinker* decision, for instance, a high school student in Sumter, South Carolina, was running for school office but suddenly found himself tossed off the ballot by the principal because in the school paper the student had written an article critical of the administration.

"You can't *do* that," the young man protested to the principal. "It's unconstitutional. You're punishing me for using my First Amendment rights."

"The constitution of this school," the principal sharply instructed the student, "takes precedence over the United States Constitution."

And that was the end of it. The young man did not know that he had the right—plus free legal resources available to him—to sue the principal and bring the United States Constitution into his school. And so he never got a chance to run in the election.

Yet, as David Ellenhorn, the American Civil Liberties Union's lawyer in the *Tinker* case, emphasizes, that decision "should bury the notion" that school officials can impose arbitrary limitations "on student expression and other First Amendment activity."

The *Tinker* decision *should* have buried that notion, and eventually will, if enough students care enough about exercising the rights they now have on paper.

II

If freedom of expression becomes merely an empty slogan in the minds of enough children, it will be dead by the time they are adults.

Priscilla Marco is a student who very much believes that spreading and testing ideas is the purpose of education.

In October 1974, Marco, a senior at Long Island City High School in New York, wrote an article for the student paper, *Skyline*. It was about the First Amendment as she had experienced it. Priscilla began by noting that the New York City Board of Education issues a pamphlet every year on the rights and responsibilities of senior high school students. That pamphlet, which is supposed to be distributed to all students and their parents, had been banned from Long Island City High School because the then principal, Dr. Howard Hurwitz, did not consider the statement on student rights suitable for student reading.

Priscilla went on to quote from the Board of Education pamphlet contrasting what *it* said students' rights were with what Dr. Hurwitz actually allowed the students in his school to do. For example, the board had ruled that official school publications were to reflect the policy and judgment of *student* editors, but at Long Island City High School, according to Marco's article, "the policy of the paper has never been determined by the students but rather by the faculty advisor and the principal." For instance: "We could not print a student's opinion in an article about the impeachment of Richard Nixon because Dr. Hurwitz did not agree with that opinion." She ended the article for *Skyline* by proclaiming, "It is illegal for us not to be informed as to what our rights are. This can not be allowed to continue. We are human beings, we have rights—they must not be ignored."

Dr. Hurwitz refused to allow Priscilla Marco's article to be printed in the student paper. Known for years as a firm disciplinarian who commanded a school free of disturbances, Dr. Hurwitz honestly and fervently believed that, as principal, he had the ultimate responsibility for everything that took place in his high school. As he said while Priscilla Marco was a student there, "First Amendment rights and censorship have nothing whatsoever to do with putting out a student newspaper. It's a matter of teaching students to write well and responsibly." Hurwitz explained that he had censored the Marco article because it was "irresponsible and badly written."

Priscilla Marco rewrote the article twice, and it was turned down each time by the principal because, he said, it was "inflammatory" and "immature." Finally, she appealed to a number of Dr. Hurwitz's superiors, including Irving Anker, then chancellor of the entire school system. Priscilla's appeal had added thrust because she had contacted the New York Civil Liberties Union, which threatened to sue the Board of Education on the ground that Priscilla's First Amendment rights were being violated.

Both because of the looming court suit and also because a number of officials at the Board of Education were genuinely concerned that the Constitution should not be locked out of Long Island City High School, Dr. Hurwitz was ordered to allow Priscilla Marco's article to be printed. The directive astonished Hurwitz because he had said confidently, when the battle first began, that "the chancellor would not dare tell me what to put in the newspaper. I run the school, not he."

Upon receiving the chancellor's order, Hurwitz simply ignored it.

On June 23, 1975, in an action unprecedented in the history of American secondary education, a group of high-level Board of Education officials, accompanied by security guards, entered Long Island City High School and distributed three thousand copies of a special edition of the school paper, *Skyline*, which they themselves had published. Dr. Hurwitz told *The New York Times* that the chancellor's action was "disgraceful, outrageous and reprehensible." Priscilla Marco cheered.

The special edition of the school paper was bannered AN ISSUE OF FREE PRESS. Included were Priscilla's original article and a revised, updated version. There was also "An Open Letter to Students, Staff and Community" from two high officials of the Board of Education. Pointing out that "even the President of the United States is criticized and praised in different newspapers, depending on the judgment of reporters about his actions," the two board members underlined that "in schools preparing young people for their responsibilities as citizens, we must be sure that the rights of the press are understood and protected."

On the second page of this truly extraordinary issue

of *Skyline* was a statement by a previous New York City chancellor, Harvey Scribner:

> Students have the right to express themselves in their press or in their comments even if their statements seem distorted to the principal or the faculty. They even have the right to be wrong in the conclusions they draw from the facts and situations they present.
>
> A student press should provide for opinions that differ, including faculty opinions. This is the place where distortions or misstatements are brought out for all to see. And this is the kind of control that the principal and faculty must exercise if the press is to be the strong educational force it can be in our high schools.

On the right-hand corner of this special edition of *Skyline* was the text of the First Amendment itself, under the headline THE LAW OF THE LAND.

Battles for freedom of the student press have also concerned publications that are not officially connected with a school. In 1972 two Illinois high school seniors, Burt Fujishima and Richard Peluso, created their own newspaper, *The Cosmic Frog,* and distributed it at school before and between classes. They were suspended for violating a Chicago Board of Education rule that no literature could be distributed on school premises without the prior approval of the superintendent of schools. In other words, the superintendent had the power to censor what he didn't like.

The students went to federal court and ultimately won a decision in the United States Court of Appeals that their suspensions had to be lifted because the Board of

Education rule was unconstitutional. Referring to the *Tinker* decision, this court declared that unless the students' actions would have disrupted school discipline—and there was no indication that handing out *The Cosmic Frog* would do that—"schools may not restrain the full First Amendment rights of their students." Accordingly, Fujishima and Peluso could not be prevented from publishing or distributing their paper in school. And they did not have to subject it to prior restraint—that is, the superintendent was not allowed to censor *The Cosmic Frog* before it could be circulated.

The Supreme Court, however, has not yet ruled on whether student publications must, in all instances, be free from prior restraint. Some lower courts have decided that if school authorities set up sufficiently precise guidelines as to what can't be published, they have a right to examine the material beforehand to see if the students are following the specific prohibitions. For instance, nearly all such guidelines insist that nothing obscene or libelous be printed in a school paper. (Material is libelous if it is so false and defamatory that it injures a person's reputation, holding him up to hatred, contempt, or ridicule. See Chapter 22 for further discussion of libel.)

Even so, it has now been generally established by the lower courts that if a school official intends to censor a student paper because of obscenity, libel, or the fear that the school will be disrupted by something about to be printed, the burden of proof is on that official to justify his action. He must show, for instance, that the material is *legally* obscene or libelous.

As for fear of disruption, the Student Press Law Center in Washington emphasizes:

Before school authorities may restrict expression on grounds of disruption, they must possess actual evidence that disruption has occurred or will occur. Unsupported apprehension or fear that student expression *might* or *could* cause disruption is not sufficient to justify censorship. Administrators must demonstrate with *concrete facts* that disruption will occur. Disagreement on the part of school officials with the student views expressed is never sufficient to permit censorship. *The fact that the views expressed may be highly controversial, critical of school officials, unpopular or in poor taste are never grounds to restrict student expression.*

If school officials do interfere arbitrarily with a student newspaper—having failed to provide valid justification for their actions—they can be taken to court by students and prevented from censoring the paper again. While student newspapers, therefore, are not yet as fully protected from censorship as their adult counterparts, high school journalists do have much more freedom than ever before. But to what extent do they use this freedom?

A grim report on this matter was made in 1974 by the Robert F. Kennedy Memorial Commission of Inquiry into High School Journalism. No previous report had ever explored student journalism through the country so thoroughly. The commission, composed of high school students, teachers, professional journalists, school administrators, and community organizers, held hearings on the freedom of the student press in various parts of the country. What it found was dismaying: "Censorship and the systematic lack of freedom to engage in open, responsible journalism characterize high school [newspapers]. Unconstitutional and arbitrary restraints [by school officials] are so deeply imbedded in high school journalism as to overshadow its achievement."

There are exceptions, the commission pointed out. "In isolated schools, students enjoy a relatively free press," and in those rather rare places "there is a healthy ferment of ideas and opinions, with no indication of disruption or negative side effects on the educational experience of the school." In other words, vigorous student use of the First Amendment's freedom of the press does not lead to riots or other disturbances.

In the majority of high schools, however, censorship is so deeply embedded in school practice that even when a court decision has affirmed students' First Amendment rights, many schools under the court's jurisdiction either ignore the decision or interpret it, says the commission, "in such a way as to continue the censorship policy. . . . The result usually is an unquestioning attitude among students, an unhealthy acquiescence in pronouncements of school authorities no matter how unfair or oppressive they may be. In such authoritarian schools, students' rights are routinely denied, with little or no protest by students. The cost of such controls is not only the absence of a free student press but also bland, apathetic students who are unaware of or uninterested in their rights."

Or, put another way, "*Self-censorship,* the result of years of unconstitutional administrative and faculty censorship, has created passivity among students and made them cynical about the guarantees of a free press under the First Amendment."

Not surprisingly, some of those students who will *not* slide into passivity get into trouble. The Commission of Inquiry heard the story of Janice Fuhrman, who had been editor of her high school paper in Novato, California. In one issue she had criticized the principal for banning from the campus another, countywide student publication of which he disapproved. The principal's reaction to Janice Fuhrman's charge of censorship was to ban *her* from the campus. He suspended her.

Because she had attended civil liberties workshops off campus, Fuhrman knew her rights and went to a lawyer. Instead of immediately filing suit against the principal, however, the lawyer used another technique that sometimes is effective in reeducating violators of the Constitution: he gave details of the Janice Fuhrman case to the *San Francisco Chronicle*, the most influential newspaper in the area. When the story was published, the principal, embarrassed by the exposure, decided it had all been "a big misunderstanding" and immediately ended Janice Fuhrman's suspension.

While Janice Fuhrman was delighted to have her First Amendment rights vindicated, what most troubled her about the controversy was that there had been so little interest in it among students in her high school. "This may sound zany," she said, "but I don't think the majority of kids in our school care that much about individuals expressing themselves. I think a lot of the problem is that they are very poorly educated on constitutional rights."

Consider, for example, an opinion survey, in the early 1970s, of ninety thousand Americans under the age of thirty-five. Conducted by the Educational Commission of the States, the poll asked if such statements as "Russia is better than America" and "It is not necessary to believe in God" should be allowed on radio and television.

A whopping 94 percent of the thirteen-year-olds surveyed answered no. Seventy-eight percent of the seventeen-year-olds gave the same reply. In the twenty-six to thirty-five age range, 68 percent said that such opinions should be banned from the air. In all three groups, the overwhelming majority favored censoring ideas with which they disagreed.

Fortunately for the future of free expression in this land, there *are* students who are passionately concerned with the First Amendment. In 1976 Lauren Boyd was editor-in-chief of *The Farm News*, the student newspaper of Hayfield Secondary School, Fairfax County, Virginia.

Boyd wrote an article for *The Farm News* based on interviews, showing that only 29 percent of sexually active Hayfield students used contraceptive devices. Most of the rest, she had discovered, just didn't know anything about birth control. In the article, Boyd told students where they could obtain such information (e.g., Planned Parenthood), and she also indicated what some of the specific contraceptive options are.

At the time the story was written, instruction in sex education in the high school was prohibited by the school board. Accordingly, the principal of Hayfield Secondary School censored Lauren Boyd's article, *Sexually Active Students Fail to Use Contraception*. The information on contraceptives, the principal told Boyd, must be removed because that section violated board of education policy and also might stir complaints from parents.

Boyd and her assistant editor, Gina Gambino, refused to submit passively to prior restraint of the newspaper.

The December 1, 1976, issue of *The Farm News* appeared with the title of the censored article followed by a blank space where the text would have run. Meanwhile, all the student editors' appeals against the principal's act of censorship, up to and including the Fairfax County School Board, were turned down.

The school board finally did adopt a sex education program, but it absolutely prohibited any instruction in birth control methods. So the offending portion of Boyd's article, the information on contraceptives, was *still* against school policy. Contraception was no more to be "taught" in the school paper than in a classroom.

Boyd and Gambino took the Fairfax County School Board into Federal District Court in Alexandria, Virginia. The essence of the school board's defense was that since the school publishes and largely pays for the paper, *The Farm News* belongs to the school and not to the students. The newspaper is also "an outgrowth of the instructional program," another reason it must be under the school's control. Furthermore, if the students should win and the paper became wholly free, *The Farm News* "could not refuse articles that were shockingly violent or disturbingly morbid, or that were clearly erroneous," such as a piece claiming that heroin was not addictive or that smoking was not hazardous to your health. In other words, the official high school paper could degenerate into a sensationalist tabloid.

"Should not," the school board asked the court, "the school administration, which is expert in educating and understanding children, be able to exercise reasonable editorial control of the official student newspaper?"

Federal Judge Albert V. Bryan, Jr., answered in favor of the students. In the first substantial court analysis of the free-press rights of students working for an official, school-funded newspaper, Bryan began by establishing the ground rules. The school board had maintained that since the school so clearly has the power to control the paper, this "does not rise to the dignity of a First Amendment case."

Wrong, said Judge Bryan. This *is* a First Amendment case. Since this public school paper was established and operates "as a conduit for student expression on a wide variety of topics, it clearly falls within the parameters of the First Amendment." The paper, then, is a "free speech forum." Accordingly, the First Amendment protects the student writers and editors, even though the part of the article dealing with contraception is objectionable "to the sensibilities of the School Board" and despite the fact that it directly violates school board policy.

As for school authorities' fears that bringing the First Amendment into the school will lead to irresponsible, sensationalistic journalism, Judge Bryan said he had found no evidence of that malady in the paper's past nor in this article. "Nor has there been any demonstrated likelihood of it in the future."

To be sure, the paper could become irresponsible. Anything is possible. "But speculation," said the judge, "is not a proper consideration in this case. *The state cannot constitutionally restrict anyone's First Amendment rights, including those of students, because of mere apprehension of what they might do with them*" (emphasis added).

When the Fairfax County School Board decided to appeal the decision, it was joined as an *amicus curiae* (friend of the court) by the National Association of Secondary School Principals. (An *amicus curiae* is not itself a party to a lawsuit but may be indirectly affected by it and wants, therefore, to urge a particular position before the court.)

The Secondary School Principals correctly considered this case to be of historic importance, although their reason for that conclusion is rather alarmingly self-revealing. Should the ruling in favor of the student press go unchallenged, said an officer of the principals' organization, it "could weaken and ultimately destroy our system of free schools."

The Court of Appeals, however, upheld Lauren Boyd and Gina Gambino. The school board decided to appeal no further—and our system of free schools is still standing.

In July 1977, three years after the Kennedy Commission report, Karen Shugrue, a reporter, investigated the high school press for National Public Radio and found that the Marcos, Boyds, and Gambinos are still a minority. A prophetic minority perhaps; but as for the present, Shugrue reported that school papers "have been censored for criticizing the dress code, the football team, and even for calling the censorship policy a bad one. Papers have been seized, shredded and burned. Students on those papers have been expelled." Or threatened with poor grades or with not being recommended for college.

Yet there has been a marked rise in students' awareness of their rights, and so court battles for First Amendment freedoms are multiplying. Said the editors of a Texas high school paper back in 1969: "To protect our rights we must understand them fully and we must be willing to work to preserve them. If we give up and knuckle under to injustice . . . what will happen later in life when we have to face abominations considerably more unbearable than the ones we face here in school? ... IT'S OUR CHOICE!"

As journalist and press historian Ben Bagdikian puts it, "If freedom of expression becomes merely an empty slogan in the minds of enough children, it will be dead by the time they are adults."

III

*What is at stake here is the right to read and be
exposed to controversial thoughts and language—a
valuable right subject to First Amendment protections.*

Bruce Severy, a teacher, was new to the small town of
Drake, North Dakota, but it was soon clear to him that
freedom of thought was hardly flourishing there. The
school librarian, for instance, was in the habit of taking
a razor blade to such magazines as *Newsweek* so that
students would be spared exposure to any "obscene"
words or pictures.

Severy, a conscientious teacher who wanted to assign
a number of lively contemporary books to his high
school students, decided to get advance clearance from
the proper authorities, just in case. The books included
Kurt Vonnegut Jr.'s *Slaughterhouse-Five*, James Dick-
ey's *Deliverance*, and a short story anthology with works
by Faulkner, Steinbeck, and Hemingway, among others.

In the spring of 1973 Severy sent the books to the
school superintendent; but neither the superintendent
nor any other administrator read them. That fall, Severy,
at the start of his first academic year in Drake's schools,
began teaching the books until a student complaint
about certain "unnecessary language" in *Slaughterhouse-*

Five led to a school board meeting at which Severy *Slaughterhouse-Five* and *Deliverance* were denounced. Several ministers, for example, indicted *Slaughterhouse-Five* as "a tool of the devil."

The school board decided that the only way to cleanse the town of Kurt Vonnegut's pernicious influence was to burn—actually burn—all the copies of *Slaughterhouse-Five* that Severy had ordered. Of the thirty-four sophomores to whom this book had been assigned, thirty-two petitioned the school board to save the life of the book and keep it in their class. (The two exceptions were the son of a school board member and the student who had made the original complaint about the book.)

Resistant to all cries for clemency, the school board did indeed burn the copies of *Slaughterhouse-Five*. Although *Deliverance* was saved from the flames, all copies had to be turned in. Unanimously, the junior class, which had been studying *Deliverance*, refused to hand over the books, and the school authorities diligently searched all the students' lockers, coming up with some of the paperbacks, but not all of them.

After the Vonnegut bonfire and the *Deliverance* locker search, it was discovered that no one on the school board had read either book.

Not surprisingly, Severy was informed that his one-year teaching contract would not be renewed. The mild-mannered teacher said, before leaving town, that he had assigned the books "to get the kids to think clearly about current problems. . . . A few four-letter words in a book is no big deal. Those students have all heard these words before; none learned any new words. I've always thought the purpose of school was to prepare these people for living in the 'big, bad world,' but it evidently isn't so."

Meanwhile, in November 1973, the Drake high school paper ran a column with these items:

What if . . .

everyone would get A's?

Wanda couldn't be with Kevin?

there wouldn't be any furnace to burn the books in?

Bruce Severy moved on to Fargo, North Dakota, where he became an orderly in the emergency room of a hospital. However, with the help of the American Civil Liberties Union, Severy brought suit against the school authorities of Drake, North Dakota, and eventually there was a settlement:

1) *Slaughterhouse-Five* and *Deliverance* could be used by teachers in the Drake High School in connection with the teaching of English in the eleventh and twelfth grades,

2) Severy's performance at Drake High School could not be described as unsatisfactory, either in writing or orally, and

3) Severy was to be awarded a judgment of $5,000.

In 1973 Avon published an original paperback, *Male & Female under 18: Frank Comments from Young People about Their Sex Roles Today*. Editors Nancy Larrick and Eve Merriam had sent circulars to schools throughout the country, inviting entries in any form that would "tell us what it is like to be a girl or a boy growing up in the 1970s."

At Hunter High School in New York, fifteen-year-old

25

Jody Caravaglia saw the notice on the bulletin board
and decided to send in a poem she had written for an
English class on what might be called the urban experience. The poem was accepted, and Jody received a
check for ten dollars, two copies of the book, and—five
years later—both national notoriety and a significant
place in the history of the First Amendment.

This is the poem:

The City to a Young Girl

The city is
One million horny lip-smacking men
Screaming for my body.
The streets are long conveyor belts
Loaded with these suckling pigs.
All begging for
a lay
a little pussy
a bit of tit
a leg to rub against
a handful of ass
the connoisseurs of cunt
Every day, every night
Pressing in on me closer and closer.
I swat them off like flies
but they keep coming back.
I'm a good piece of meat.

For more than a year Jody Caravaglia's poem became
the inflammatory center in Chelsea, Massachusetts, of a
classic battle over censorship in school libraries.

Wars over students' rights to read what librarians
have made available to them are perpetual. Every month,
in American towns and cities, controversial books are

hauled off school library shelves. As the National Council of Teachers of English has pointed out, "any roster of authors whose works are sometimes considered unsuitable for school use begins to read like a random sampling from a *Who's Who* of distinguished literary figures of the Western world." (Among authors banned, for instance, have been Mark Twain, Ernest Hemingway, Alexander Solzhenitsyn, Ralph Ellison, Malcolm X, Herman Hesse, and J. D. Salinger, whose *Catcher in the Rye* is the book most frequently expelled by the nation's school boards.)

The short, fierce history of Jody Caravaglia's poem is best understood in this context:

1. The Supreme Court has never directly ruled on a case of censorship in a school library.

2. The two leading lower court cases, before the decision on Jody's poem, resulted in contradictory decisions.

In *President's Council, District 25 v. Community School Board No. 25* (1972), the Second Circuit Court of Appeals upheld the right of a school board to remove Piri Thomas's *Down These Mean Streets* from junior high school libraries because some of the language and scenes in the book were "ugly and violent." The United States Supreme Court refused to review the case, although Justice William O. Douglas vehemently disagreed with his brethren:

> What else can the School Board now decide it does not like? How else will its sensibilities be offended? Are we sending children to school to be educated by the norms of the School Board or are we educating our youth to shed the prejudices of the past, to explore all

forms of thought, and to find solutions to our world's problems?

In *Minarcini v. Strongsville City District* (1974), on the other hand, the Sixth Circuit Court of Appeals overturned a Federal District Court ruling and denied a school board's right to remove Joseph Heller's *Catch-22* and Kurt Vonnegut's *Cat's Cradle* from a high school library in Ohio. The appeals court said that while a school board was under no obligation to set up a library, once it did so it could not "place conditions on the use of the library which were related solely to the social or political tastes of the school board members." Such acts of censorship, said the court, violated the First Amendment rights of both students and librarians: the students' right to receive information; the librarians' right to disseminate it.

Nonetheless, elsewhere in the country, school board censorship of library books goes on, as well as attempts by various pressure groups (such as conservatives, feminists, religious fundamentalists, blacks) to get books thrown out which offend their particular criteria of what is suitable for young readers.

Then came Jody Caravaglia's poem.

This First Amendment battlefield was Chelsea, a working-class city of thirty thousand northeast of Boston. At the time, the chairman of the school committee was Andrew Quigley, publisher and owner of the *Chelsea Record* (the town's daily paper), and a former mayor. On May 19, 1977, Quigley received a telephone call from James McCarthy, father of a fourteen-year-old girl at Chelsea High School. Mr. McCarthy was about to explode. His daughter had borrowed the paperback anthology *Male & Female Under 18* from the school library, read Jody's poem, and had become so distraught as a result that McCarthy was on the verge of going down to the high school and punching out the headmaster. "I pay $2,012 in taxes to this city," the father roared, "and I just can't believe this kind of poem is available to my child."

As Quigley was later to point out at a tumultuous school hearing, this greatly aggrieved father "was not a professor, nor was he a graduate of a great university. He was a member of that great body of people, the common working folk." Has he no right to protect his daughter from contamination by the "slime," as a Boston columnist was to put it, in this poem?

Quigley promptly got a copy of the poem, found the language "filthy" and "offensive," and called an emergency meeting of the school committee to consider the subject of "objectionable, salacious and obscene material being made available in books in the high school library." The only hearing to this point had been held in Quigley's head. If the poem had already been found guilty, what was to be the purpose of the emergency school committee meeting? It was essential, said Quigley, to find out how the book had gotten on the library shelves and "to make certain that no such filth" will ever again be "distributed in our schools."

Prior to that meeting, Quigley distributed copies of the Caravaglia poem to the three other male members of the committee, but not to the three female members. A gentleman of the old school, he considered the language too "crude" and "offensive" for their eyes.

The emergency meeting was followed by other school committee sessions on Jody's poem. At one of them,

Lisa Jarvis, sixteen, a Chelsea High student, urged the committee not to ban the book and noted that the language in the poem was hardly unknown to the young women of her city. "Mr. Quigley," said Lisa Jarvis, "should walk through Chelsea square with a girl some time and just listen to what the guys say."

And Sharon Ultsch, president of the junior class, told the school committee members, "I'm not here tonight to defend this poem, for in my opinion the language used is vulgar. But I am here to express my concern for the right of any student to read what he or she desires. To take a book out of the Chelsea High School library is unjust, unlawful, and against the First Amendment, for this is censorship."

Andrew Quigley was not persuaded. "To the average working-class Chelsea people," he shouted at one point, "this is dirty rotten filth." Calming down, Quigley insisted that he was by no means a prude, but "I agree with the old Boston lady when she said, 'People can do what they want so long as they don't do it out on the streets where they can frighten the horses.' "

Another member of the school committee, Anthony Tiro, astonished that anyone would try to justify keeping so foul an object in the library, exclaimed, "Thank God our forefathers are not here to see this!"

As infuriated as the school committee was by Jody Caravaglia's poem, it was even more outraged by Sonja Coleman, Chelsea High's librarian. Coleman had ordered the book and from the start of the ferocious controversy had not diluted her First Amendment position, although it was clear that if she persisted she would be turned down for a permanent position at the school. Coleman's view, as she kept saying amid the Chelsea clamor, was that any parent has the right to question the suitability of a book for his *own* child, but that no book in the library should be denied to any of the other students in the school who want to read it.

To gather their forces for the coming right-to-read Armageddon, Sonja Coleman, two teachers, three students (including Lisa Jarvis and Sharon Ultsch), and the parents of one of the students formed the Right to Read Defense Committee of Chelsea.

At this point the author of the by now famous poem was heard from. Since leaving Hunter High School, Jody Caravaglia had spent three years in college and then had become a professional photographer, whose work appeared in *Rolling Stone, The Village Voice, Esquire, Saturday Review,* and other publications. On hearing of the great trouble her poem was causing, Jody sent a telegram to Sonja Coleman: "The poem expresses feminine outrage against public lechery, an obscene, dehumanizing situation. It is antipornographic. Censorship is a gross injustice as awareness is our greatest asset in combating sexism."

Nonsense, said Andrew Quigley: "A girl reading that without proper instruction could arrive at the opinion that every man walking down the street is considering her only as a sex object to be violated. It is not good education, and it is not something to found in the halls of a school."

The fateful day came. On July 28, 1977, the Chelsea School Committee banned Jody's poem. The anthology itself could stay on the shelves provided that the page containing the poem was ripped out of every copy. On August 3 the Right to Read Defense Committee, along with the Massachusetts Library Association, filed suit in federal court against the Chelsea School Committee. Sonja Coleman and her allies asked for a preliminary injunction to prevent the banning or censoring of the book, an action to prohibit reprisals against Sonja Coleman, and a judgment that removing this book and poem from the library violated the rights of students, teachers, and librarians "to receive and communicate ideas and information." Also being abused was the right "to academic freedom."

On August 19, Federal Judge Joseph Tauro issued a temporary order. The book went back on the shelves, but no student could read it unless he had written permission from a parent. Furthermore, there was to be no retaliation against Sonja Coleman or any of the other plaintiffs on the faculty.

The six-day trial took place in November. More than a hundred Chelsea High School students eagerly crowded into the courtroom as if it were the site of a rock concert. Taking every available seat, sitting cross-legged on the floor, cracking chewing gum, they watched in fascination the intense play of forces contesting whether they, as students, had a First Amendment right to read Jody's poem that was stronger than the school committee's power to tell them they could not read it.

A number of experts in adolescent literature testified to the poem's bracingly frank educational value. The other side pointed out, however, that none of these so-called experts lived in Chelsea. Were the educational wishes of this working-class community to be wholly ignored because *outside* specialists thought filth was good for Chelsea schoolchildren?

"Look," Andrew Quigley said after the trial, "they were *all* outsiders. Sonja Coleman didn't live in Chelsea, and neither did any of the other teachers who got involved in the suit. They're floating freethinkers is what they are. And there's nothing wrong with that in places like Newton or Marblehead, where the parents are the same way. But it doesn't go in Chelsea, nor should we be forced to accept it if this is a democracy."

Months went by, and there was no word from Judge Tauro. In March 1978 the school committee, emboldened by the silence, voted 7 to 0 to deny Sonja Coleman a permanent position. Immediately, Coleman and the Right to Read Defense Committee went to court asking that the school committee be held in civil contempt for refusing job tenure to the librarian and thereby defying the judge's order that there be no retaliation against her. The school committee reversed itself (4–3), not wishing to bear the expense of yet another lawsuit.

At last, on July 5, 1978, Federal Judge Joseph Tauro delivered his opinion. An eight-column banner headline on the front page of the *Chelsea Record* reported:

JUDGE RULES "POEM" STAYS IN CHS LIBRARY

. . . The defendants are enjoined from removing, or causing to be removed, in whole or part, the anthology *Male & Female Under 18* from the Chelsea High School Library because of the theme of or language of the poem "The City to a Young Girl." Said anthology shall be made available to all students at Chelsea High School in accordance with the standard library procedures.

The lead editorial was bordered in black. "The people to feel sorry for," wrote Andrew Quigley, "are the parents of the children who are going to be subjected to this filth."

But what did Federal Judge Joseph Tauro actually say? To start with, "Clearly a school committee can determine what books will go into a library and, indeed, if there will be a library at all. But the question presented here is whether a school committee has the same degree of discretion to order a book *removed* from a library" (emphasis added).

Yet, is it not true, as the Chelsea School Committee claimed, that the committee is in charge of the schools, under state statute, and so has the power to remove as well as select books? True, up to a point, said the judge, and that point is when basic constitutional values are involved. That's when the courts can intervene.

In this case, Judge Tauro pointed out, there is no doubt that the school committee banned the book because "it considered the theme and language" of the poem at issue "to be 'filthy,' 'obscene,' 'disgusting.'" But these were the personal judgments of the members of the committee. Tauro recalled the 1976 Court of Appeals ruling (*Minarcini v. Strongsville City School District*) that it is unconstitutional for school board members to censor books on the basis of their own social or political tastes.

Therefore, members of the Chelsea School Committee cannot censor library books unless they can demonstrate "some substantial and legitimate government interest" in doing so. Simply citing their own outraged tastes won't do. There could be a substantial government interest, said the judge, in preventing harm from being done to the students by the presence of the book, but there was no evidence at the trial that the poem could cause any damage at all.

On the other hand, Judge Tauro continued, Jody Cara-vaglia's poem might do the kids some good. "Whether or not scholarly, the poem is challenging and thought-provoking. It employs vivid street language, legitimately offensive to some, but certainly not to everyone. The author is writing about her perception of city life in rough but relevant language that gives credibility to the development of a sensitive theme. *City's* words may shock, but they communicate."

Isn't that where education begins?

Judge Tauro, warming to his First Amendment theme, became quite blunt. "The committee claims an absolute right to remove *City* from the shelves of the school library. It has no such right, and compelling policy considerations argue against any public authority having such an unreviewable power of censorship.

"There is more at issue here," he continued, "than the poem, *City*. If this work may be removed by a committee hostile to its language and theme, then the precedent is set for removal of any other work. The prospect of successive school committees 'sanitizing' the school library of views divergent from their own is alarming, whether they do it book by book or one page at a time."

That, of course, is the unending danger of giving school committees the absolute power to censor. Each will have its own *Index Librorum Prohibitorum*, and the library shelves may well be arranged to accommodate each new orthodoxy. This is hardly education for freedom of thought.

The judge then came to the core of his ruling, a declaration with emancipatory overtones for every public library in the country: *"What is at stake here is the right to read and be exposed to controversial thoughts and language—a valuable right subject to First Amendment protection"* (emphasis added).

To support his unprecedentedly clear affirmation of a student's right to read, Tauro went to the text of the Supreme Court's decision in the 1969 *Tinker* case: "In our system, students may not be regarded as closed-circuit recipients of only that which the State chooses to communicate. They may not be confined to the expression of those sentiments that are officially approved."

And the most stimulating place for exposure to all kinds of ideas and sentiments is the school library. "There," Judge Tauro noted, "a student can literally explore the unknown, and discover areas of interest and thought not covered by the prescribed curriculum. The student who discovers the magic of the library is on the way to a life-long experience of self-education and enrichment. That student learns that a library is a place to test or expand upon ideas presented to him, in or out of the classroom."

But this only works if the library is not controlled by authoritarian hands, even if those hands belong to members of an elected school committee. The library is violated even if "just one poem is excised." Said the judge: "It would be no less offensive to First Amendment principles for a School Committee to bowdlerize an anthology by removing one poem, than it would be for it to excise objectionable passages in a novel."

Tauro's decision ended emphatically: "The most effective antidote to the poison of mindless orthodoxy is ready access to a broad sweep of ideas and philosophies. The danger is in mind control." No judge in all of American history had ever before so clearly and vigorously set forth the First Amendment right-to-read of public school students.

Because of the expense involved, the Chelsea School Committee decided not to appeal, and so Judge Tauro's decision stands.

The librarian, Sonja Coleman, points out that the battle resulted in more than the return of Jody Caravaglia's poem to the school library shelves. "More of the kids," she says, "became aware that they have rights, and they became aware of what those rights are.

"For the first time in the history of the school, for instance, some thirty of the kids formed a students' rights association as a direct result of the case. And one of the things the group did last spring was to fight the school committee's refusal to let a student newsletter be distributed in the school. They got the American Civil Liberties Union involved, a lawsuit was filed, and the school committee backed down. I think the students learned a lot from the fight over the poem."

What had Sonja Coleman, who chose to leave the school, learned? For one thing, that it is sometimes hard for a dissenter—even one, like Coleman, who has been honored by librarians' groups for her courage in this fight—to find another job. Sonja Coleman was unemployed for a long time after leaving Chelsea High School. Also, she is under no illusion that school library censorship will soon end. "It'll keep on happening," she says, "as it has in other parts of the country since the decision. And what I have learned most of all is that the First Amendment is *never* abstract. It's always *this* book, *this* poem. So, anyone who cares about students' right to read will have to keep on doing battle one book at a time, sometimes one page at a time."

IV

Maybe one student will see how as a result of all this that (a teacher) has a right to stand up for what he believes in.

When attempts are made to censor books in school libraries, the First Amendment rights of students, teachers, and librarians intersect. But what of those First Amendment conflicts that involve primarily teachers? To what extent are they, at their jobs, full "persons" under the Constitution?

From the beginning of the nation's history, teachers were expected to conform to much stricter moral standards than the rest of the populace. Since the nation's future was entrusted to them, teachers had to be constantly careful that their influence over the young, within and outside the classroom, was in no way harmful. Philosopher Josiah Royce, for instance, pointed out in 1883 that a teacher might well find that "his non-attendance in church, or the fact that he drinks beer with his lunch, or rides a bicycle, is considered of more moment than his power to instruct." Nor did this attitude end in the nineteenth century. In 1956 a teacher hired in a small Oklahoma town was ordered by school officials not to get involved in politics, to attend church regularly, and not to use tobacco or alcohol.

Even as late as 1969 education professors David Schimmel and Louis Fischer had the following dialogue with a California school superintendent:

> *Superintendent*: Teaching is a privilege, not a right. If one wants this privilege, he has to give up some of his rights.
>
> *Questioners*: Just what constitutional rights does one have to give up in order to enter teaching?
>
> *Superintendent*: Any right his community wants him to give up.

There are still some places where teachers are treated as inferior citizens, but by and large they have achieved their rights, or most of them. This has been due to a combination of strong teacher unions, the increase in tenure laws (guaranteeing teachers their jobs after a probationary period), and a series of clarifying court decisions.

In a 1952 case (*Wieman v. Updegraff*), in which a loyalty oath required of college teachers was struck down by the Supreme Court, Justice Felix Frankfurter said in his concurring opinion:

> To regard teachers—in our entire educational system, from primary grades to the university—as the priests of democracy is . . . not to indulge in hyperbole. It is the special task of teachers to foster those habits of open-mindedness and critical inquiry which alone make for responsible citizens, who, in turn, make possible an enlightened and effective public opinion.

To encourage open-mindedness in their students, Frankfurter continued, teachers must themselves have the right to free inquiry and not be bound to orthodox ideas.

But what about decidedly unorthodox words? The case, for instance, of a high school teacher assigning a senior English class an article that includes one or more "dirty" words? *Keefe v. Geanokos* (1969) concerned just such an article in the *Atlantic Monthly*. The teacher, in assigning it, said that any student finding the article distasteful could have the choice of another assignment. Written by a psychiatrist and a medical school professor, the essay was an analysis of dissent, protest, and radicalism in the society at the time. There were frequent references to the word *motherfucker*. In discussing the assignment with his class, the teacher, Keefe, examined the word, its origin, the context in which it was used, and the reasons the authors had included it.

The school committee objected to the word and demanded that the teacher agree never again to use it in the classroom. Keefe refused and was suspended, preparatory to being fired. The United States Court of Appeals ruled that the teacher's First Amendment right to academic freedom made it unlawful for the school committee to dismiss him. The article in question, said the court, was "in no sense pornographic." Instead, it was "scholarly, thoughtful and thought-provoking." Moreover, the "single, offending word, although repeated a number of times, is not artificially introduced, but on the contrary, is important to the development of the thesis."

In another case, *Parducci v. Rutland* (1970), a high school teacher in Montgomery, Alabama, assigned her eleventh-grade English class a short story, "Welcome to the Monkey House," by Kurt Vonnegut. The principal vigorously objected to some of the language in the story as well as its "philosophy." (He interpreted this "literary garbage," as he called it, as condoning "the killing off of elderly people" and the advocacy of free sex.)

Upon being ordered not to use the story again, the teacher told the principal that indeed she had a professional obligation to teach it again and that furthermore he had thoroughly misinterpreted the story. Fired for "insubordination," she sued in federal court to get her job back.

The court ruled, first of all, that nothing in the story would make it obscene under standards developed by the Supreme Court, and also agreed with the teacher that the principal had misunderstood the story. Finally, the court said that school officials had not shown that the story was inappropriate for the eleventh grade, nor had they proved that it significantly disrupted the school's educational processes. The teacher's firing had therefore been "an unwarranted invasion of her First Amendment right to academic freedom."

Teachers, however, cannot use absolutely any kind of language in class with impunity. If brought up on such charges, the teacher's case could depend, as one appeals court put it, "on the age and sophistication of the students." Also figuring in the judgment, to be made on a case-by-case basis, is "the context and manner of presentation." If a teacher habitually used vulgarity in class, without relating "dirty" words to a specific educational objective, he might be fired, after a hearing, on the basis of his teaching competence (that is, his sense of judgment).

There is also the thorny question of the extent to which a teacher's speech is protected when he deals with controversial issues, rather than just words, in the class-room. A 1972 case, *Sterzing v. Fort Bend Independent School District,* involved a high school civics teacher who had been fired for "insubordination" by the school board after parents complained he had taught a project on race relations "propagandistically." Another charge was that the teacher, in answer to a student's question, had said he was not against interracial marriages.

The court decided that the teacher had been reason-ably fair in the way he handled those controversial is-sues and that his teaching methods were within "ac-cepted professional standards." The court then emphasized a vital principle of academic freedom: "The freedom of speech of a teacher and a citizen of the United States must not be so lightly regarded that he stands in jeopardy of dismissal for raising controversial issues in an eager but disciplined classroom."

On the other hand, a teacher who proselytizes (tries to gain converts for a cause or a political organization) in the classroom is likely to be in trouble. In 1970 (*Knarr v. Board of School Trustees*), a federal court ruled that a teacher had been rightly denied renewal of his contract because he had used his classroom "as his personal forum to promote union activities, to sanction polygamy, to attack marriage, to criticize other teachers and to sway and influence the minds of young people without a full and proper explanation of both sides of the issue."

And in 1924 a California court noted that a teacher advocating "the election of a particular candidate for public office" in a classroom "introduces into the school questions wholly foreign to its purposes and objects."

What about a teacher's beliefs and political associations *outside* the classroom? Can he be disciplined or dismissed, for instance, solely for being a member of the Communist party, even if he does not proselytize for its goals in the classroom?

A key case on teachers' First Amendment rights of free association was *Keyishian v. Board of Regents,* decided by the Supreme Court in 1967. The state of New York had devised a plan to get rid of any "subversive" teachers in the public schools (including state universities and colleges). Under this plan every teacher had to sign a certificate saying that he or she was not a member of the Communist party. There was also an official list of other "subversive" organizations (groups accused of advocating the overthrow of the government). Anyone belonging to one of those groups would not be hired as a teacher—or, if already in a school, would be fired.

By a 5 to 4 vote the Supreme Court struck down the New York "loyalty" plan. Said Justice William J. Brennan, Jr., speaking for the majority:

> Our nation is deeply committed to safeguarding academic freedom, which is of transcendent value to all of us and not merely to the teachers concerned. That freedom is therefore a special concern of the First Amendment, which does not tolerate laws that cast a pall of orthodoxy over the classroom. "The vigilant protection of constitutional freedoms is nowhere more vital than in the community of American schools."

It is true, said Brennan, that in 1952 the Supreme Court had held that a teacher could be fired just for being a member of the Communist party (*Adler v. Board of Education*). But constitutional doctrine had changed since then, rejecting the major premise of the *Adler* decision. That premise used to be, Brennan pointed out, that anyone who wanted to get public employment, including teaching, might have to surrender certain of his constitutional rights. For instance, his First Amendment right to belong to the political party of his choice—if that were the Communist party. The Supreme Court, in a series of decisions since *Adler*, had come to the opposite conclusion, said Brennan, and it is now unconstitutional for the state to fire anyone just for membership in the Communist party.

This *Keyishian* decision vindicated Justice William O. Douglas's forceful dissent during the *Adler* case fifteen years earlier:

> I cannot . . . find in our constitutional scheme [Douglas had said then] the power of a state to place its employees in the category of second-class citizens by denying them freedom of thought and expression. The Constitution guarantees freedom of thought and expression to everyone in our society. All are entitled to it; and no one needs it more than the teacher. The public school is in most respects the cradle of our democracy. . . .
> What happens under this law is typical of what happens in a police state. Teachers are under constant surveillance; their pasts are combed for signs of disloyalty; their utterances are watched for clues to dangerous thoughts. . . . There can be no real academic freedom in that environment. Where suspicion fills the air and holds scholars in line for fear of their jobs, there can be no exercise of the free intellect. Supineness and dogmatism take the place of inquiry. A "party line"—as dangerous as the "party line" of the Communists—lays hold. It is the "party line" of the orthodox view, of the conventional thought, of the accepted approach. A prob-

lem can no longer be pursued with impunity to its edges. Fear stalks the classroom. The teacher is no longer a stimulant to adventurous thinking; she becomes instead a pipe line for safe and sound information. A deadening dogma takes the place of free inquiry. Instruction tends to become sterile; pursuit of knowledge is discouraged; discussion often leaves off where it should begin.

This, I think, is what happens when a censor looks over a teacher's shoulder. . . . It produces standardized thought, not the pursuit of truth. Yet it was the pursuit of truth which the First Amendment was designed to protect. A system which directly or inevitably has [the opposite] effect is alien to our system and should be struck down. Its survival is a real threat to our way of life. We need be bold and adventurous in our thinking to survive. A school system producing students trained as robots threatens to rob a generation of the versatility that has been perhaps our greatest distinction. The Framers of our Constitution knew the danger of dogmatism; they also knew the strength that comes when the mind is free, when ideas may be pursued wherever they lead. We forget these teachings of the First Amendment when we sustain this law.

Of course the school systems of the country need not become cells for Communist activities; and the classrooms need not become forums for propagandizing the Marxist creed. But the guilt of the teacher should turn on overt acts. *So long as she is a law-abiding citizen, so long as her performance within the public school system meets professional standards, her private life, her political philosophy, her social creed should not be the cause of reprisals against her.* [Emphasis added]

Pursuit of "subversives" in the public schools took place in the 1950s, when there was much obsession with communism in the nation. Russia was expanding her influence in various parts of the world, and there was fear that members of the American Communist party were engaged in a conspiracy to so weaken this government as to lead eventually to its overthrow. In the 1960s and early 1970s there was another kind of unrest in the land. The Vietnamese War created deep divisions, and many of those in positions of authority, such as school officials, regarded those protesting the war as "subversive" and furthering the aims of communism, whether or not they were Communists themselves.

From these strong feelings, on both sides, concerning the Vietnamese War came a celebrated case, *James v. Board of Education.* Like the *Tinker* case it had to do with the wearing of a black armband, but this time it was a teacher who chose to use that form of symbolic speech.

In November 1969, the year of the *Tinker* decision, at a Quaker meetinghouse in Elmira, New York, a group opposing the Vietnamese War met to figure out how to best take part in a local peace vigil and then a national rally in Washington. Available for those who wanted them were armbands of black silk. The wearers—like Mary Beth Tinker in Des Moines—would thereby symbolically express their refusal to support or condone the killing in Vietnam.

One of those taking a black armband was forty-one-year-old Charles James, a teacher of eleventh-grade English in the small nearby village of Addison. (The full story of what happened to James thereafter is in "A Scrap of Black Cloth," a chapter of Richard Harris's 1976 book, *Freedom Spent: Tales of Tyranny in America.*)

Charles James, who had been a minister before becoming a teacher, decided to wear the armband to school because, he told Richard Harris, "if my wearing it could bring someone, anyone, to consider that some people do believe in the preciousness of life and dare to say so, then our world would have a better chance of surviving."

The high school's principal told James to remove the armband because it would create controversy among parents and other citizens whose taxes paid for the school and its faculty. "You mean," said the teacher, "they'd be upset by my asserting my rights but they wouldn't be upset if you took my rights away?"

The principal insisted that James make a decision; the teacher said he would continue to wear the armband. James was then sent to the principal of the entire school district. This school official ordered James to take off the armband because wearing it, he maintained, was a political act and indeed an "illegal act." Said the district principal, "You are acting against the President of the United States, Mr. Nixon." Furthermore, said the district principal, it was unethical for a teacher to use a classroom as a forum for his political views. To be sure, he could discuss a controversial subject in his classroom, but he was required to present all points of view on that subject objectively. And here was Charles James, wearing his black armband, which represented only one side of the issue. Finally, said the district principal, this piece of black silk could well lead to student disruptions in the school and to divisiveness among the faculty.

When James refused to remove the armband, he was suspended, and later fired. The school board backed that decision. Yet the teacher was sure he would be vindicated. "I just assumed," he says, "that I had some kind of right to express my conscience."

Charles James's vindication took three years, and it was so destructive financially for James, his wife, and their four daughters that the family was forced to go on welfare from time to time. There were also intense emotional pressures on everyone in the family. But James insisted on continuing to fight for the right to follow his conscience.

"They should have had a better chance to be children and grow up more slowly," James's wife, Neva, said to Richard Harris about the four James daughters. "I know they thought their father was right, and were proud of him. But I also know—I can see it in their faces sometimes when they look at Charles—that they're thinking, If it wasn't for your armband, we could have had some new sneakers." One daughter, an eleven-year-old, stopped pledging allegiance to the flag in school because her father's ordeal had shown her, she said, that it was not true that in America "liberty and justice" is "for all."

James's own colleagues in the Addison Teachers Association voted in favor of the school board's backing of James's suspension for refusing to remove the armband. In January 1970 the school board fired James.

With the aid of the New York Civil Liberties Union, James appealed to Ewald Nyquist, the New York State commissioner of education and generally considered sensitive to the civil liberties of students and teachers. Nyquist, however, ruled against the teacher, holding that James had provided his students with "only one point of view on an important public issue." The wearing of the black armband had therefore violated "sound educational principles" and was not "constitutionally protected." According to the commissioner, Charles James's First Amendment rights had not been violated. Said James's wife,

"The irony of the situation is that quite likely Charles, for the first time in Addison, presented the other side of the issue of war and peace."

A long court battle began. In Federal District Court in Buffalo the judge decided against James, ruling that he had been "insubordinate" in refusing to remove the black armband. Why? Because by wearing it in the classroom James had ignored state education policy mandating "neutrality and objectivity" in dealing with such issues as the Vietnamese War and protests against it. James's dismissal "did not violate his rights under the First Amendment." Nor had he been entitled to a hearing prior to his summary dismissal.

Finally, *James v. Board of Education* reached the Second Circuit Court of Appeals, which in a unanimous three-judge decision ruled in favor of the teacher. Speaking for the court, Chief Judge Irving Kaufman noted that James's wearing of the armband did not threaten to disrupt classroom activities or create any disruption in the school as a whole. James had met the test of the *Tinker* decision: his exercise of symbolic speech "would [not] materially and substantially disrupt the work and discipline of the school."

In this case, therefore, "we cannot countenance school authorities arbitrarily censoring a teacher's speech merely because they do not agree with the teacher's political philosophies or leanings. This is particularly so when that speech does not interfere in any way with the teacher's obligations to teach, is not coercive and does not arbitrarily inculcate doctrinaire views in the minds of the students."

Furthermore, said Judge Kaufman, "we cannot ignore the fact that James was teaching 11th grade (high school) English. His students were approximately 16 or 17 years of age, thus more mature than those junior high school students in *Tinker*. . . . Recently, this country enfranchised 18-year-olds. It would be foolhardy to shield our children from political debate and issues until their first venture into the voting booth. Schools must play a central role in preparing their students to think and analyze and to recognize the demagogue. *Under the circumstances here, there was a greater danger that the school, by power of example, would appear to the students to be sanctioning the very 'pall of orthodoxy' . . . which chokes freedom of dissent"* (emphasis added).

But what of the high school principal's concern that the teacher's wearing of a black armband might well create controversy among many of the parents and other adults in the community? On a First Amendment matter, said the chief judge, "the prejudices of the community" cannot be allowed to prevail. Indeed, "the will of the transient majority can prove devastating to freedom of expression."

The court also noted that, according to James, another teacher in the same school, " 'without incurring any disciplinary sanction, prominently displayed the [pro-Vietnamese War] slogan "Peace with Honor" on a bulletin board in his classroom.' " The fact that the school board allowed *that* slogan but fired James because of the black armband "would indicate that its regulation against political activity in the classroom" may be no more than a way of censoring "only that expression with which it disagrees." (Similarly, Kaufman noted, in the *Tinker* case, Mary Beth Tinker and her associates "were barred from wearing black armbands, but other students were allowed to wear political campaign buttons and the Iron Cross, a traditional symbol of Nazism.")

The significance of the decision was not only vindication for Charles James but also the clear extension of the *Tinker* ruling to teachers as well as students. In terms of their First Amendment rights, teachers, like students, are entitled to freedom of expression, provided it does not lead to "material and substantive disruption" of the work and discipline of the school.

When the school board asked the Supreme Court to review the case, it refused. The Court of Appeals decision stood.

The teacher's ordeal, however, was not yet over. A federal district judge ordered James reinstated in the high school, but school authorities made life very difficult for him, continually harassing him in the hope that he would finally explode and so justify his being dismissed once again.

There was also the question of back pay due the teacher. The school board had made no move to fulfill that obligation, and it looked as if James would have to go to court again. Meanwhile, though he had continued teaching and had been careful to obey all his superiors' directives, the school board nonetheless informed James in June 1973 that his appointment at Addison High School would not be renewed. What kind of victory had he actually won?

All the parties went back to court, and finally, in July 1974, a federal district judge awarded Charles James $27,000 in back pay and interest plus "reasonable" legal fees. Pending was another action by James against three school officials for illegally and intentionally depriving him of his First Amendment rights and also of his rights to due process of law. (When he was first fired for refusing to remove the black armband, James had received no notice of the charges against him, no chance to see the evidence against him and to present evidence of his own, no right to cross-examine witnesses or bring forward witnesses on his own behalf. Nor had he been given the right to be represented by a lawyer.)

In this suit against the three school officials, James was asking for a total of $225,000 in damages. Meanwhile, however, he had at least been awarded the $27,000 in back pay. But the board of education appealed that decision, James had still received nothing, and he had lost his job again.

Before arguments were heard in the Court of Appeals on the school board's move to overturn the back pay award, the board finally offered to settle all the cases and claims by paying James $55,000. There was no mention, however, of giving him back his job. Since James had decided not to return to the school anyway, he accepted the settlement.

At great cost, financial and emotional, to himself and his family, Charles James had finally established his right to express his conscience. "Maybe," his wife told Richard Harris when it was all over, "one student will see now, as a result of all this, that [a teacher] has a right to stand up for what he believes in." James himself added that, after all, he had worn the armband "only as a symbol of conscience. I didn't do it so I would lose my job, or to hurt my family, or to be a martyr. I did it because I had to live with myself."

If, said James, he had taken off his armband when ordered to, "I would have been without identity and self-respect. And if I hadn't fought on, I never would have felt free again."

If a teacher has the First Amendment right to bear silent witness to his convictions by wearing a black armband, does he also have the right to another kind of highly expressive silence—refusing to take part in the Pledge of Allegiance to the flag?

Just such a case came into the courts during the same period that Charles James was fighting for self-vindication. In 1970 Mrs. Clinton Hanover, an eighth-grade teacher in Connecticut, refused to lead her class in the Pledge. Instead, she arranged for a student to do it while she, head bowed, remained seated at her desk. Mrs. Hanover refused to lead the Pledge because, she said, the state of the country at the time made it impossible for her to say in conscience that "liberty and justice" did indeed exist for all. Particularly with regard to the black citizens of America.

A number of Mrs. Hanover's students thereupon decided that they too could not, in conscience, take part in the pledge to the flag. The teacher was fired.

Ordering Mrs. Hanover reinstated, a federal court declared: "There is no question but that Mrs. Hanover's refusal to recite or lead recitation of the pledge of allegiance is a form of expression protected by the First Amendment which may not be forbidden at the risk of losing her job. It does not matter that her expression took the form of silence." Although some students also refused to recite the Pledge, the teacher's expression of conscience, said the court, had not disrupted school activities nor interfered with the rights of other teachers or students.

The James and Hanover victories are among many signs that teachers' First Amendment rights are steadily being strengthened in the courts. There have been setbacks, but by and large it is becoming clearly recognized that teachers, along with students, are "persons under the Constitution." As such, teachers and students ought to be in a natural alliance in support of the indivisibility of First Amendment freedoms.

Indeed, the more deeply one explores the continually embattled history of free expression, the clearer it is that, as Aryeh Neier, formerly executive director of the American Civil Liberties Union, says, "The only social order in which freedom of speech is secure is the one in which it is secure for everyone."

With that in mind, let us begin the journey that led to the creation of the First Amendment.

From "Imagining the Death of the King" to the Birth of the First Amendment

"'By no means,' exclaimed Hamilton, in his clear, thrilling, silvery voice. 'It is not the bare printing and publishing of a paper that will make it a libel: the words themselves must be libelous, that is, false, scandalous, and seditious, else my client is not guilty.'" (Andrew Hamilton defending Zenger at his trial for seditious libel in 1735; nineteenth century wood engraving.) (The Granger Collection)

V

Whoever would overthrow the liberty of a nation must begin by subduing the freeness of speech.

In 1579 John Stubbs, a critic of certain royal policies, wrote a fierce attack on the proposed marriage between Queen Elizabeth and the Duke of Anjou. Agents of the queen ordered that all copies of the book be burned in the kitchen stove of Stationer's Hall. As for the author, his punishment for the crime of dissent was the loss of his right hand—a cleaver having been driven through his wrist by a mallet. The unfortunate Mr. Stubbs, mindful now of the painful hazards of free thought, raised his hat with his remaining hand and cried, "God save the Queen!"

Twenty-four years later, in London (as reported by Anne Lyon Haight in *Banned Books*), a printer was hanged, drawn, and quartered because of a book he had published opposing the succession of James I to the throne after the death of Queen Elizabeth. The printer having been terminated, the book itself was suppressed by Parliament, which decreed that "whosoever should be found to have it in their house should be guilty of high treason."

The suppression of books—and sometimes the extinction of their authors—by the state was rooted in a grim tradition, as Irving Brant details in *The Bill of Rights*. In fifteenth-century Britain, for example, it was treasonable and punishable by death not only to war on the king but also to call him a fool, to publish poems or ballads ridiculing him or his council, or even to imagine his death. Then, after the death of Henry VIII, halfway through the next century, it became an act of treason for anyone to say that the new king, Edward VI, was not entitled to be head of the Church of England. It was also an act of treason, of course, to express the *opinion* that the new king ought not to be king at all.

Such talk or writing was considered seditious speech (language inciting the people to rebellion against the authority of the state). These were the penalties for such speech after Henry VIII's death:

First offense: Jail and confiscation of the offender's property.

Second offense: Life imprisonment.

Third offense: Death.

In the time of Queen Elizabeth, who came to the throne in 1558, "it was made high treason," as Irving Brant points out, "to imagine bodily harm to the queen, or to call her a tyrant, usurper or heretic." An overt act of treason against the queen did not have to be proved. "Mere expression of an opinion was enough for conviction and death."

Printed seditious speech was considered the most dangerous of all because a pamphlet or book could keep on stirring up dissent as long as it circulated. Accordingly, soon after the introduction of the printing press in England in 1476 the Crown had moved to control the printed word. The basic method was by licensing both presses and books. What the Crown or its agents did not officially approve of could not legally be printed.

In 1538 the Star Chamber (a powerful court that sat in closed session and dealt with state security) explicitly forbade printers to put out any book in English without prior examination by the king's officials and without a license. Eighteen years later it was decreed that unlicensed books and presses would be searched out and destroyed. In 1558 a royal proclamation warned that those caught with books proclaimed to be "wicked and seditious . . . shall without delay be executed." (Also to be killed were those who found such books and did not burn them immediately—without showing them to anyone—so as to prevent the spread of seditious ideas.)

In order to tighten the screws of censorship, Queen Elizabeth and the lords of the Privy Council set up new regulations in 1585. Except for one press in Oxford and one in Cambridge, all printing was to be done in London, and nothing would be printed unless first approved by the Archbishop of Canterbury and the Bishop of London. As Irving Brant notes, "Book publishers violating the decree were to be punished by six months' imprisonment and banned from printing; their equipment to be destroyed." Authors caught violating the decree had to face trial for seditious libel or, if the work was religious, for heresy. They might also be charged with treason or with other crimes that could bring the death penalty. Writers often tried to flee or to hide behind a false name to avoid punishment. But one intent of the laws was to place so much pressure on the printer that he would become an informer and tell the authorities where to find the criminal author.

Of particular interest to American students of those chilling times is a 1663 case in which John Twyn, a printer, was tried for sedition because a book he had published maintained—as its most treasonous idea—that a king was accountable to the people. The three judges emphasized that printing so wicked a notion was indeed an overt act declaring the treason of "compassing and imagining" the king's death. Convicted and sentenced to death, Twyn was told by the prison chaplain that he might live if he disclosed the name of the book's author. Twyn refused: "Better one suffer, than many." And he was executed.

The licensing of publication ended in England in 1695. Prior censorship by the state was thereby ended, but the press could still be punished *after* publication, under the laws of seditious libel. Indeed, in the thirty years before the adoption in the United States of the First Amendment, some seventy prosecutions for seditious libel took place in England, most of them brought by whatever political party was in power. Of the seventy defendants, fifty were convicted.

A 1719 case demonstrates how pernicious, let alone lethal, the laws of seditious libel still were. As told by Donald Thomas in *A Long Time Burning: The History of Literary Censorship in England,* John Matthews, a nineteen-year-old printer, was arrested in London. Found in his pocket was a copy of a single-sheet pamphlet advocating the claim of James Francis Edward Stuart to the throne of England.

Matthews's rooms were searched and a few more copies of the pamphlet were found. Charged with treason, the young printer swore—and there was no evidence to the contrary—that he was unaware of the significance of the pamphlet and indeed could not remember what was in it. Nonetheless John Matthews was hanged.

In the New World, meanwhile, colonists concerned with freedom of speech and press were well aware of the English history of suppression. They also knew their own. The first public burning of a book in America, for instance, took place in 1650, when Thomas Pynchon's *The Meritorious Price of Our Redemption* was ignited in the marketplace of Boston by the common executioner. The author's religious ideas, declared the authorities, differed from the colony's established religion and so had to be obliterated.

Practically from the beginning, prosecutions for seditious libel had been taking place. As American constitutional historian Leonard Levy points out, "Each community, outside the few 'cities,' tended to be a tight little island clutching its own orthodoxy and willing to banish unwelcome dissidence or punish it."

With regard to the press, for example, the first newspaper in the colonies was officially suppressed after only one issue. Its publisher was Benjamin Harris, who had previously been arrested in London for printing a "seditious" pamphlet, imprisoned, and set in the pillory. One of the charges against Harris in that instance was that he had printed the pamphlet "without authority."

In Boston, on September 25, 1690, Harris introduced a newspaper, *Publick Occurrences Both Foreign and Domestic*. It would be a monthly, he announced, "or if any Glut of Occurrences happen, oftener."

Once again Benjamin Harris had printed without a license, a requirement imposed in 1662 on printing in Massachusetts. Enraged, the governor and his council closed down the paper. What had primarily infuriated them were some of the stories Harris had printed. One had been sharply critical of certain Indian allies of the English in the war against the French: the Indians had neglected to show up for an important attack. Another story accused the French king of having slept with his daughter-in-law; this report greatly upset the Puritan clergy, who did not believe that such lascivious tales should be set before the people of Boston. After *Publick Occurrences* was shut down, there was no new paper in Boston for ten years.

Another illustration of the often sizable obstacles to a free press in prerevolutionary America was the experience of James Franklin, a Boston printer-editor, who began to publish the *New England Courant* in August 1721. At first, although the paper was not "published by Authority," it was allowed to continue. But in June 1722 James Franklin was imprisoned because the government considered itself highly insulted by his criticism of its ineffective defense against pirates preying on shipping in the area.

While James Franklin remained behind bars for a month, the paper was put out by his younger brother Ben, who was sixteen and was later to be renowned far beyond the calling of journalism. While Ben Franklin did not directly attack the authorities for punishing freedom of discussion—not wishing to join his brother in jail— he pointedly published excerpts from the work of two London essayists who used the collective pseudonym Cato:

> Without freedom of thought, there can be no such thing as wisdom; and no such thing as public liberty without freedom of speech. . . . This sacred privilege is

so essential to free government that the security of property and the freedom of speech always go together; and in those wretched countries where a man cannot call his tongue his own, he can scarce call anything else his own. Whoever would overthrow the liberty of a nation must begin by subduing the freeness of speech.

After James Franklin was released from jail, he continued criticizing both political and religious officialdom. The General Court thereupon ordered that "James Franklin be strictly forbidden . . . to print or publish the New England Courant or any Pamphlet or paper of the like Nature, Except it be first Supervised, by the Secretary of the Province."

Actually, formal licensing laws were technically no longer in effect in the colonies, since the Crown had lost its power to license the press in England in 1695. But on occasion publishers in the colonies had continued to yield to official insistence that they get permission to print. Franklin, however, fought the royal governor's attempt to reinstitute licensing, and a grand jury refused to indict him for contempt of court for continuing to publish without permission. The authorities gave up.

James Franklin, therefore, became a significant figure in the history of a free press in America. By defying the royal governor and the General Court, Franklin established the principle that the government cannot censor *before* publication. And the grand jury, by allowing his defiance to succeed, affirmed the concept of an independent press responsible to its readers, not to government authority.

The most renowned and resounding battle over freedom of the press in prerevolutionary America was con-

63

ducted by John Peter Zenger in the city of New York in
1735. Zenger's *New York Weekly Journal* had been criticizing the haughty, willful royal governor, William
Cosby. In two particular issues of the paper Cosby and
his administration were attacked in a number of articles
for incompetence, favoritism, and inattention to the defense of the colony against the French. Most gravely, the
paper had charged the government with endangering the
rights and property of the people by, among other things,
tampering with trial by jury and rigging elections.

Acting on instructions from the governor, Chief Justice
James De Lancey urged the grand jury to indict Zenger
for the "seditious libels," which "with the utmost virul-
ency have endeavored to asperse his Excellency and vilify
his Administration" and "have gain'd some credit among
the common people."

After the grand jury had twice refused to indict Zenger
and the elected assembly had declined to bring charges
against him, the governor's council issued a warrant for
Zenger's arrest on the charge of "raising sedition."

The *New York Weekly Journal* missed one issue and
then reappeared with a notice from the jailed Zenger that
the paper would continue to be edited "thro' the Hole of
the Door of the Prison." Actually, Zenger's wife and
friends kept the paper alive for the nine months he was
behind bars, but Zenger's thrust of defiance entertained
the city and further infuriated the royal governor and his
courtiers.

At the trial John Peter Zenger was defended by one of
the most eminent lawyers in the colonies, Andrew Hamilton of Philadelphia. Nearly eighty, with white hair down
to his shoulders, Hamilton had journeyed to New York to
brave the authorities there because he considered the case

crucial to the future of liberty in this still new land—so crucial that Hamilton would accept no fee from Zenger.

The prosecutor—the attorney general—stated the traditional British rule of seditious libel. All that had to be proved was that Zenger had indeed published the "libels" (that is, the criticism of the royal governor and his administration). It would then be up to the court to decide whether that criticism was "*seditious* libel" (whether it tended to stir the people to rebellion). Zenger could not, said the attorney general, claim in his defense that what he had published was true. If the criticisms were found to be seditious, the prosecutor pointed out, "the law says their being true is an aggravation of the crime." (True attacks on the government would all the more lead people to distrust the government and incline them to commit acts of sedition. Therefore, if the libel were true, the damage to authority would be all the greater.)

Andrew Hamilton startled the court and the spectators by confessing for his client that Zenger *had* printed the particular two editions of the paper which brought about his indictment. "I cannot think it proper," said the elderly lawyer, "to deny the Publication of a Complaint which I think is the right of every free born subject to make." But the question of criminality, Hamilton went on, does not depend simply on the act of publishing. "The words themselves must libelous—that is, false, scandalous, and seditious, or else we are not guilty."

In his red robe and great wig, Chief Justice De Lancey, the governor's man, sharply instructed the defense attorney, "You cannot be admitted, Mr. Hamilton, to give the truth of a libel in evidence."

The Philadelphia lawyer bowed to the chief justice. "I thank your honor." Hamilton proceeded to ignore him, turning instead to the jury: "Then, gentlemen of the jury, it is to you we must now appeal [as] witnesses to the *truth of the facts* we have offered and are denied the liberty to prove. . . . You are citizens of New York [and the facts] are notoriously known to be true; and therefore in your justice lies our safety" (emphasis added).

"No, Mr. Hamilton," the chief justice interrupted. The jury, he instructed the lawyer for the defense, could decide *only* whether or not Zenger had published the criticisms. (Zenger had already admitted that much.) Now, the chief justice continued, it was up to the court to judge whether they were seditiously libelous—whether, true or false, Zenger's criticisms could lead to sedition.

Hamilton courteously disagreed again, claiming that the jury had "the right, beyond all dispute," to determine both the law and the fact. That is, both the *fact* as to whether Zenger published the material and the *law* as to whether what he had printed was actually seditious libel.

"As you see," Andrew Hamilton continued, speaking to the jury as if the judges were not even in the room, "I labor under the weight of many years, and am borne down with great infirmities of body; yet old and weak as I am, I should think it my duty, if required, to go to the utmost part of the land where my service could be of any use in assisting to quench the flame of prosecutions by the Government to deprive a People of the right of remonstrating (and complaining too), of the arbitrary attempts of men in power. Men who injure and oppress the people under their administration; provoke them to cry out and complain; and then make that very complaint the foundation for new oppressions and prosecutions."

The jury was clearly impressed by what the old man was saying, all the more so when Andrew Hamilton concluded: "The question before the court and you gentlemen of the jury is not of small nor private concern. It is not the cause of the poor printer, nor of New York alone, which you are now trying. No! It may in its consequence affect every freeman that lives under a British government on the main of America. It is the best cause. It is the cause of Liberty."

The jury assumed the powers Hamilton said it had and found John Peter Zenger not guilty. "Upon which," wrote a chronicler of the time, "there were three huzzas in the Hall, which was crowded with people." Chief Justice De Lancey could have set aside the verdict but decided not to further arouse public opinion.

Though a most popular victory, the outcome of the Zenger case had no immediate effect on libel law in the colonies. It was not until after the Revolution that a state, Pennsylvania, accepted the principles of truth as a defense and the jury's right to decide both the law and the fact. Pennsylvania put those principles into its 1790 constitution. New York followed fifteen years later.

Yet in the minds of the people the principles of Andrew Hamilton's defense were established as essential goals. That is, truth was to be a defense against charges of seditious libel, and the jury was to have the right to decide whether the publication at issue met the test of seditious libel.

The key psychological significance of the Zenger victory was its proclamation that the press had the right to criticize public officials, even if that criticism made the people distrustful of the government. All in all, the impact of Zenger's acquittal was such that Gouverneur Morris, a leading figure in the American Revolution, once said that American liberty dated back to the persecution of John Peter Zenger, because that event so embodied the philosophy that freedom, both of thought and speech, was an inborn human right.

In England too, where a stenographic record of the Zenger trial was printed, its editor noted that the trial and its outcome had "made a great noise in the world."

VI

The censorial power is in the people over the Government, and not in the Government over the people.

While it had been the royal governor of New York who tried to punish John Peter Zenger for engaging in free speech, the weapon of seditious libel was more often used in the colonies by the popularly elected assemblies. As a historian of the period, Mary Patterson Clark, has noted, "Literally scores of persons, probably hundreds, throughout the colonies were tracked down by the various messengers and sergeants [of the assemblies] and brought into the house to make inglorious submission for words spoken in the heat of anger or for writing which intentionally or otherwise had given offense." Those who did not submit were subjected to criminal penalties.

Given this intolerance of criticism among the people's representatives in colonial assemblies, it is not entirely surprising to find hostility to certain dissenters among the people themselves. In a cartoon printed shortly before the American Revolution, a troupe of patriots are tarring and feathering a Tory printer under the banner "In Liberty's Cause." As a Massachusetts judge said of some of the patriots during the 1760s, "They are contending for an unlimited Freedom of Thought and Action which they would confine wholly to themselves."

On the other hand, there was a lively countertradition that held freedom of thought and of the press to be fundamental rights. In 1734, for instance, Andrew Bradford, founder of *The American Weekly Mercury,* Pennsylvania's first newspaper, defined "freedom of the press" as meaning "a liberty of detecting the wicked and destructive measure of certain politicians, of dragging villainy out of its obscure lurking holes and exposing it in its full deformity to open day; of attacking wickedness in high places, of disentangling the intricate folds of a wicked and corrupt administration, and pleading freely for a redress of grievances. . . . As therefore you love your liberties, my dear countrymen, support and defend the liberty of the press."

In 1776 George Mason, on framing Virginia's Declaration of Rights—from which Thomas Jefferson drew in drafting the Declaration of Independence—inserted a clause maintaining that "freedom of the press is one of the great bulwarks of liberty and can never be restrained but by despotic governments."

Four years later, in a draft of the Massachusetts Declaration of Rights, John Adams too emphasized: "The liberty of the press is essential to the security of freedom in a state; it ought not, therefore, to be restrained in this commonwealth."

Yet there was no explicit protection of free speech and a free press in the United States Constitution that was approved by the Constitutional Convention in 1787 and ratified by the states in 1788.

Such language was not needed, insisted Alexander Hamilton. Writing in the *Federalist Papers,* Hamilton said there was no way to secure such a concept as freedom of the press by *words*. "Whatever fine declarations may be inserted in any constitution respecting it," Hamilton insisted, the protection of free speech and a free press, like all our rights, "must altogether depend on public opinion, and on the general spirit of the people and of the government." If the people want these freedoms, it will have them.

Others, however, aware of the vulnerability of dissent in England and the colonies, strenuously urged that these protections be spelled out. James Madison, in a letter to Thomas Jefferson, pointed out that those rights which were *solely* dependent on majority public opinion could be snuffed out whenever that opinion changed.

"In Virginia," Madison wrote, "I have seen the [state] bill of rights violated in every instance where it has been opposed to a popular current. . . . Wherever the real power in a Government lies, there is the danger of oppression. *In our Government, the real power lies in the majority of the Community,* and the invasion of private rights is chiefly to be apprehended not from acts of Government contrary to the sense of its constituents but *from acts in which the Government is the mere instrument of the major number of the Constituents*" (emphasis added).

In sum, when it comes to the rights and liberties of *individual* dissenters, a democratic majority can be as represssive as a king.

Indeed, James Madison himself, one of the preeminent civil libertarians of the early years of this nation, had not always favored the right to free expression of unpopular minority views. Historian Richard Morris writes that "so far as freedom of the press was concerned," the Madison of the revolutionary years "only wished that he could get his hands on New York's notorious Tory printer, James Rivington, 'for 24 hours in this place.' Here in Virginia he could be sure of being adequately punished [Madison felt], unlike New York, where Tories were permitted to 'insult the whole Colony and Continent with impunity.' "

Madison came to believe, however, that with regard to freedom of the press and of religion "it is proper that *every* Government should be disarmed of powers which trench upon those particular rights" (emphasis added). He pressed for the addition of a bill of rights to the Constitution—including what was to become the First Amendment.

He was not alone. When the Constitution was sent out to the states to be considered for ratification, protests of varying degrees were heard in all thirteen of them about the absence of a bill of rights. Some of the complainants, to be sure, hoped only that the controversy would lead to the defeat of the Constitution, which they themselves objected to on other grounds. (Fear, for instance, that the individual states would be surrendering too much sovereignty, fear that lands would be heavily taxed by a central government, fear that Northern shipowners would secure a monopoly of Southern agricultural exports, and fear that property rights in slaves would be threatened.)

On the other hand, among those opposing a bill of rights were supporters of the Constitution who were convinced there was no need for these amendments because the individual states had already adopted declarations of rights. Madison disagreed. Some states, he pointed out, "have no bills of rights, there are others provided with very defective ones, and there are others whose bills of rights are not only defective, but absolutely improper."

Yet another argument against a bill of rights was

that nowhere in the newly adopted Constitution had any authority been given the federal government to suppress speech or to violate any other basic rights. As Alexander Hamilton put it, "Why declare that things shall not be done which there is no power [in Congress] to do? Why, for instance, should it be said that the liberty of the press shall not be restrained when no power is given by which restrictions may be imposed?"

Natural rights, inherent rights, said these objectors to Madison's proposal, were beyond the scope of the national government. That's why the Constitution gives the national government no power to interfere with them. Some opponents of Madison and his allies became almost contemptuous in their arguments. You might as well, said one member of the new Congress, write into the Constitution that a man has the right to go to bed when he feels like it and to wear his hat when he feels like it.

Similarly, Noah Webster observed that if it really was necessary to write into the Constitution such obvious inherent rights as freedom of speech, one might as well also include a provision "that everybody shall, in good weather, hunt on his own land, and catch fish in rivers that are public property . . . and that Congress shall never restrain any inhabitant of America from eating and drinking, at seasonable times, or prevent his lying on his left side in a long winter's night, or even on his back, when he is fatigued by lying on his right."

Madison was not particularly amused, pointedly reminding his newly independent fellow citizens that "the freedom of the press and rights of conscience, those choicest privileges of the people, are unguarded in the British constitution." And, as we have seen, those unguarded "privileges" were regularly abused for centuries.

73

("For hundreds of years," as Irving Brant has put it, "Englishmen had been fined, whipped, pilloried, imprisoned, and had their ears cut off for speech and writings offensive to government or society.")

So it *is* essential, Madison persisted, to add these protections to the Constitution so that "the great rights," such as freedom of speech and freedom of the press, can be placed beyond the reach of any branch of government. In addition, these "great rights" must be protected, when need be, against shifting popular tides. In this new America, Madison reemphasized, the greatest danger to liberty is to be found "in the body of the people, operating by the majority against the minority."

The minority, even of one, must have its liberty protected.

Madison prevailed. The Bill of Rights was adopted by the First Congress in 1789, then ratified by the states, and on December 15, 1791, became the first ten amendments to the Constitution.

One amendment, which Madison had considered "the most valuable in the whole list," was not ratified. It was the proposal that "no *state* shall violate the equal rights of conscience, or of the freedom of the press . . . because it is proper that *every* Government should be disarmed of powers which trench upon those particular rights" (emphasis added). That is, not only shall the federal Congress make no law abridging the freedom of the press, but none of the individual states shall make such a law.

"I cannot see any reason," Madison said, "against obtaining even a double security on these points. . . . It must be admitted on all hands that the State Governments are as liable to attack these invaluable privileges as the General Government is, and therefore ought to be as cautiously guarded against."

A majority of the House, after adding a clause concerning free speech as well as a free press, approved this Madison amendment. In the Senate, however, it failed to get a two-thirds majority, its opponents having claimed that the Constitution already included too many limitations on the powers of the individual states. (It was not until 1925 that the Supreme Court barred the individual states in the union from violating the provisions of the Bill of Rights, including the First Amendment.)

There was yet another vital element lacking in the First Amendment as adopted in 1791. When Virginia ratified the Constitution, it proposed additional language that would have protected First Amendment rights absolutely. The declaration said that "the liberty of Conscience and of the press cannot be cancelled, abridged, restrained, or modified *by any authority of the United States*" (emphasis added). Not only the Congress but the executive and judiciary as well would be forbidden from limiting any of the guarantees in the First Amendment. When the First Amendment was adopted, however, that clause was not present. And so, from time to time, freedom of the press in the United States has indeed been constricted by the courts. And, during the Civil War, by a president.

Nonetheless, the First Amendment, as finally added to the Constitution, at first appeared strong enough to support James Madison's declaration in 1794 that in this new American democracy, "we shall find that the censorial power is in the people over the Government and not in the Government over the people."

The First Amendment was not absolute, to be sure. It did not prevent the individual states from tampering with freedom of speech and freedom of the press. But at least so far at the powers of Congress were concerned, surely such prerevolutionary dangers to free thought as laws of seditious libel were done with for good. Yet, only seven years after the ratification of the First Amendment, it was to be sorely tested by just such laws.

The Hard, Early Times of the First Amendment: From the Alien and Sedition Acts of 1798 to the "Red Scare" of the First World War

A Wobbly "free speech" campaign in San Diego runs into ferocious opposition. (*Industrial Worker*, May 9, 1912)

VII

Downfall to the Tyrants of America!

In 1798 Congress, dominated by the Federalist party, enacted the Alien and Sedition Acts, making political dissent against government policy as dangerous as if there were no First Amendment in the new republic.

The Federalists believed that the nation should be directed by an elite, people of marked talent and wealth. Their opposition, the Democratic-Republicans (of whom Thomas Jefferson was a leader), were both suspicious of centralized authority and insistent that government must be responsive to the people at large. The Republicans also saw America as a sanctuary for the oppressed and a symbol to the world of the self-governing liberty of free men.

When France declared war on Great Britain in 1793, the Republicans tended to favor the French while Federalist sympathies were with the British. As time went on, relations between the American and French governments steadily deteriorated, and war between France and the new nation seemed imminent. Adding to the rising tension at home were rumors of French espionage and of French plots against the republic, along with great outrage over French attacks on American shipping.

With fear and anger in the land, the Federalists saw a chance to beat down their Republican opposition, including the aggressive Republican press that was continually attacking the Federalist government. Federalist Alexander Hamilton warned that many of the Republicans so fiercely opposed to the anti-French policy of President John Adams would ultimately be regarded by the people as similar to "the Tories of our Revolution." And, in 1798, the Federalists pushed the Alien and Sedition Acts through Congress.

Three of the laws were mainly directed against French and Irish immigrants, most of them Republicans. The government was empowered to arrest and deport any foreigner judged "dangerous" to the nation's peace and safety or suspected of "secret machinations." Although these provisions dealing with aliens were not enforced, many aliens, in acute apprehension, either went into hiding or fled the country.

The statute dealing with seditious speech *was* enforced, mostly against the Democratic-Republican citizens of the new nation. This act punished, by fine and imprisonment, anyone who uttered, wrote, or published "any false scandalous and malicious [speech] against the government of the United States," including the President and the Congress. It was now seditious to use speech that would bring the President or Congress "into contempt or disrepute" or that might excite against them "the hatred of the good people of the United States," thereby stirring up "sedition within the United States."

If convicted of exercising this kind of speech—which had presumably been protected by the First Amendment

—the miscreant could be fined up to two thousand dollars and could be imprisoned for up to two years. As one legacy of the John Peter Zenger case, however, the Sedition Act did specify the right of the accused to plead the truth of what he had said or written as a defense against the charge of seditious libel. Moreover, the jury would have the right to determine both the law and the facts of the case.

On the passage of the Sedition Act, the Republican press was understandably outraged. The *Boston Independent Chronicle*, for instance, sternly reminded its readers that in a free country it remained the *duty* of citizens to speak their minds, "and may the hand be palsied that shrinks back from its duties." The very day President John Adams signed the bill, the Philadelphia *Aurora*—the nation's leading Republican journal, edited by Benjamin Franklin Bache, grandson of Benjamin Franklin—ran this "Advertisement Extraordinary!!!":

> *Orator Mum* takes the very orderly method of announcing to his fellow citizens that a thinking Club will be established in a few days at the sign of the *Muzzle* in *Gag* street. The first subject for cogitation will be:
> "Ought a Free People to obey the laws which violate the constitution they have sworn to support?"
> N.B. No member will be permitted to think longer than fifteen minutes.

The wit was defiant, but those enforcing the Sedition Act were sufficiently impervious to such wit to have brought about at least twenty-five arrests, fifteen indictments, and ten convictions within the two years it was in force.

To give a sense of the vengeful spirit of that period,

there is the case of the Sedition Act's first victim, Congressman Matthew Lyon of Vermont. Born in Ireland, Lyon had come to America as an indentured servant, earned his freedom, and fought in the Revolution. Having prospered in the state of Vermont, he had published a newspaper, among his other enterprises there, from 1773 to 1775.

Among the charges leveled against Lyon under the Sedition Act was a letter he had writted to the *Vermont Journal* in Windsor in answer to a vehement attack on him by that Federalist paper. In the letter Lyon said that John Adams's administration had entirely forgotten the public welfare "in an unbounded thirst for ridiculous pomp, foolish adulation, and selfish avarice." Another alleged crime was Lyon's having quoted, during a reelection campaign, from a letter by American poet John Barlow, then in France. Barlow had wondered that Congress, in response to a "bullying speech" by President Adams, had not given "an order to send him to a mad house."

On these charges of malicious sedition, Lyon was tried, fined, and jailed. On hearing the news, Thomas Jefferson, in Virginia, wrote, "I know not which mortifies me most, that I should fear to write what I think or that my country bear such a state of things. Yet Lyon's judges . . . are objects of national fear."

In October 1798, seven years after the First Amendment's addition to the Constitution, Matthew Lyon, in punishment for expressing his ideas, was paraded through the town of Vergennes, Vermont, on his way to a twelve-by-sixteen cell, "the common receptacle for horse-thieves, money-makers, runaway-negroes, or any kind of felons." As described by historian James Morton Smith, the cell contained "an indoor toilet in one corner of the room [which] perfumed the air with a stockyardlike aroma. Light and air came through a small window, which was crossed by nine iron bars. The cell had neither fireplace nor stove." There the Revolutionary patriot remained until the following February, when a group of his constituents raised the money to pay Lyon's fine. (He had been reelected to Congress while in jail.)

Republicans throughout the new nation toasted his release, and at a Liberty Tree celebration in Bridgehampton, New York, tribute was paid to "Colonel Matthew Lyon, the martyr to the cause of Liberty and the Rights of Man: may his suffering bring good out of evil by arousing the people to guard their rights and oppose every unconstitutional measure."

Among others imprisoned under the Sedition Act were the editors of four of the five most important Republican newspapers in the country. There were less influential targets as well. A town drunk, for instance, who was on hand when President Adams came through to the accompaniment of a sixteen-gun salute, said, "I do not care if they fired through his ass." He was found guilty of contempt of the President under the Sedition Act.

The prosecution that resulted in the longest prison sentence under the act took place in Dedham, Massachusetts, where a number of people had set up a Liberty Pole to which they attached a sign reading "No Stamp Act, No Sedition, No Alien Bills, No Land Tax; downfall to the Tyrants of America."

Outraged over this "outbreak of sedition" (as one Federalist paper called it), the authorities arrested and indicted two of those responsible for this criminal act of free expression. One expressed deep repentance. The spirit of the other, however, would not be broken. Nor would he name his associates in this seditious enterprise because, he told the judge, if he did so, "I would lose all my friends." Accordingly, the culprit, a veteran of the Revolutionary Army and a common laborer with little formal schooling, was convicted of having created a "rallying point of insurrection and civil war." He languished in jail for two years.

Many Republican politicians and journalists defied the Sedition Act, and popular opinion was so shocked by it that the presidential victory of Thomas Jefferson in 1800 was due in considerable part to the citizenry's abhorrence of this Federalist legislation. The Sedition Act expired on March 3, 1801; Jefferson pardoned everyone who had been convicted under it. In time Congress also repaid most of the fines.

No case under the Sedition Act ever reached the Supreme Court, but ominously, the constitutionality of the act *was* sustained by lower federal courts, including three Supreme Court Justices riding circuit (hearing cases, individually, away from Washington). Indeed, it was not until 1964 that the Supreme Court, in effect, struck down that anti–First Amendment legislation, declaring:

> Although the Sedition Act was never tested in this Court, the attack upon its validity has carried the day in the court of history. . . . [There has been] a broad consensus that the Act, because of the restraint it imposed upon criticism of government and public officials, was inconsistent with the First Amendment.

Jefferson and Madison, of course, had immediately come to that conclusion when the Alien and Sedition Acts were passed. Jefferson called them an unconstitutional "reign of terror," and Madison charged that Congress's promulgation of the Alien and Sedition Acts "ought to produce universal alarm because it is levelled against the right of freely examining public characters and measures, and of free communication among the people thereon, which has ever been justly deemed *the only effectual guardian of every other right*" (emphasis added).

To insure that there could be no possible doubt as to what the framers of the Constitution and the Bill of Rights had intended, Madison asked the fundamental question: "Is then the federal government destitute of every authority for restraining the licentiousness of the press, and for shielding itself against the libellous attacks which may be made on those who administer it?"

The clear answer is in the First Amendment. Said Madison, "The answer must be that the federal government is destitute of all such authority." The censorial power is in the people over the government, not in the government over the people. Accordingly, the Alien and Sedition Acts profoundly violate the Constitution.

VIII

The very act of retreating will embolden the mob to follow me wherever I go.

Although Thomas Jefferson vehemently opposed the Alien and Sedition Acts, even this paladin of free thought was not an absolutist on the matter of freedom of the press. In *Jefferson and Civil Liberties: The Darker Side*, Leonard Levy, while noting that "repression was certainly not congenial to Jefferson's temperament or ideals," adds that in 1803 President Jefferson wrote "an entirely confidential letter" to Governor Thomas McKean of Pennsylvania about punishing the press.

Furious at the attacks on him and his government by Federalist newspapers ("Tory presses" he called them), Jefferson accused these journals of such licentiousness, lying, and prostitution as to deprive them "of all credit." He went on to remind the governor that while the First Amendment prevented the federal government from moving against the press, the individual states still had that power.

"I have therefore long thought," Jefferson continued, "that a few prosecutions of the most prominent offenders would have a wholesome effect in restoring the integrity of the presses. Not a general prosecution, for that would look like persecution; but a selected one. The paper I now inclose appears to me to offer as good an instance in every respect to make an example of, as can be selected. . . . If the same thing be done in some other of the states it will place the whole band more on their guard."

For much of the rest of his life Jefferson was quite ambivalent about the press, saying in an 1819 letter that he had come to the point of reading only one newspaper, the *Richmond Enquirer*, "and in that chiefly the advertisements for they contain the only truths to be relied on in a newspaper."

Nonetheless, in 1823, three years before his death, Jefferson told a French correspondent that freedom of the press was a basic American principle, essential to public and personal liberty. "This formidable censor of the public functionaries," Jefferson said, "by arraigning them at the tribunal of public opinion, produces reform peaceably, which must otherwise be done by revolution."

Even Jefferson, when he felt kindly toward the press, did not go so far as such libertarian Republicans as George Hay, a fellow Virginian who later became a federal judge. Hay claimed that freedom of the press was like chastity, in that it was either "absolute" or did not exist. The press was to be free not only from prior restraint [censorship by government] but also from punishment for anything it published. That is, there was to be no punishment *after* publication. As Hay said, "If the words 'freedom of the press' have any meaning at all, they mean a total exemption from any law making any publication whatever criminal."

George Hay and other early Americans who believed as he did helped create the absolutist theory of the First

Amendment. This concept has never carried a majority of the Supreme Court or a majority of the country, but it remains a challenge to the logic of those who claim that the state has power under the Constitution to punish certain kinds of expression.

"To Hay," Leonard Levy notes, "the concept of a *verbal* political crime was abhorrent. He explicitly favored complete freedom of all political expression, including licentiousness, falsehood, and error, even if maliciously motivated and harmful. And he meant freedom from all state as well as federal laws" (emphasis added).

In the twentieth century, Supreme Court Justice Hugo Black advocated complete freedom for all expression (not only political speech) in the conviction that "it is time enough for government to step in to regulate people when they *do* something, not when they *say* something, and I do not believe myself that there is *any* halfway ground if you enforce the protections of the First Amendment."

Yet the history of free speech in the United States abounds in halfway grounds because the absolutist position has always been held only by a minority. For instance, while it is true that Congress passed no more sedition acts between 1800 and 1917, threats to freedom of the press continued throughout the nineteenth century. They came from individual state legislatures and also from nongovernmental sources—mobs and murderously incensed individuals.

During the 1812–14 war with England, for example, when a Baltimore newspaper, the *Federal Republican*, came out strongly against the declaration of war, an angry mob destroyed the presses and tore down the very building in which the newspaper was housed.

In addition to the occasional possibility of violent dissent by mobs, newspaper editors (particularly in the South and in the West) sometimes had to deal with readers bent on challenging them to a duel for what they had printed. One such editor, Joseph Street of the *Western World* (Frankfort, Kentucky), received so many urgent invitations to duels that he listed them regularly in his paper. Street actually fought only one duel but eventually was seriously wounded in an attempted assassination. His paper finally went under, not because of dueling threats but as the result of a number of libel verdicts that went against it.

Despite the not-so-distant oppressive experience of the Alien and Sedition Acts and despite the regeneration of the First Amendment by those who had courageously opposed those acts, many nineteenth-century Americans continued to reject the essence of that amendment, as once distilled by Supreme Court Justice Oliver Wendell Holmes: "If there is any principle of the Constitution that more imperatively calls for attachment than any other, it is the principle of free thought—not free only for those who agree with us, but freedom for the thought we hate."

In the white South, before the Civil War, the most hateful of all possible ideas was the abolition of slavery. In *Fettered Freedom: Civil Liberties and the Slavery Controversy, 1830–1860*, Russell Nye points out that "with the exception of Kentucky, every Southern state eventually passed laws controlling and limiting speech, press, and discussion." An 1849 Virginia Code, for example, mandated imprisonment of up to a year and a fine of up to five hundred dollars for anyone who "by speaking or writing maintains that owners have no right of property in slaves." In Louisiana anyone caught indulging in conversation having "a tendency to promote discontent among free colored people, or insubordination among slaves" was liable to a sentence ranging from twenty-one years at hard labor to death.

It should be noted, Russell Nye adds, that "though these statutes served to hamper free expression of antislavery opinion in the South, they did not fully suppress it. Most of the laws dealt out punishment for ' incendiary' talk, of 'opinions tending to incite insurrection'—terms vaguely defined and charges difficult to establish—a fact recognized by Southern courts, whose verdicts were usually lenient." Nonetheless, the laws did cast a pall on "the freedom of speech" supposedly guaranteed in the Constitution as well as on freedom of the press.

Thickening that pall, many Southern postmasters, defying federal law but backed by *local* laws permitting censorship of "incendiary" material in the mails, suppressed the circulation of abolitionist literature in their sections of the South. And of course it was exceedingly difficult in the South for homegrown opponents of slavery to gain access to the press. Academic freedom was also gravely curtailed. At most Southern educational institutions a faculty member speaking out against slavery had a better than excellent chance of losing his job.

Often during this period the most effective enemy of free expression was what had been known on the frontier as "lynch law." That is, mob law. In response, for instance, to his abolitionist writings, a Boston mob dragged William Lloyd Garrison half-naked through the streets in 1835. His publication, *The Liberator*, nonetheless remained the most effective of all the antislavery papers, and Garrison, undaunted by mobs, kept it alive. Equally courageous but ultimately destroyed was the Reverend

Elijah Lovejoy, whose paper, *The Observer*, functioned as an antislavery religious journal in Alton, Illinois.

Three times in one year Lovejoy's press was torn apart and thrown into the river by mobs. When a group of Alton's citizens passed a resolution instructing Lovejoy that the First Amendment guarantee of free expression did not apply to an editor who was endangering the peace of the community, Lovejoy replied that no public resolution could tell an editor what to do. When a meeting of the town's most prominent citizens—"the wise and the good" of Alton, as a contemporary observer described them—rejected Lovejoy's argument that he had a constitutional right to publish his newspaper, he said:

> I do not admit that it is the business of this assembly to decide whether I shall or shall not publish a newspaper in this city. . . . I know I am but one and you are many. My strength would avail but little against you all. You can crush me if you will; but I shall die at my post, for I cannot and will not forsake it. . . . The very act of retreating will embolden the mob to follow me wherever I go. . . .
>
> And now you come together for the purpose of driving out a confessedly innocent man, for no cause but that he dares to think and speak as his conscience and his God dictate. . . . Pause, I beseech you, and reflect. The present excitement will soon be over; the voice of conscience will at last be heard. And in some season of honest thought, even in this world, as you review the scenes of this hour, you will be compelled to say, "He was right; he was right!"
>
> I am hunted as a partridge upon the mountains. I am pursued as a felon through your streets; and to the guardian power of the law I look in vain for that protec-

tion against violence which even the vilest criminal may claim. . . .

I dare not flee away from Alton. . . . The contest has commenced here; and here it must be finished. Before God and you all, I here pledge myself to continue it, if need be, till death. If I fall, my grave shall be made in Alton.

And so it was. On November 7, 1873, when Elijah Lovejoy brought to town his fourth press, which he vowed to defend by force, yet another mob attacked, and Lovejoy was shot to death.

Many other abolitionist editors, printers, and speakers learned the fragility of freedom of speech and press in the baleful face of mobs bearing guns, whips, clubs, and firebrands.

IX

A clear, flagrant, and gigantic case of Rebellion.

It was the government, in addition to mobs, that threatened freedom of expression during the Civil War. At the start of the war President Lincoln closed the mails to "treasonable correspondence" and also suspended the writ of habeas corpus. (This is the right of anyone imprisoned to obtain a court order requiring him to be taken before a judge who will decide whether he is legally being held in custody.)

By doing away with the writ of habeas corpus Lincoln was able to order the arrest, by special civil as well as military agencies, of people suspected of being involved (or about to be involved) in disloyal and treasonable practices. They were confined in military prisons without charges, without trial, and with no fixed date for their release. It is estimated that some thirty-eight thousand of these executive arrests were made before the war ended. There is no telling, of course, how many of Lincoln's critics, aware of other dissenters being suppressed, censored themselves to avoid prison.

Much criticism of the President, however, remained

free and virulent, and among its sources were certain newspapers. Lincoln, mindful of the First Amendment, was hesitant to act against that part of the press he believed to be actively and dangerously aiding the Confederate rebellion but, reluctantly, he did order some newspapers closed and some editors jailed. As Lincoln wrote to Erastus Corning, a New York political leader, "Must I shoot a simple-minded soldier boy who deserts, while I must not touch a hair of a wily agitator who induced him to desert?"

Other newspapers were shut down by Northern military commanders, and the postmaster general barred a number of papers from the mails. Meanwhile, mobs were attacking editors or burning print shops, or both. On occasion, Union soldiers were among the mobs marching on the "seditious" press.

The Supreme Court did not rule as a body on Lincoln's restrictions of constitutional liberties—habeas corpus and the First Amendment—until 1866, the year after Lincoln's death. Chief Justice Roger B. Taney, however, sitting in circuit court in Baltimore, did hold in 1861 that the President had no authority to suspend the writ of habeas corpus. His opinion was ignored by Lincoln and the military, and in 1863 Congress ratified the suspension of habeas corpus.

In the 1866 case, *Ex parte Milligan*, when the High Court finally did address the constitutionality of Lincoln's suspension of habeas corpus, a majority decided that it cannot be suspended so long as the nation's courts are open and functioning. "Martial law," said the Court, "cannot result for a *threatened* invasion. The necessity must be actual and present; the invasion real, such as effectually closes the courts and deposes the civil administration."

At issue—and this debate has occurred during a number of periods of American history—is whether government can justify limiting freedom of expression in a time of danger to its very survival. Lincoln claimed that he had to jail those suspected of treason without offering them habeas corpus and that he had to shut down certain newspapers in the face of a "clear, flagrant, and gigantic case of Rebellion." As a twentieth-century Supreme Court Justice, Arthur Goldberg, has put it in another context, "While the Constitution protects against the invasion of individual rights, it is not a suicide pact."

There were those, Lincoln pointed out, whose use of free expression was actually causing desertions from the Union Army. Should they be allowed to continue, unpunished, in these acts of disloyalty that might well destroy the government and the Constitution that is its foundation? In defending his suspension of the writ of habeas corpus, Lincoln argued that he had to violate this one law in order to prevent the overthrow of all the laws. ("Are all the laws but one to go unexecuted, and the government itself go to pieces, lest that one [law] be violated?")

When, however reluctantly, he moved—or had others move—against the press, Lincoln was operating on the same survival principle. Consider E. N. Fuller, editor of the *Newark Evening Journal*. In 1864 he was arrested, prosecuted, and fined on charges of inciting to insurrection and discouraging enlistments in the army. This case, as Robert S. Harper notes in *Lincoln and the Press*, "was singular in that the action was civil, not military. In many other cases of a similar nature, the editors had been arrested and taken off to a Federal prison on orders from Washington."

Fuller was fined rather than imprisoned, but the fundamental issue is that he was punished for exercising his First Amendment rights. This, in part, was Fuller's offending editorial:

> It will be seen that Mr. Lincoln has called for another half million of men. Those who wish to be butchered will please step forward. All others will please stay home and defy old Abe and his minions to drag them from their families. We hope that the people of New Jersey will at once put their feet down and insist that not a man shall be forced out of the state to engage in the Abolition butchery, and swear to die at their own doors rather than march one step to fulfill the dictates of the mad, revolutionary fanaticism which has destroyed the best government the world ever saw, and now would butcher its remaining inhabitants to carry out a more fanatical sentiment. This has gone far enough and must be stopped. Let the people rise as one man and demand that this wholesale murder shall cease.

Most newspapers that agreed with E. N. Fuller were afraid to reprint his editorial for fear of also being indicted. One paper, the Somerville, New Jersey, *Messenger*, did run the editorial, and its editor, O. C. Cone, was arrested, convicted, and fined.

E. N. Fuller, it should be noted, was not intimidated by having been prosecuted and convicted. He wrote later that year, in another editorial:

> We have no honeyed words for such a ruler as Abraham Lincoln who, if we read, is a perjured traitor, who

has betrayed his country and caused the butchery of hundreds of thousands of the people of the United States in order to accomplish either his own selfish purpose, or to put in force a fanatical, impractical idea.

Although there is no evidence that Fuller was punished for *that* broadside, it was because of his previous conviction—and the fining and jailing of other editors—that some other newspapers were eventually frightened into self-censorship. The First Amendment, as a number of jurists have emphasized, is not only for the brave. It was meant to create and sustain a climate in which all citizens would be free to comment, however critically, about their government. For all that some of the press was let alone during the Civil War, the overall climate during those years was not such as to nourish the First Amendment.

Yet, in a time such as the Civil War—and later, during World Wars I and II and the American involvement in Vietnam—is there not a serious danger that an unbridled First Amendment may indeed help turn the Constitution into a "suicide pact"? Is not the maintenance of national security more vital than keeping the First Amendment intact when the nation is imperiled? This question in various forms has continued to enmesh legislators, judges, journalists, presidents, and other citizens. The First Amendment says Congress shall make *no law* limiting freedom of speech or of the press. Yet this guarantee has been broken, from time to time, in the name of national security.

X

They're jailing men and women for speaking on the street.

From the Civil War to the First World War, freedom of expression became downright dangerous for certain groups of Americans. After 1877, when federal troops were withdrawn from the South, blacks in that region had practically no right of expression at all. They may no longer have been slaves, but they surely were not free American citizens.

Back in 1787, during the Constitutional Convention, George Mason of Virginia, one of the delegates most sensitive to individual liberties, had denounced "this infernal traffic" of slavery and then warned that "by an inevitable chain of causes and effects, providence punishes national sins by national calamities." The national sin of racism, including but not limited to slavery, did indeed lead to a "national calamity," the Civil War. But racism was hardly ended, and blacks continued to be suppressed.

Meanwhile, in the decades preceding the First World War, others were excluded from the protection of the Bill of Rights. Not as continuously and as wholly as Southern blacks, but sometimes just as devastatingly. This was a period during which such "outsiders" as aliens, immigrants, workers trying to organize into unions, and political radicals served as primary targets for those, in and out of government, who were engaging in the grand old American hunt for "un-Americans."

In one particular event, the fatal explosion of a bomb at Chicago's Haymarket Square in 1886, the worst popular stereotypes of these "outsiders" converged.

On May 3, 1886, a mass meeting of workers striking against the McCormick Harvest Company was held near the plant. It had been a peaceful gathering until a group of nonunion strikebreakers came out of the factory and were attacked by those whose jobs they had taken. Police shot into the melee and killed two union members.

In protest, some anarchists (people who believe that all forms of government should be abolished) called a rally the next night at Haymarket Square to support the strikers. At first there had been no violence; nonetheless, a police captain ordered a squadron of 176 men to break up the demonstration. As the detachment moved toward the speaker's stand, a bomb exploded, killing a sergeant and causing injuries to more than sixty men. An exchange of gunfire followed. This time ten workers and seven policemen were killed and more than fifty from both sides were injured.

No one ever discovered who threw the bomb. As Leon Friedman writes in *The Wise Minority*, "It could have been an agent provocateur, a citizen with a nonlabor grievance against the police, or a madman. However, the police and the public assumed immediately that the anarchists, and therefore the labor movement, were to blame."

The police raided the homes and gathering places of

radicals, having been instructed by the state's attorney: "Make the raids and look up the law afterward."

Eight anarchists were tried for murder. Five had not even been in Haymarket Square the night of the explosion. The government argued, however, that these anarchists had, after all, *advocated* violence against the police, including the use of bombs. That advocacy alone —even though it was speech and not an overt act—was sufficient for them to be held responsible for the murders. Even though the actual bomb-thrower remained unknown. Of the eight defendants, seven were sentenced to be hanged; four were actually executed, one committed suicide in prison, and the remaining three were pardoned three years later by Governor John Peter Altgeld of Illinois.

At the trial, Judge Joseph E. Gary stressed that the anarchist defendants' very utterances had been their crime because they "had generally by speech and print advised large classes to commit murder and had left the commission, the time, the place, and when [to commit murder] to the individual will, whim or caprice . . . of each individual man who listened to their advice."

As Ray Ginger has pointed out in *Altgeld's America*, "The defendants were tried, not for a specific murder, but for their general views about society, and they could not overcome the prejudicial effect of the wild statements that most of them made."

Although the eight men tried were indeed anarchists, only one of them was new to the country, having arrived from Germany the year before. The others were either native Americans or had been in the country a long time. Yet the large segment of the American public that was already fearful of insidious foreign influences saw radicals and immigrants and labor organizers as one and the same. The Haymarket bombing had been further, and particularly alarming, proof of the rising danger posed by this hydra-headed menace.

Fifteen years after the Haymarket bomb went off, President William McKinley was assassinated by a young man, Leon Czolgosz, who was instantly indentified in the public mind as an anarchist although he had had only the sketchiest association with anarchism. Indeed, there was evidence that it had been insanity, not politics, which triggered Czolgosz's act. However, in vehement reaction to the murder of the President, there was a wave of sedition laws aimed at anarchists and the foreign born.

In 1902, the year after McKinley's assassination, New York passed a criminal anarchy act. According to this statute, "criminal anarchy" was defined as "the doctrine that organized government should be overthrown by force and violence . . . or by any unlawful means." And it also became a crime under the New York law to join any organization that *taught* or *advocated* "criminal anarchy," or to teach or advocate it oneself by speech or writing. New Jersey and Wisconsin followed with similar statutes. Thus, little more than a hundred years after the Alien and Sedition Acts of 1798, new sedition legislation was on the books of a number of states.

Furthermore, reflecting the degree to which Americans across the nation identified "criminal anarchists" with aliens, in 1903 Congress passed an immigration act which, for the first time, forbade entry into the United States of certain immigrants because of their associations and beliefs.

Among those ineligible for entry were anarchists or other persons believing in or advocating the overthrow by force and violence of the United States government. Also excluded were those believing in or advocating the assassination of public officials (a provision inserted in remembrance of the assassination of President McKinley). Nor could any foreigner be admitted if he was opposed to all organized government, or belonged to a group that taught this doctrine.

The 1903 Immigration Act did not exclude, however, those who believed in or advocated the overthrow of *any* government by force and violence. One senator had this provision removed from the law because of his belief that there are governments in the world that *ought* to be overthrown by force and violence.

In any case, the bill did not require that any *acts* of violence be proved against these would-be immigrants. Sufficient for exclusion were certain *beliefs*. Moreover, if an "anarchist" slipped into this country despite the safeguards in the law, he was subject to deportation if arrested within three years after his date of entry.

Meanwhile, adding to the public disquiet about the apparent rise of criminal anarchy and sedition, often linked to rebellious labor, was a distinctly homegrown group, the Industrial Workers of the World (IWW). Founded in 1905, it evolved into the largest and most visible band of radicals in the country and was therefore considered the most dangerous.

The program of the IWW, whose members were known as "the Wobblies," was the abolition of capitalism and the establishment of an egalitarian socialism under which hunger and want would also be abolished. The Wobblies organized those workers whom other unions ignored or just didn't want—among them, as historian Melvyn Dubofsky has noted, " 'timber beasts' (lumber workers), hobo harvesters, itinerant construction hands, the exploited East and South European immigrants, racially excluded Negroes, Mexicans, and Asian Americans." And women. Feeling themselves "marginal, helpless, dependent, inferior," these chronic outsiders were assured by the IWW: "We shall conquer the world for the working class." Added one of its organizers, "We are the modern abolitionists fighting against wage slavery."

Although there was much talk of force in the IWW, the Wobblies essentially focused on nonviolent direct action in trying to gain their objectives. They were not pacifists, but they did believe they could take power peaceably. For a time, however, the Wobblies saw the Constitution, particularly the First Amendment, as a most powerful weapon. This despite the fact that their leader, "Big Bill" Haywood, had been a member of the Western Federation of Miners, which had been violently crushed in the first years of the century by the Colorado state militia—one of whose officers had said, "To hell with the Constitution. We aren't going by the Constitution."

From 1909 to 1916, mostly in the West, the Wobblies made free speech the basic engine of their organizing drives by capitalizing on attempts to shut off their own speech.

As the Wobblies grew in numbers, government officials in various towns and cities, often prodded by businessmen who saw the IWW as a looming threat, would pass ordinances prohibiting public speech and assembly in areas where migrant workers and other potential IWW recruits were used to gathering.

Characteristic of the laws aimed at the Wobblies was this Los Angeles ordinance:

It shall be unlawful for any person to discuss, expound, advocate or oppose the principles or creed of any political party, partisan body, or organization, or religious denomination or sect, or the doctrines of any economic or social system in any public speech, lecture, or discourse, made or delivered in any public park in the City of Los Angeles.

The authorities were well aware that the IWW vitally depended on the soapbox—free open-air speech—to gather new members. Every winter, coming from fields and construction camps, migratory workers appeared by the thousands in western cities. To try to attract them as members, IWW organizers had to be free to expound their ideas as well as to distribute the Wobbly newspaper and other literature. Since the Wobblies needed the use of the streets in order to survive, they launched a series of "free speech fights."

Part of the Wobblies' strategy was to defy the ordinances against them by continuing to speak, continuing to be arrested, and having new speakers immediately ready to take the place of those arrested, with yet more speakers on hand to replace each wave taken away by the police. Thereby, having clogged the jails and courts and having become so stubborn and expensive a nuisance, the Wobblies would be given back their free speech rights.

The Wobblies waged this war for free expression in some twenty-six cities, primarily in Washington, Oregon, and California. In a sizable number of speech clashes, they won. On the other hand, they often had to pay hard dues for their actual as well as strategic devotion to freedom of speech and assembly. Not only were there mass arrests but also, on occasion, torture. In Spokane, for example, a reporter said that "if men had murdered my own mother, I could not see them tortured as I saw IWW men tortured in the city jail."

As brutal as the police frequently were, even worse outrages were committed by vigilante committees, which operated without interference from local officials—and sometimes in conjunction with them. More often than not, these committees were composed of the more respectable elements of the community—lawyers, doctors, bank workers, real estate men. As an official of the Second National Bank of Minot, North Dakota, said at the time, "There ain't no use in treating these fellows with kindness. The only thing to do is club them down. Beat them up. Drive them out of the city."

Here, in bloody action, was the tyranny of the majority over *individual* rights and liberties that James Madison had so feared but had thought he had been able to prevent by getting the Bill of Rights into the United States Constitution.

In *The Industrial Workers of the World, 1905–17,* Philip S. Foner quotes from an unpublished memoir by a Wobbly free-speech fighter in San Diego. Forced by a posse of vigilantes to kiss the American flag, he was hit with a wagon spoke all over his body. Then, as was the custom after the ritual of the forced kissing of the flag, the trapped Wobbly had to run a gauntlet:

> 50 men being on each side and each man being armed with a gun and a club and some had long whips. . . . I got about 30 feet when I was suddenly struck across the knee. I felt the wagon spoke sink in, splitting my knee. I reeled over. As I was laying there I saw other fellow workers, running the gauntlet. Some were bleeding freely from cracked heads, others were knocked down

to be made to get up to run again. Some tried to break the line only to be beaten back. It was the most cowardly and inhuman cracking of heads I have ever witnessed.

Even though some of their members were killed, the Wobblies would not be stopped. As soon as one group in the union became involved in a free speech fight in a particular town or city, word would go out to the general IWW office, which then spread the news along the entire network of IWW unions. Thereupon, Wobblies from all around would converge on the town where their colleagues were being beaten up, along with free speech. The news of each free speech battle was spread by leaflet and talk and song:

> Out there in San Diego
> Where the western breakers beat,
> They're jailing men and women
> For speaking on the street.

As the free speech fights intensified, the Wobblies picked up some middle-class supporters who were also serious about protecting the most basic of American freedoms, the right to speak one's mind.

In *Bread and Roses Too: Studies of the Wobblies*, Joseph Robert Conlin tells of Herman Tucker, an employee of the United States Forestry Department in Missoula, Montana:

> During the free speech fight there in 1909, Tucker was watching from the window of his second-story office when a young logger was arrested on the corner below for reading from the Declaration of Indepen-

dence. Although not especially sympathetic to the Wobblies, Tucker was incensed by the mockery of the arrest,
rushed downstairs, mounted the vacant platform, and
continued the reading. He too was arrested.

Eventually the Wobblies won the right to speak in the
open in Missoula, in Spokane (where the city also agreed
to stop interfering with the distribution of their newspaper, *The Industrial Worker*), and in a number of additional cities. In other places they were routed. Losers and
winners, the Wobblies dramatically added to the battered
heritage of Americans who have sufficiently prized their
rights of speech and assembly to risk being beaten and
going to jail for asserting those rights.

Said a constitutionalist of the time in *Pearson's Magazine:*

> Whether they agree or disagree with its methods and
> aims, all lovers of liberty everywhere owe a debt to this
> organization for its defense of free speech. Absolutely
> irreconcilable, absolutely fearless, and unsuppressibly
> persistent, it has kept alight the fires of freedom, like
> some outcast vestal of human liberty. That the defense
> of traditional rights to which this government is sup-
> posed to be dedicated should devolve upon an organiza-
> tion so often denounced as "unpatriotic" and "un-
> American," is but the usual, the unfailing irony of
> history.

XI

*Who does not put the flag above the church had
better close his church and keep it closed.*

The Wobblies were finally destroyed, except for a few
who persisted in limbo to bear witness to the lost dream.
They became victims of the fierce pressures against radicals and other "subversive" nonconformists that kept es-
calating during the First World War and in the years
immediately after. A combination of state and federal sedition laws, together with a direct assault on the IWW
by the Justice Department, did the Wobblies in.

A number of state statutes, for example, were directed,
in part, specifically at the Wobblies. In 1917 the Wobblies
were threatening strikes in mining, lumber, and wheat,
sticking to their antimilitarism while continuing to stress
the class war, and all in all showing none of the "patriotism" demanded by most Americans while the country—
as of April 1917—was at war.

Accordingly, in Idaho, South Dakota, Montana, Minnesota, Nebraska, and other states, bills were passed punishing seditious speech and writing. (Sedition was usually
defined as the advocacy of violence to bring about industrial or political change.) Before this wave of repressive

patriotism had receded, thirty-five state legislatures had put such laws on the books. But they were not aimed solely at the Wobblies, since all manner of radicals were being targeted.

Essentially, as Robert K. Murray points out in *Red Scare*, "although such laws varied slightly from state to state, the effect was generally the same. *Opinions* were labeled as objectionable and punished for their own sake *without any consideration of the probability of criminal acts;* severe penalties were imposed for the advocacy of small offenses; and a practical censorship of speech and press was established" (emphasis added).

Lacking the patience to wait for the crippling of the IWW by sedition laws, the Justice Department in September 1917 raided Wobbly offices throughout the country. The government agents confiscated literature from which "evidence" was obtained that led to trials of IWW leaders on charges of sedition, obstruction of the war effort, and espionage. (Most of the "seditious" utterances used to convict the Wobblies at their trials had been made *before* America's entry into the war, many of them dating back before 1914.) By the end of 1917 just about every important official of the IWW was in prison.

Meanwhile, a new federal law, the Espionage Act of 1917, was making it much easier to jail Wobblies and other radicals. Although ostensibly designed to punish treason in time of war, the law was primarily used to ferret out "disloyalty."

Under the Espionage Act it became a crime punishable by a twenty-year jail term or a ten thousand dollar fine or both to "willfully convey false reports or false statements with intent to interfere with the operation or success of the military or naval force of the United States or to promote the success of its enemies . . . or attempt to cause insubordination, disloyalty, mutiny, or refusal of duty, in the military or naval forces of the United States, or . . . willfully obstruct the recruiting or enlistment service of the United States."

Eleven months after it was passed, the Espionage Act was expanded further to punish "disloyal" speech even more broadly. A 1918 amendment, often called the Sedition Act, made it a crime to "utter, print, write, or publish any disloyal, profane, scurrilous, or abusive language about the form of government of the United States, or the Constitution of the United States, or the uniform of the Army or Navy of the United States." It was also made criminal to engage in "any language intended to . . . encourage resistance to the United States, or to promote the cause of its enemies."

These measures, the harshest national laws against speech since the Alien and Sedition Acts of 1798, clearly reflected the will of the majority of Americans. Again, as James Madison had foreseen, even a democratic government can try mightily to stifle dissent when it reflects fearful majoritarianism.

During this period that formidable patriot, Theodore Roosevelt, issued a warning directed at pacifists in various church groups. "The clergyman," Roosevelt said, "who does not put the flag above the church had better close his church, and keep it closed." So much not only for freedom of speech but also for the "free exercise" of religion clause in the First Amendment.

In some cases pacifist ministers were abused or imprisoned. In December 1917 Reverend Samuel Siebert of Carmel, Illinois, was imprisoned because of a sermon in which he preached against all wars. In Audubon, Iowa, a crowd grabbed a preacher and another man and dragged them with ropes around their necks to the public square. After the layman signed a check for a thousand-dollar Liberty Bond he was let go, and the minister was later released because of the intervention of his wife. The *Sacramento Bee* headlined its report of this exemplary event: NEAR LYNCHINGS GIVE PRO-GERMANS NEEDED LESSON.

In this kind of atmosphere, with dissent often being equated with treason, it is not surprising that there were some two thousand prosecutions under the Espionage Act and thousands more under various state sedition laws. The many convictions included almost half of those charged with violating the Espionage Act.

As Zechariah Chafee has emphasized in *Free Speech in the United States* "almost all the convictions were for expressions of *opinion* about the merits and conduct of the war" (emphasis added). Despite the First Amendment, "it became criminal to state that conscription was unconstitutional though the Supreme Court had not yet held it valid . . . to urge that a referendum should have preceded our declaration of war, to say that war was contrary to the teachings of Christ."

Under the Minnesota Espionage Act it was held that a crime had been committed when someone told a group of women knitting for the war that "no soldier ever sees these socks." The comment, interpreted as an attempt to discourage the women from continuing to knit, was judged to be obstructive of the war effort.

As for those charged with fomenting insubordination and disloyalty in the armed forces, it was not necessary to prove that they had specifically addressed soldiers or men about to go into the service. "Most judges," Chafee writes, "held it enough if the words might conceivably reach such men. They have made it impossible for an opponent of the war to write an article or even a letter in a newspaper of general circulation because it will be read in some training camp where it might cause insubordination or interfere with military success.

"He cannot address a large audience because it is liable to include a few men in uniform, and some judges have held him punishable if the audience contains men between eighteen and forty-five, since they may be called into the army eventually; some have emphasized the possible presence in the audience of shipbuilders and munition-makers. All genuine discussion among civilians of the justice and wisdom of continuing a war thus becomes perilous."

With the war over, the First Amendment did not soon recover. There was still rampant fear of radicals, aliens, and labor agitators (who were still widely considered interchangeable). Moreover, there was now the rising specter of Russian Bolshevism under Lenin and Trotsky.

Attorney General A. Mitchell Palmer warned of the pervasive dangers of this most pernicious of foreign ideologies; "The chief evil of the Red movement, both here and abroad, consists in the fact that it accomplishes a constant spread of a disease of evil thinking." It was this evil *thinking* that had to be punished and, in so far as possible, eradicated from American society.

XII

A disease of evil thinking

Attorney General A. Mitchell Palmer, in hot pursuit of malignant Reds, ordered in 1919 that a labor paper, *The Seattle Union-Record*, be raided and its offices closed. The newspaper had been urging workers to vote against the candidates of the capitalists in the next election, and it otherwise took positions that decidedly did not reflect "respectable opinion" of the time. (Palmer was able to move against this arm of the press because technically the war was still on and the Espionage Act still in effect.)

Palmer was operating in a climate of near-hysteria about the "Red menace," which has been described by Murray Levin in *Political Hysteria in America: The Democratic Capacity for Repression*:

> In 1920, a salesman in Waterbury, Connecticut, was sentenced to six months in jail for having remarked to a customer that Lenin was "the brainiest" or "one of the brainiest" political leaders in the world. In 1919, a citizen of Indiana, in a fit of rage, shot and killed an alien who yelled, "to hell with the United States." The jury deliberated for two minutes before acquitting the killer.

In Weirton, West Virginia, during the great steel strike of 1919, a mob of enraged citizens forced 118 aliens, who were on strike, to kiss the American flag. . . . In the state of Washington, school teachers were forbidden to answer students' questions concerning Bolshevism or "any other heresies." Twenty-eight states passed laws banning the display of Red flags. . . . In 1920, the legislature of the state of New York expelled five duly elected members of the Socialist party. [The Socialist Party, a legal organization, did not advocate violence, but its name alone inspired fear.]

This is not to say that the "Red menace" was entirely imaginary. There were some Communists in the land, and there were some believers in violent revolution. Yet the actual extent of violent revolutionary activity was small and in no reasonable way justified the huge, raging, indiscriminate repression of "radicals" by public officials and by many of the citizenry. In Syracuse, New York, for example, three men were arrested in the fall of 1919 for distributing circulars. The circulars described the allegedly poor treatment of political prisoners, called for a meeting to generate requests that the prisoners be given amnesty, and urged that letters of protest be sent to the President and to members of Congress. Quoted in the circulars—which these men were later tried for distributing—was the First Amendment.

The three men were found guilty and sentenced to eighteen months in prison on the grounds that they had violated the Espionage Act (still on the books) by using language disloyal to the American form of government and its military forces. Moreover, the court claimed that their seditious language had brought the government and the Constitution into contempt, with consequent obstruction of recruiting.

Of all the repressive actions of this "Red scare" period, the most terrifying phenomena were the "Palmer raids," carried out on the night of January 2, 1920. This Department of Justice expedition, directed against the recently formed Communist and Communist Labor parties, cast a dragnet over thirty-three cities in twenty-three states. Fished up were more than four thousand suspected radicals.

The main quarry consisted of aliens allegedly afflicted with what Attorney General Palmer had called "a disease of evil thinking." He wanted to deport as many of them as possible. Palmer ordered those conducting the raids to search everyone picked up and to collect all documentary evidence at the sites of the raids: "charters, meeting minutes, membership books, dues books, membership correspondence, etc." In addition to the four thousand people scooped up on the night of January 2, the Justice Department arrested another six thousand in a second expedition four days later.

Both sets of raids had been conducted so carelessly, however, that among those seized were many American citizens—not aliens at all—and many who belonged neither to the Communist nor the Communist Labor parties, nor to any political party. In the course of the raids, moreover, government agents enthusiastically engaged in such massive violations of the Constitution as unlawful searches and seizures, holding prisoners incommunicado and thereby denying their right to a lawyer, making arrests without warrants, and detaining prisoners for excessive periods of time without their having a chance to be heard by a judge.

Indeed, during the Palmer raids there were many scenes in which law-enforcement agents made the United States resemble the kind of ruthless authoritarian Communist state which Attorney General Palmer so zealously condemned. For example, Massachusetts Federal District Judge George Anderson, in his opinion on a case that grew out of the raids, observed:

> Pains were taken to give spectacular publicity to the raid, and to make it appear that there was great and imminent public danger, against which these activities of the Department of Justice were directed. The arrested aliens, *in most cases quiet and harmless working people,* many of them not long ago Russian peasants, were handcuffed in pairs, and then, for the purposes of transfer on trains and through the streets of Boston, chained together. . . . In the early days at Deer Island [where many prisoners were initially taken] one alien committed suicide by throwing himself from the fifth floor and dashing his brains out in the corridor below in the presence of other horrified aliens. One was committed as insane; others were driven nearly, if not quite, to the verge of insanity. [Emphasis added]

In *Red Scare*, Robert K. Murray tells of the Detroit raid:

> About 800 persons were arrested and imprisoned from three to six days in a dark, windowless, narrow corridor in the city's antiquated Federal Building. The prisoners were forced to sleep on the bare floor and stand in long lines for access to the solitary toilet. Some, unable to wait, were forced to urinate in the corridor itself, and, as the custodian later testified, "Before many days . . . the stench was quite unbearable." It was later discovered that the prisoners were denied all food for the first

twenty-four hours and thereafter were fed largely on what their families brought to them. Including among their number "citizens and aliens, college graduates and laborers, skilled mechanics making $15 a day and boys not yet out of short trousers," these 800 prisoners were closely questioned by bureau agents who finally released 300 by the end of the sixth day when it was proved that they had not even a cursory interest in the domestic radical movement.

As for the "dangerous radicals" who remained in custody under these wretched conditions, a Detroit citizens' committee finally concluded that most were, as Robert K. Murray points out, just "plain, ignorant foreigners who were completely unaware of why they were being so treated."

So out of control was the Red scare that in Lynn, Massachusetts, when thirty-nine bakers met on the night of the raids to organize a cooperative bakery, they were picked up by Lynn police as Communists. In Newark, a man was hauled in merely because he "looked like a radical."

Attorney General Palmer, commenting on those caught in the raids, provided actual descriptive guidelines so that patriotic citizens could, in the future, more readily identify dangerous radicals: "Out of the sly and crafty eyes of many of them leap cupidity, cruelty, insanity, and crime; from their lopsided faces, sloping brows, and misshapen features may be recognized the unmistakable criminal type."

The Palmer raids—with their mass arrests, ransacking of homes, confiscation of literature and letters, and other wholesale violations of individual liberties—were directed against "evil," un-American, dangerous radical *thought*. Not actions but suspected ideas were being punished.

Although there was some protest against the Palmer raids, the great majority of Americans applauded the attorney general. Among many newspapers supporting the roundups, *The Washington Post*, answering minority complaints that the Bill of Rights had been violated, lectured: "There is no time to waste on hairsplitting over infringement of liberty."

Symbolic speech was also a casualty of the Red scare. In 1919, for example, the mere display of a red flag was declared to be illegal by twenty-four state legislatures (with eight more passing similar legislation the next year). A number of cities also made it criminal to show a flag that had been subversively colored red. The usual penalty, on conviction, was a fine of up to five hundred dollars and a jail sentence of up to six months. While these red-flag laws were being actively enforced, some fourteen hundred people were arrested for breaking them, with about three hundred winding up in prison.

By the end of 1920 the Red scare was losing its momentum. In *Political Hysteria in America*, Murray Levin advances a number of intersecting reasons for the cooling of the national hysteria: All of Europe had not become infected with bolshevism, as had originally been feared when Lenin came to power; no huge Red conspiracy in America had been revealed; labor unrest, including the number of strikes, had declined; radicals had by and large been successfully intimidated and their forces weakened; and a number of prominent citizens had finally spoken out publicly in defense of the constitutional rights and liberties of even radicals. These rather belated advocates of everyone's right to free speech emphasized primarily that the surest way to bring about a dangerous radical movement, in the long run, was to create an atmosphere of suppression. As Albert Beveridge, a former senator from Indiana, put it, "Attempts to smother thought by force only make converts to the very doctrines thus sought to be destroyed. . . . Denial of lawful free speech is the noxious culture in which crazy radicalism is propagated most rapidly."

The First Amendment, though wounded, had once more survived. Nonetheless, there were still people in jail for what they had said or written rather than for anything they had actually done. Around 1923 a pamphlet put out by the Wobblies noted that every country involved in World War I had freed all the spies and insurrectionists in its prisons except for the United States, where some fifty-nine people were still locked up.

Forty-three of these abandoned souls were Wobblies who had been imprisoned for the crime of sedition. And what was the evidence against them? Only that they possessed paid-up "little red cards" in the IWW. They were languishing in jail only because of their thoughts, their ideas. Indeed, as historian Joseph Robert Conlin has emphasized, "despite dozens of prosecutions and the investigative powers of a dozen states, the Federal Bureau of Investigation, the Immigration Bureau, and the Justice Department, *no Wobbly was ever proved to have committed an act of violence*."

Some of those long-incarcerated Wobblies may have remembered such vintage free-speech songs of their union as the 1912 "We're Bound for San Diego" (sung to the Irish tune "The Wearing of the Green"):

In that town called San Diego when the workers
    try to talk
The cops will smash them . . . and tell 'em
    "take a walk."
They throw them in a bull pen, and they feed
    them rotten beans.
And they call that "law and order" in that city,
    so it seems.

The Supreme Court of the United States Confronts Criminal "Seditious" Speech

"How Long Would Germany Stand for It?" (*Life*, December 13, 1917)

XIII

The most stringent protection of free speech would not protect a man in falsely shouting fire in a theatre and causing a panic.

It was not until after the First World War that the Supreme Court began to hear cases involving the various espionage, sedition, criminal anarchy, and other laws aimed at limiting and punishing speech. Then, in a series of important decisions, the Court shook up the First Amendment, broadening it in some rulings, narrowing its protections in others.

The first notable—and to some, dismaying—decision was *Schenck v. United States* (1919). Charles Schenck, general secretary of the Socialist party, had been convicted, under the Espionage Act of 1917, of conspiracy to print, mail, and circulate material aimed at causing insubordination among those drafted for military service in World War I.

What did the offending material in the fifteen thousand leaflets circulated by Schenck actually say? That the Conscription Act was unconstitutional and that those wishing to oppose the draft had a constitutional right to do so. Surely this was protected speech under the First Amendment.

Justice Oliver Wendell Holmes, delivering the unanimous opinion of the Court, said that Schenck's leaflets *would* have been protected speech "in many places and in ordinary times." But *not* in time of war. In wartime, speech aimed at obstructing the war effort is "a clear and present danger" to the nation, and under such circumstances First Amendment protections can be limited. In this case, the Court held, Schenck's speech was clearly an incitement to injure the war effort and his punishment had therefore been proper. It was in this opinion that Holmes used an illustration of "clear and present danger" that has been widely quoted ever since: "The most stringent protection of free speech would not protect a man in falsely shouting fire in a theatre and causing a panic."

Another 1919 case, *Abrams v. United States,* was based on the harshly sweeping 1918 amendments to the Espionage Act. The defendants had been indicted for publishing leaflets intended to encourage resistance to the United States government in time of war, to incite the curtailment of production of war materials, and to bring the American form of government into contempt.

The actual crime had been the printing and distributing (by throwing from the window of a building) of two sets of leaflets. One, in English, protested the sending of American troops in the summer of 1918 to help the enemies of the Russian Revolution. Among other things, the leaflet proclaimed: "There is only one enemy of the workers of the world and that is CAPITALISM."

The second set of leaflets, in Yiddish, was directed to workers in munitions factories and urged them to engage in a general strike because "you are producing bullets, bayonets, cannons, to murder not only the Germans, but also your dearest, best, who are in Russia and are fighting for freedom."

Military intelligence police seized those responsible for printing and distributing the leaflets. Without a warrant, the police took away all the papers and records they found during the arrests. Diverse sentences were handed out to the convicted leafleteers; three of them, including Abrams, were sentenced to twenty years in prison.

The Supreme Court ruled that the kind of speech contained in the two sets of leaflets was an incitement to sedition and revolution and that the defendants were therefore guilty of having violated the 1918 amendments to the Espionage Act. Justices Louis Brandeis and Oliver Wendell Holmes dissented.

Holmes, who had written the Court's opinion against Schenck, said he continued to believe that in certain circumstances proof of a "clear and present danger" could outweigh the First Amendment. But in *Abrams*, "sentences of twenty years imprisonment have been imposed for the publishing of two leaflets that I believe the defendants had as much right to publish as the Government has to publish the Constitution of the United States now vainly invoked by them."

The difference was that in the Schenck case circulars had been mailed directly to draftees, urging them to resist going into the armed forces. To Holmes, that was an unmistakable incitement which in time of war presented "a clear and present danger" of bringing about "substantive evils." In *Abrams* the defendants had thrown leaflets indiscriminately out the window. Yes, it had happened in time of war, but even in time of war, said Holmes, "Congress certainly cannot forbid *all* effort to change the mind of the country" (emphasis added).

Holmes went on to formulate a classic statement on the nature of free speech:

> The best test of truth is the power of the thought to get itself accepted in the competition of the market. . . . That at any rate is the theory of our Constitution.
>
> It is an experiment, as all life is an experiment. . . . While that experiment is part of our system, I think that we should be eternally vigilant against attempts to check the expression of opinions that we loathe and believe to be fraught with death, unless they so imminently threaten immediate interference with the lawful and pressing purposes of the law that an immediate check is required to save the country.

The defendants in *Abrams*, Holmes emphasized, had engaged only in "expressions of opinion and exhortations." When they were convicted for just that, they "were deprived of their rights under the Constitution of the United States."

The *Schenck* and *Abrams* cases had been brought by the federal government. In 1920, however, the Supreme Court heard *Gilbert v. Minnesota*, involving limitations on speech by an individual state. Soon after the United States entered the war in 1917, and before the passage of the Federal Espionage Act, the state of Minnesota had passed a law making it a crime to advocate in vocal, written, or printed speech "that men should not enlist in the military or naval forces of the United States or the state of Minnesota."

As further illustration of the perniciousness of sedition laws, this particular statute, Zechariah Chafee points out in *Free Speech in the United States*, "could be violated although not a single person was dissuaded from enlisting

[and] even though the jury found and believed that the speaker had not the slightest intention of hindering enlistment or any other war service." Indeed, the speaker need not have said a word about enlisting.

There was enough cause to convict, Chafee pointed out, if it appeared that "the natural and reasonable effects of the statements uttered" was to deter those who heard or read them from helping in the war effort. Freedom of speech thereby had been put into a deep freeze in Minnesota.

Meanwhile, an organization, the Non-Partisan League, had been formed in the state. The league opposed the war, claiming that the American government had intervened against the will of its people in order "to protect the investments of Wall Street." Gilbert, the leader of the league, was indicted and convicted for a speech in which he questioned how much democracy actually exists in the United States: "Have you had anything to say as to whether we would go into this war? You know you have not." Gilbert had also said that "if they conscripted wealth like they have conscripted men, this war would not last over forty-eight hours."

The United States Supreme Court sustained Gilbert's conviction under the Minnesota sedition law, but in an important dissent Mr. Justice Brandeis became the first member in the history of the Court to say flatly that the First Amendment to the Constitution protects freedom of speech against abridgement *by the individual states.* (Until then no Justice had gone against the traditional interpretation that the Bill of Rights restricted only *federal* action.)

Here was Gilbert, convicted of expressing his views about the federal conscription law. Surely, said Brandeis, in a democracy every citizen has a right to "teach the truth as he sees it," and that includes his opinions on the conduct of government. Actually, it is his duty, for the citizen's exercise of this right "is more important to the nation than it is to himself. . . . In frank expression of conflicting opinion lies the greatest promise of wisdom in governmental action; and in suppression lies ordinarily the greatest peril."

The Minnesota law under which Gilbert was convicted, said Brandeis, "affects rights, privileges and immunities of one who is a *citizen of the United States;* and it deprives him of an important part of his liberty. *These are rights which are guaranteed protection by the Federal Constitution, and they are invaded by the [state] statute in question*" (emphasis added).

What about "clear and present danger" to the nation in time of war? If a time of emergency does come, said Brandeis, when the government must suppress "divergent opinion," only Congress has the right to do so, because only Congress is charged with the conduct of war and with the preservation of government, both state and federal. Accordingly, Gilbert should have been released because the state of Minnesota had had no right to violate his freedom of speech.

It was not until five years later, in *Gitlow v. New York,* that Brandeis's views prevailed concerning the power of the First Amendment over the individual states—a vital advance in First Amendment law. Benjamin Gitlow and three associates had published a "Left Wing Manifesto" which ran afoul of a New York State criminal anarchy law making it a crime to advocate or teach the overthrow of the government by force "or by any unlawful means." Indeed, the manifesto proposed "revolutionary mass action" to replace the present government with a Communist state.

Although finding no evidence that the sixteen thousand copies of the manifesto which were distributed had had any effect at all, the Supreme Court upheld Gitlow's conviction. But in doing so the Court broke new First Amendment ground, because the majority of the Justices declared that freedom of speech and of the press had to be respected by the individual states as well as by the federal government.

Why was Gitlow's conviction allowed to stand? After all, Gitlow had been convicted only for his ideas, not his acts. There had been no proof that his advocacy of those ideas had turned out to be a "clear and present danger." Furthermore, he had been punished under a New York State sedition law, and since the Court now said that none of the individual states could violate the First Amendment, why didn't the Supreme Court let Gitlow go?

There are times when the reasoning of the High Court is not particularly lucid, and this was one of those instances. First of all, said the majority, freedom of speech is not an absolute right. *All* speech is not protected by the First Amendment. Even though the First Amendment does now apply to the individual states, New York could still limit freedom of speech if its very existence were endangered by a publication, as here, that urged the masses to overthrow the government.

Since, however, there was no indication Gitlow's writings had constituted a "clear and present danger" that a revolution would take place, the Court came up with what it called the "bad tendency" test. If certain speech *tends* to corrupt public morals, incite to crime, or disturb the public peace, that speech is not protected by the First Amendment. In this case, although Gitlow's manifesto had no effect, it *tended* to incite "breaches of the peace and ultimate revolution."

Fortunately, the "bad tendency" test did not last long in the deliberations of the Supreme Court. It was so broad, so vague, that a judge or a jury who despised certain ideas of a defendant could easily come to the conclusion that these views were so dangerous—even if no overt acts had been proved—that they *tended* to create great harm to government.

Gitlow was a victim of the "bad tendency" test; his case is important in First Amendment law not because of what happened to him but because of one brief paragraph in the majority opinion: "For present purposes we may and do assume that freedom of speech and of the press— which are protected by the First Amendment from abridgement by Congress—are among the fundamental personal rights and 'liberties' protected by the due process clause of the Fourteenth Amendment from impairment by the states."

James Madison had finally been vindicated. When the Bill of Rights was being formulated, he had tried and failed to get an amendment through to insure that, along with Congress, each of the states would be prevented from violating its citizens' First Amendment rights. Now, in 1925, the First Amendment was finally whole, applying to every state in the nation.

How did the High Court come to use the Fourteenth Amendment to make this possible? And why did it take so long for this vital expansion of the First Amendment to happen?

XIV

*Citizenship of the United States is the primary
citizenship in this country; and . . . State citizenship
is secondary and derivative.*

The Fourteenth Amendment was ratified in 1868; its first clause says: "No State shall make or enforce any law which shall abridge the privileges or immunities of citizens of the United States; nor shall any State deprive any person of life, liberty, or property, without due process of law; nor deny to any person within its jurisdiction the equal protection of the laws."

The writer of that first clause, Congressman John Bingham of Ohio, fully intended that the Bill of Rights should limit the power of the individual states as well as that of the federal government. And the majority of Congress apparently agreed when the amendment was passed in 1866. During a debate in the House in 1871, Bingham emphasized that before the Fourteenth Amendment had gone into effect, "the States did deny to citizens the equal protections of the laws, they did deny the rights of citizens under the Constitution. . . . They denied trial by jury and he [the wronged citizen] had no remedy. They took property without compensation and he had no remedy. They restricted the freedom of the press and he had no remedy. . . . Who dare say now, now that the Constitution has been amended, that the nation cannot by law provide against all such abuses and denials of right as these in States and by States?"

As Irving Brant underlines in *The Bill of Rights,* during the entire 1866 United States Senate debate on what was to become the Fourteenth Amendment, "not a single senator challenged Senator [Jacob] Howard's declaration that Section 1 [of the Fourteenth Amendment] made the first eight amendments [of the Bill of Rights] enforceable against the states."

In 1873, however, by a 5 to 4 vote, the Supreme Court (*Slaughterhouse Cases*) interpreted the Fourteenth Amendment quite differently—so differently that it was not until 1925 (*Gitlow v. New York*) that the Court returned to the intentions of the framers of the Fourteenth Amendment. (The case had to do with butchers protesting a Louisiana law that forced them to deal with only one slaughterhouse. They claimed that, as citizens of the United States, they had been deprived of equal protection of the laws under the Fourteenth Amendment.)

The majority of the Court in that 1873 ruling held that there is a difference between "a citizenship of the United States" and "a citizenship of a State." What the Fourteenth Amendment deals with, the majority said, is only United States citizenship. It does not provide any further protections for those living in, and thereby being citizens of, a particular state. Otherwise, the effect of this amendment would be to "fetter and degrade the State governments by subjecting them to the control of Congress" in all things, thereby stripping the states of certain powers they had universally been acknowledged to possess.

What does all this mean? What is left, then, of each person's "privileges and immunities" that no individual state can abridge? All that is left, said the Court, are those privileges and immunities which "owe their existence to the Federal government, its national character, its Constitution, or its laws." For instance: the right to hold federal office; the right of free access to national seaports and federal courts; the right to care and protection on the high seas and in foreign countries; the right to assemble to petition Congress; the right to the writ of habeas corpus; the right to use the navigable waters of the United States; the right to become a citizen of any state by means of a bona fide residence therein.

By this tortured reading of the first section of the Fourteenth Amendment—apparently without the Justices having consulted or paid attention to congressional debate on what was really intended—the 1873 Supreme Court, as one commentator later noted, overthrew "the Congressional ideal for the Fourteenth Amendment within five years after its victorious adoption."

One of the dissenting Justices, Joseph Bradley, insisted that "it was now settled by the Fourteenth Amendment itself that citizenship of the United States is the primary citizenship in this country; and that State citizenship is secondary and derivative." The latter, after all, only has to do with where a citizen chooses to live. Among the privileges of an American citizen—which no state may now violate—are (Bradley said) "the right of free exercise of religious worship, the right of free speech and a free press . . . and above all, and including almost all the rest, the right of not being deprived of life, liberty, or property, without due process of law."

Clearly, Bradley continued, the purpose of the Fourteenth Amendment was to "provide National security against violation by the states of the fundamental rights of the citizen," including "that intolerance," by some states, "of free speech and free discussion, which often rendered life and property insecure, and led to much unequal legislation."

The majority decision, however, applying the Bill of Rights only to the federal government, was the law of the land until the Supreme Court changed its mind fifty-two years later.

In the *Slaughterhouse* decision the Fourteenth Amendment took a wrong turn five years after it was ratified. In the 1925 *Gitlow* case the Court unanimously set that amendment in the right direction again, declaring freedom of speech to be among "the fundamental personal rights and 'liberties' protected [by that amendment] from impairment by the states." (Only three years before, Justice Mahlon Pitney of the High Court had said flatly that "the Constitution imposes on the States no obligation to confer upon those within their jurisdiction . . . the right of free speech.")

With the Supreme Court having turned itself around, Zechariah Chafee regarded this breakthrough in the *Gitlow* decision as the greatest victory for free speech in his lifetime. Eventually, he predicted, future Courts "could prevent the United States from becoming a checkerboard nation, with ultra-conservative states into which moderately radical Americans could come at peril of imprisonment for sedition."

That is, once it was established that the First Amendment applied equally to all the citizens of all the states, no single state, however gripped by a "Red" or any other kind of scare, could get away with enacting a law tampering with the First Amendment.

XV

Communism Will Not Go to Jail with
These Communists

The First Amendment is usually most endangered when the nation is most fearful: in time of war, for instance, or during a period when there is much anxiety about an outside menace, such as Russian Communism, that is thought to be seeding the nation with agents committed to destroying it from within.

During the First World War the anxious national mood manifested itself in federal and state sedition laws as well as through informal hunting of "subversives" by aroused citizens. The climate during the Second World War was less poisonous for dissenters. There was some chilling of speech and one entirely disgraceful act of governmental suppression—the exiling from the West Coast of people of Japanese ancestry, including citizens, and their imprisonment in "relocation centers."

Otherwise there were few excesses, in large part because the terrifying specter of Hitler produced relatively few dissenters to that war. As for the earlier "Red scare," this time Russia and the United States were allies.

Soon after the Second World War, however, dissent

again became perilous. It was an increasingly uneasy peacetime. Relations with Russia had stiffened into the Cold War, and renewed hysteria about domestic Communists was nurtured by this grim global tension between the "Free World" and what lay behind the Iron Curtain. In Congress and in state legislatures "investigative" committees began to search out Communists (some real, many imagined). This form of thought-policing reached its most dangerous stage with the emergence in 1950 of Senator Joseph McCarthy as the most ferocious and reckless of the Communist-hunters.

Even before McCarthy, considerable damage was being done to the First Amendment. In 1948, for example, the federal government indicted the twelve members of the Communist party's Central Committee for conspiracy to violate the advocacy-and-organizing sections of the Smith Act. Named after its sponsor, Congressman Howard W. Smith, the act had been passed by Congress in 1940 as Title I of the Alien Registration Act. As Zechariah Chafee has pointed out, this bill was "no more limited to the registration of aliens than the Espionage Act of 1917 was limited to spying." Actually, the Smith Act was a *peacetime* sedition law. It applied to everybody, said Chafee, "especially United States citizens." Not since the Alien and Sedition Acts of 1798 had there been such a peacetime *federal* statute.

(As an illustration of malign historical fallout, the Smith Act was modeled on New York's Criminal Anarchy Act of 1902, passed after the assassination of President McKinley, and the basis for the conviction of Benjamin Gitlow of *Gitlow v. United States*.)

One of the Smith Act's provisions made it a crime to advocate or teach the overthrow or destruction of any government in the United States by force or violence (from a village to the federal government). Accordingly, it was also made a crime to print, edit, publish, circulate, sell, distribute, or publicly display any written or printed material in furtherance of such advocacy. If two or more people conspired to commit any of these offenses, they too were subject to the criminal penalties of the act.

Another provision held that violators of this law would include "whoever organizes or helps or attempts to organize any society, group, or assembly of persons who teach, advocate, or encourage the overthrow of any such government by force or violence." If two or more people joined to violate any part of the law, they could be charged with conspiracy.

That wasn't all; anyone just belonging to a group calling for the overthrow of the government was liable under the Smith Act if he knew the purposes of the group he had joined.

In 1940, when the Smith Act was being considered by Congress, only three people testified against it—representatives of the American Civil Liberties Union, the CIO Maritime Union, and the American Federation of Labor. Nor was there substantial opposition in the press, on the radio, or at public meetings. It was one of those periods in the history of the republic when neither the people nor their representatives in Congress were alert to a truly subversive attack on their liberties.

Because the national mood had not been harshly punitive toward dissenters during the Second World War, the Smith Act was largely dormant during that time. But in 1948, with the Cold War gathering momentum, the government moved against the twelve leading domestic Communists. (The number of defendants was reduced to eleven when the case of William Z. Foster was severed because of his ill health.)

What were these defendants charged with? That they had engaged in a conspiracy to organize the Communist party of the United States and to teach and advocate the overthrow of the government by force and violence. All this was illegal under the Smith Act.

The eleven Communists were convicted, and the verdict was sustained by the Court of Appeals for the Second Circuit. The fiercely contentious trial in the lower Federal District Court had lasted nine months, and the record consisted of a whopping sixteen thousand pages.

Finally, in 1951, the Supreme Court voted, 6 to 2, against the defendants (one Justice did not participate). There was division even among the majority, however, and the overall debate shows how difficult it can be for the ultimate arbiters of our laws to agree on how free the First Amendment meant speech to be.

In *Dennis v. United States* Chief Justice Fred M. Vinson's opinion, in which three other Justices joined, rejected "any principle" that would leave the government helpless "in the face of preparation for revolution." Therefore, the "overthrow of the Government by force and violence is certainly a substantial enough interest for the Government to limit speech . . . for if a society cannot protect its very structure from armed internal attack, it must follow that no subordinate value can be protected."

What of the contention that "a conspiracy to advocate" cannot be punished constitutionally because it is "only the preparation"? These are utterances—not *acts*—of rebellion.

Not so, said Vinson. "It is the existence of the conspiracy which creates the danger." The lower court judge had been correct, he added, in pointing out that the utterances, the language, used by the defendants had been calculated to incite persons to action—that is, overthrow of the United States government. Accordingly, these defendants had created a "clear and present danger" to the United States.

In a concurring opinion, Justice Felix Frankfurter did not use the "clear and present danger" test but rather the "balancing test." He balanced First Amendment rights against other competing vital interests. Here the interest to be balanced against the First Amendment was national security.

On the one hand, said Frankfurter, "the Communist party was not designed by these defendants as an ordinary political party. It is revolutionary and international in scope." Therefore, organizing and advocacy leading to "recruitment of additional members for the Party would create a substantial danger to national security."

On the other hand, when balancing national security interests against the value of free speech, it is important, Frankfurter continued, to recognize that "it is self-delusion to think that we can punish them [the Communist defendants] for their advocacy without adding to the risks run by loyal citizens who honestly believe in some of the reforms these defendants advance. It is a sobering fact that in sustaining the conviction before us, we can hardly escape restriction on the interchange of ideas." In fact, suppressing those urging overthrow of the government "inevitably will also silence critics who do *not* advocate overthrow but fear that their criticism may be so construed."

What, then, is to be done? Well, Frankfurter concluded, it was Congress that decided the Smith Act should become law. "Can we say that the judgment Congress exercised was denied it by the Constitution? . . . Can we hold that the First Amendment deprives Congress of what it deemed necessary for the Government's protection?" Frankfurter's answer was to yield to the judgment of Congress, thereby avoiding answering for himself whether, in this case, free speech should be subordinated to national security.

In another separate opinion, Justice Robert H. Jackson, while agreeing with the majority, went on to pay troubled tribute to the power of speech, even when it has been punished, as in this instance: "I have little faith in the long-range effectiveness of this conviction [of the Communist party leadership] to stop the rise of the Communist movement. *Communism will not go to jail with these Communists.* No decision by this Court can forestall revolution wherever the existing government fails to command the respect and loyalty of the people and sufficient distress and discontent is allowed to grow up among the masses" (emphasis added).

In dissent were the two most passionate defenders of the First Amendment in the history of the Court, Hugo Black and William O. Douglas. Said Black: "These [defendants] were not charged with an attempt to overthrow the Government. They were not charged with overt acts of any kind designed to overthrow the Government. They were not even charged with saying anything or with writing anything designed to overthrow the Government. The charge was that they agreed to assemble and to talk and to publish certain ideas at a later date: The indictment is that they conspired to organize the Communist Party and to use speech or newspapers and other publications in the future to teach and advocate the forcible overthrow of the

Government. No matter how it is worded, this is a virulent form of *prior censorship of speech and press,* which I believe the First Amendment forbids" (emphasis added).

"Undoubtedly," Black wrote, "a governmental policy of unfettered communication of ideas does entail dangers. To the Founders of this Nation, however, the benefits derived from free expression were worth the risk." That is why the First Amendment was intended to protect all views, not just "those 'safe' or orthodox views which rarely need its protection."

Black was aware that his interpretation of the First Amendment was a minority view not only on the Court but among the populace as a whole. But he also knew that, from the Alien and Sedition Acts of 1789 on, climates of opinion had changed. He kept hoping that the Founders' approach to the First Amendment would again prevail: "Public opinion being what it now is, few will protest the conviction of these Communist petitioners. There is hope, however, that in calmer times, when present pressures, passions and fears subside, this or some later Court will restore the First Amendment liberties to the high preferred place where they belong in a free society."

Justice William O. Douglas began his dissent by conceding that "the freedom to speak is not absolute." If these defendants had been claiming protection under the First Amendment for "teaching the techniques of sabotage, the filching of documents from public files, the planting of bombs, the art of street warfare, and the like, I would have no doubts [that their convictions should be affirmed]. No such evidence, however, was introduced at their trial.

"So far as the present record is concerned," Douglas

went on, "what these petitioners did was to [teach and] organize people to teach . . . the Marxist-Leninist doctrine obtained chiefly in four books: Stalin, *Foundations of Leninism* (1924); Marx and Engels, *Manifesto of the Communist Party* (1848); Lenin, *The State and Revolution* (1917); *History of the Communist Party of the Soviet Union* . . . (1939)."

To be sure, Douglas said, the defendants "preached the creed [contained in these books] with the hope that someday it would be acted on." However, "the opinion of the Court does not outlaw these texts nor condemn them to the fire, as the Communists do literature offensive to their creed. But if the books themselves are not outlawed, if they can lawfully remain on library shelves, by what reasoning does their use in a classroom become a crime?"

This is a case, said Douglas, that has to do not with acts, "but with speech, to which the Constitution has given a special sanction. . . .

"We have deemed it more costly to liberty to suppress a despised minority than to let them vent their spleen. We have above all else feared the political censor. We have wanted a land where our people can be exposed to all the diverse creeds and cultures of the world."

In this case, Douglas wrote, there is no evidence at all in the record that "the acts charged . . . have created any clear and present danger to the Nation." Indeed, "I would doubt that there is a village, let alone a city or county or state [in this country] which the Communists could carry. Communism in the world scene is no bogey-man; but communism as a political faction or party in this country plainly is. Communism has been so thoroughly exposed in this country that it has been crippled as a political force. *Free speech has destroyed it as an effective political party.* It is inconceivable that those who went up and down this country preaching the doctrine of revolution which petitioners espouse would have any success" (emphasis added).

At the end of his dissent, Douglas quoted from a 1938 book by the chief Soviet prosecutor, Andrei Vishinsky, *The Law of the Soviet State:* "In our state, naturally, there is and can be no place for freedom of speech, press, and so on for the foes of socialism."

"Our concern," Douglas warned, "should be that we accept no such standard for the United States. Our faith should be that our people will never give support to these advocates of revolution, so long as we remain loyal to the purposes for which our Nation was founded."

Nonetheless, the conviction of the eleven Communist defendants was affirmed, and they went to jail for what they thought, not for any acts they had committed.

In 1969, looking back at the *Dennis* case, Justice Douglas said that "the trial of those teachers of Marxism" had been "an all-out political trial which was part and parcel of the cold war that has eroded substantial parts of the First Amendment."

In 1973, still incensed at what had been done to freedom of speech in this case, Douglas told students at Staten Island Community College that the defendants in *Dennis* "were not plotting revolution, handing out grenades, making caches of rifles and ammunition and the like. They were teachers only—men teaching Marxism."

XVI

I would leave the Communists free to advocate their beliefs in proletarian dictatorship publicly and openly among the people of the country.

As a result of the Supreme Court's decision in *Dennis v. United States*, the government was encouraged to indict an additional 129 people under the Smith Act for having, as Mr. Justice Black had put it, views that were not "safe." Six years after *Dennis*, however, another case, *Yates v. United States*, put an end to these prosecutions, although the Court's majority opinion did not appear to break sharply from what had been ruled in *Dennis*.

The basic issue in both cases was the same. At what point, if any, is advocacy—speech—to be punished? On trial in *Yates* were fourteen second-string Communist leaders. The result, unlike *Dennis*, was a reversal of their convictions, by a vote of 6 to 1.

Speaking for the majority, Justice John Marshall Harlan tried to explain why the trial in *Yates* had been different from the trial in *Dennis*. In *Yates* the lower court judge had committed error in his instructions to the jury by failing to make it clear that under the Smith Act it was not illegal to advocate an *abstract* doctrine of forcible overthrow of the government. Advocacy becomes *crim-*

inal under the Smith Act only when it promotes unlawful *action* to forcibly overthrow the government.

"The essential distinction," Harlan wrote, "is that those to whom the advocacy is addressed must be urged to *do* something, now or in the future, rather than merely to *believe* in something."

Is that distinction confusing? Harlan conceded that this line between abstract and action-directed advocacy is "often subtle and difficult to grasp." That's why in the *Yates* case it was all the more essential for the lower court judge to have given very precise and understandable instructions to the jury on the differences between those two kinds of advocacy. The record of that trial, Harlan added, shows very few "instances of speech that could be considered to amount to 'advocacy of action.'" On the other hand, there were hundreds of instances of vague, abstract speech very "remote from action." By contrast, said Harlan, in *Dennis* there was clear advocacy of violent action to be taken sometime in the future.

Among those critical of Harlan's majority decision in *Yates* was Professor Thomas Emerson, an expert on First Amendment law and theory. In *The System of Freedom of Expression,* Emerson pointed out that "advocacy of ideas" (protected by the Court in *Yates*) and "advocacy of *action*" (not protected in *Yates*) are both forms of "expression." And all expression must be protected by the First Amendment until and unless it becomes so intertwined with action that it is no longer only expression.

For example, says Emerson, "advocating in general terms the use of force or violence at some time in the future must be considered expression. Advocacy of legal forms of action which would put an organization in a more favorable position for later utilization of force and violence—such as forming labor unions in industrial plants—would remain expression. As the communication approached the point of urging immediate and particular forms of violence, it would come closer to being classifiable as action. If such advocacy became merely an incidental part of a program of overt acts, the total conduct would cross the boundary line. Instructions on techniques of sabotage, street fighting, or specific methods of violence are well into the area of action. . . . Training in paramilitary groups to engage in acts of violence would fall within the action category.

"In essence, the line would be drawn between the *ideological* preparation or indoctrination in the use of violence on the one hand, and participation in *overt acts* of preparation or *actual use* [of violence] on the other" (emphasis added).

Emerson's distinction, therefore, is indeed between *expression* (protected by the First Amendment) and *action* (not protected). In Yates, however, the majority of the Supreme Court blurred the issue by trying to draw a line between two forms of expression: *advocacy* of ideas and *advocacy* of action. In a separate opinion joined by Justice William O. Douglas, Justice Hugo Black's thinking was very much like Emerson's. "I believe," said Black, "that the First Amendment forbids Congress to punish people for talking about public affairs, *whether or not such discussion incites to action, legal or illegal*" (emphasis added). So long as it remains speech, advocacy is protected.

Although the reasoning of the majority opinion in *Yates* did not please Justices Black and Douglas because it did not go far enough to completely protect the advocacy of all ideas, the result of *Yates* was to end government prosecution of Communists under the Smith Act. In the *Yates* case itself, the Court had ordered five of the defendants immediately acquitted because there was no evidence that they had done anything unlawful. The other nine were remanded for a new trial, but the lower court dismissed the indictments because the government said it did not have the kind of evidence against the defendants that the *Yates* decision now required for convictions under the Smith Act. In other words, the government admitted it did not have sufficient basis to charge the remaining defendants with advocacy of action rather than only ideas.

After the *Yates* decision, no new prosecutions were instituted under the Smith Act. The law was still on the books, but inactive. All told, 141 persons had been indicted under the Smith Act, and 29 of them served prison terms.

Meanwhile, there were other congressional attempts to severely hamper the functioning of the Communist party. One law, for instance, required that members of a "Communist-action" group be officially designated by the Subversive Activities Control Board—thereby making each such member vulnerable to considerable public contempt in view of the general attitude in the United States toward Communists. Indeed, people thus publicly labeled "Reds" were highly likely to suffer professional and personal injury.

The constitutional issue in this and other such laws was the First Amendment right of association. As Thomas Emerson has pointed out, "The right to form, join, and participate in an association is a crucial aspect of any freedom of expression. Increasingly in modern times the only way an individual can be effectively heard is through membership in an organization. Associations perform other significant functions also, such as affording their members access to information or providing forums for developing and testing ideas."

Freedom of association became perilous, however, when a member of the Communist party could be publicly pilloried as such by the government. But in 1969 the Court of Appeals for the District of Columbia ruled (*Boorda v. Subversive Activities Control Board*) that it was unconstitutional to punish a Communist party member by "exposing" that member's affiliation in public.

"It seems clear to us," said the court, "that mere membership in the Communist party is protected by the First Amendment" as "an individual's right of association." The court emphasized its point by quoting an earlier decision: "Assuming that some members of the Communist Party . . . had illegal aims and engaged in illegal activities, it cannot automatically be inferred that all members shared their evil purposes or participated in their illegal conduct." No one, therefore, can be punished, or singled out for special exposure, just because he is a member of the Communist party. The government appealed that decision to the Supreme Court, which refused to review it, and the Court of Appeals ruling stood.

Those Supreme Court Justices, primarily Black and Douglas, who had been arguing all along for the First Amendment rights of Communists finally saw the judicial tide going their way. Eight years before, a majority of the High Court had decided that the government could constitutionally require the Communist party to register as a "Communist-action" organization and to list its members (*Communist Party v. Subversive Activities Control Board*). Dissenting then, Black said:

I realize that these laws are aimed only at the Communist Party. No one need console himself, however, that the policy of using governmental force to crush dissident groups . . . can or will be stopped at that point. The weakening of constitutional safeguards in order to suppress one obnoxious group is a technique too easily available for the suppression of other obnoxious groups to expect its abandonment when the next generally hated group appears. . . .

I would . . . leave the Communists free to advocate their beliefs in proletarian dictatorship publicly and openly among the people of this country with full confidence that the people will remain loyal to any democratic Government truly dedicated to freedom and justice—the kind of Government which some of us still think of as being "the last best hope of earth."

Freedom of—and from —Religion under the First Amendment

After the 1962 and 1963 Supreme Court decisions declaring prayer recitations in public schools to be unconstitutional, as well as school Bible readings in a religious context, some schools "adjusted" to these rulings by scheduling silent prayers. Here, first graders in South Carolina start their school day in this manner in 1966. To those who adhere to strict separation of church and state, even silent prayer in a public school classroom breaches the wall. Their opponents, on the other hand, intermittently work toward getting a constitutional amendment passed to allow both verbal prayers and Bible readings in public schools. Their chances appear slim. (UPI photo, September 7, 1966)

XVII

It does me no injury for my neighbor to say there are twenty gods, or no God. It neither picks my pocket nor breaks my legs.

While the nation and its Supreme Court have long been embattled over the limits, if any, that can be imposed on "seditious speech" and the political parties disseminating it, there have been just as bitter battles concerning another section of the First Amendment—the clauses guaranteeing freedom of religious belief.

The words would seem to be very clear:

"Congress shall make no law respecting an establishment of religion, or prohibiting the free exercise thereof."

Yet these two brief clauses have led to fierce lawsuits and embattled Supreme Court decisions.

One of the most inflammatory High Court rulings concerning the First Amendment and religion came down on June 25, 1962. At issue was a simple prayer that the Board of Education in New Hyde Park, New York, had ordered each class to say aloud, in the presence of a teacher, at the start of each school day.

This was the prayer:

"Almighty God, we acknowledge our dependence upon

Thee, and we beg Thy blessings upon us, our parents, our teachers, and our Country."

It had been made clear that this was a nondenominational prayer. That is, the prayer, composed by state education officials, was not identifiable as belonging to any particular religion. It was intended to be a general affirmation of belief in God, an affirmation to which Protestants, Catholics, Jews, and other believers could subscribe. Moreover, the prayer had been made part of the school day on the recommendation of the New York State Board of Regents, a governmental agency charged with supervising all public schools in the state. The regents considered the prayer an important part of their program for "Moral and Spiritual Training in the Schools."

Students who did not want to recite the prayer or whose parents disapproved were allowed to remain silent or to be excused from the room. Nonetheless, five parents with children in the New Hyde Park schools brought suit to abolish this prayer reading in the public classrooms on the ground that it violated the part of the First Amendment which says that Congress—and the states by virtue of the Fourteenth Amendment—"shall make no law respecting an *establishment* of religion" (emphasis added).

This prayer, the protesting parents said, was written and implemented by government officials in order to further religious beliefs. But in our constitutional system, the parents added, there must be a wall of separation between church and state. A prayer is on the church side of that wall and should remain out of the state's schools.

The objecting parents lost, 5 to 2, in New York's Court of Appeals. But when the case, *Engel v. Vitale*, reached the United States Supreme Court, the Court's 6 to 1 decision held that the parents were right. The recitation of the regents' prayer in the public schools violated the Establishment Clause of the First Amendment ("Congress shall make no law respecting an establishment of religion").

Speaking for the majority, Justice Hugo Black explained that there can be "no doubt that New York's program of daily classroom invocation of God's blessings as prescribed in the Regents' prayer is a religious activity. It is solemn avowal of divine faith and supplication for the blessings of the Almighty."

That avowal of divine faith has no place in a public school because, said Justice Black, "the constitutional prohibition against laws respecting an establishment of religion must at least mean that in this country *it is no part of the business of government to compose official prayers for any group of the American people to recite as a part of a religious program carried on by government*" (emphasis added).

The prestige and power of the government, said Black, cannot be used to influence, support, or control the kinds of prayers to be said by the American people. The Establishment Clause was written into the First Amendment because the founders of our constitution knew, from history, that "a union of government and religion tends to destroy government and to degrade religion." They also knew that "religion is too personal, too sacred, too holy, to permit its 'unhallowed perversion' by a civil magistrate. . . .

"The First Amendment, which tried to put an end to governmental control of religion and of prayer, was not written to destroy either. [The founders] knew rather that it was written to quiet well-justified fears which nearly all of them felt arising out of an awareness that governments of the past had shackled men's tongues to make them speak only the religious thoughts that government wanted them to speak and to pray only to the God that government wanted them to pray to. It is neither sacrilegious nor antireligious to say that each separate government in this country should stay out of the business of writing or sanctioning official prayers and leave that purely religious function to the people themselves and to those the people look to for religious guidance."

In furious reaction to the decision in *Engel v. Vitale,* there were demands across the nation that the six Justices in the majority resign. When they did not oblige, there were demands that they be impeached. Ironically, Mr. Justice Black, a devout Baptist and long-time Sunday school teacher, was attacked in letters branding him "Communistic," "Godless," and "atheistic."

On the other hand, President John Kennedy, the first Roman Catholic elected to that office, urged public support of the decision, calling it "a welcome reminder to every American family that we can pray a good deal more at home and attend our churches with a good deal more fidelity, and we can make the true meaning of prayer much more important in the lives of all of our children."

If prayers in schools are unconstitutional, what about readings from the Bible? In 1963 the Supreme Court handed down a decision involving two cases dealing with that issue (*School District of Abingdon Township v. Schempp* and *Murray v. Cortleff*). One case had to do with a Pennsylvania law saying that "at least ten verses from the Holy Bible shall be read, without comment, at the opening of each public school on each school day." In the other, an atheist mother and her son had challenged a Baltimore school rule, based on Maryland law, requiring that "each school, collectively or in classes, shall be opened by the reading, without comment, of a chapter in the Holy Bible and/or the use of the Lord's Prayer." In both situations a child could be excused from the readings at the request of a parent.

Speaking for a majority of the Court, Justice Tom C. Clark declared that the school readings of the Lord's Prayer and the Bible are forbidden by the Establishment Clause of the First Amendment. They are religious exercises, "prescribed as part of the curricular activities of students who are required to attend [public] school. They are held in the school buildings under the supervision and with the participation of teachers employed in those schools." Therefore, these readings have been "required by the States in violation of the command of the First Amendment that the Government maintain strict neutrality, neither aiding nor opposing religion."

Justice Clark went on to deal with the charge that unless those readings of the Bible and the Lord's Prayer were permitted, a "religion of secularism" would be established in the schools. "We agree, of course," said Clark, "that the State may not establish a 'religion of secularism' in the sense of affirmatively opposing or showing hostility to religion, thus 'preferring those who believe in no religion over those who do believe.' . . . We do not agree, however, that this decision in any sense has that effect" (emphasis added).

Insisting that the state be strictly neutral is not at all the same as permitting the state to be hostile to religion.

Did this decision mean that the Bible is entirely excluded from public school classrooms? Not at all, said Clark. "The Bible is worthy of study for its literary and historic qualities. Nothing we have said here indicates that such study of the Bible or of religion, when presented objectively as part of a secular program of education, may not be effected consistently with the First Amendment." The difference in these cases, said Clark, is that Bible readings were being used as *religious* exercises.

In a concurring opinion, Justice William J. Brennan, Jr., noted that although both laws permitted children to be excused from the readings if a parent so requested, it was quite possible that some children would feel too intimidated to ask to be excused. The very setting up of these religious exercises in a public school creates a "cruel dilemma" for children who do not want to participate. They are allowed to be excused, but if they actually do get excused, they may be "stigmatized as atheists or nonconformists simply on the basis of their request. Such reluctance to seek exemption seems all the more likely in view of the fact that children are disinclined at this age to step out of line or to flout 'peer-group norms.' "

In another concurring opinion, Justice William O. Douglas observed that these Bible readings were unconstitutional because the First Amendment's Establishment Clause "forbids the State to employ its facilities or funds in a way that gives any church, or all churches, greater strength in our society than it would have by relying on its members alone. . . . [Here] public funds, though small in amount, are being used to promote a religious exercise. Through the mechanism of the State, all of the people [all the taxpayers] are being required to finance a religious exercise that only some of the people want and that violates the sensibilities of others. . . .

"It is not the amount of public funds expended; as this case illustrates, it is the use to which public funds are put that is controlling. For the First Amendment does not say that some forms of establishment are allowed; it says that 'no law respecting an establishment of religion' shall be made."

The First Amendment's firm rejection of any state support of any religion was rooted in what had happened in the American colonies before the Revolution.

In his decision in *Engel v. Vitale,* Justice Black noted:

> By the time of the adoption of our Constitution, our history shows that there was a widespread awareness among many Americans of the dangers of a union of Church and State. These people knew, some of them from bitter personal experience, that one of the greatest dangers to the freedom of the individual to worship in his own way lay in the Government's placing its official stamp of approval upon one particular kind of prayer or one particular form of religious services. They knew the anguish, hardship and strife that could come when zealous religious groups struggled with one another to obtain the Government's stamp of approval from each King, Queen, or Protector that came to temporary power.

Much of the history of religion, after all, had consisted of merciless warfare between divergent sects. As Irving Brant had noted about seventeenth-century England: "Gallows, pillory, knotted whip and prison were used, by every faction that gained power, in an effort to determine which Christian denomination best represented the loving spirit of the Nazarene and the merciful benignity of God."

Although religious dissidents fled England to America in order to secure their own freedom of conscience, many were sternly disinclined, once in power themselves, to allow religious liberty to those with whom they disagreed. The Puritans' colony at Massachusetts Bay, for instance, was a theocratic state which severely punished such "damnable heresies" as the beliefs of Catholics and Quakers. When four Quakers returned to the Massachusetts Bay colony after having been banished from it because of their religious convictions, they were put to death.

Also in Massachusetts, Anne Hutchinson was convicted in 1638 for being a seducer of the faithful and a blasphemer because she had held religious meetings in her home, where she spoke of the "covenant of grace." (This was the belief that salvation was to be found through faith and direct, intuitive knowledge of God—not, as the Puritans held, through obedience to the strict laws of the Church.) Upon conviction Anne Hutchinson was excommunicated and banished. When she was killed by Indians on New York's Long Island in 1643, her former neighbors in Massachusetts proclaimed her demise to have been an act of divine judgment.

In Maryland—founded by Catholics who had suffered under Anglican persecution in England—there was no freedom of religion for those heretics who denied that Jesus was the son of God or who rebelled against the doctrine of the Trinity.

Constitutional historian Leo Pfeffer reports that in Virginia one of the "Lawes Divine, Moral and Martial," adopted in 1614, provided that "every person in the colony, or who should come into it, was required to repair to the Minister for examination in the faith. If he should be unsound, he was to be instructed. If any refused to go to the minister, he should be whipt; on a second refusal he should be whipt twice and compelled to 'acknowledge his fault on Saboth day in the assembly of the congregation';

for a third refusal he should be 'whipt every day until he makes acknowledgement.' "

It was indeed dangerous in Virginia to have no religious faith. For instance, the penalty for breaking the Sabbath for the third time was death. Pfeffer adds that the code also included the death penalty for speaking "impiously of the Trinity or one of the Divine Persons, or against the known articles of Christian faith."

In early Virginia, moreover, Quakers were banished, Catholics were forbidden to hold office, and priests were not even allowed to set foot in the colony. In most of the colonies, in fact, there was no wall of separation between the state and the particular religious establishment that the state supported.

In Colonial America, according to Justice Black, "Catholics found themselves hounded and proscribed because of their faith; Quakers who followed their conscience went to jail; Baptists were peculiarly obnoxious to certain dominant Protestant sects; men and women of varied faiths who happened to be in a minority in a particular locality were persecuted because they steadfastly persisted in worshipping God only as their consciences dictated. And all of these dissenters were compelled to pay tithes and taxes to support government-sponsored churches whose ministers preached inflammatory sermons designed to strengthen and consolidate the established faith by generating a burning hatred against dissenters."

Two of the colonies, Pennsylvania and Rhode Island, came much closer than the others to understanding and allowing for religious freedom. William Penn, a Quaker who had been imprisoned in England because of his beliefs, designed in 1683 a "Frame of Government" for Pennsylvania which proclaimed that anyone believing in

"One Almighty God" should be free to worship as he liked. However, a requirement for holding civil office was a belief in "Jesus Christ, the Savior of the World." Jews, agnostics, and atheists, among others, were not first-class citizens, even in Pennsylvania.

Roger Williams, who had been exiled from the Massachusetts Bay Colony in 1635 for unorthodox religious views, founded a community of free conscience in Providence, Rhode Island. In 1663 the "Charter of Rhode Island and Providence Plantation" clearly separated church and state, but after the death of Roger Williams there was some backsliding. In 1762, for instance, a Rhode Island court turned down a petition by two Jews for naturalization. To grant them full membership in the community, said the court, would be "inconsistent with the first principles on which the colony was founded."

Yet in the 1663 "Charter of Rhode Island and Providence Plantation"—secured by Roger Williams from Charles II—it had been clearly stated that no person within this colony "shall be in any wise molested, punished, disquieted, or called in question for any difference of opinion in matters of religion . . . and every person . . . may . . . freely and fully have and enjoy his . . . own judgements and consciences, in matters of religious concernments."

Although Roger Williams's insistence on separation of church and state was hardly the norm in the colonies, more and more colonists came to resent those laws which made taxpayers share in the financial support of an established church regardless of whether or not they subscribed to the doctrines of that church.

This resentment continued into the early years of the new republic. In 1784, for example, a Virginia Assessment Bill, supported by Patrick Henry, would have required that everyone pay taxes to support the churches. Aware of the opposition to this commingling of church and state, the drafters of the bill made it possible for every taxpayer to choose the church to which his tax would be paid. Or if he did not want his money to go to any specific church, he could specify that it be used "for the encouragement of seminaries of learning."

The protest continued anyway. Anticipating the First Amendment, the Presbytery of Hanover declared: "Religion is altogether personal; and the right of exercising it is inalienable; and it is not, cannot, and ought not to be, resigned to the will of the society at large; and much less to the Legislature."

Among those agreeing with the fundamental need to prevent any state involvement with religion were Thomas Jefferson, James Madison, and Tom Paine. In *Common Sense* (1776) Paine wrote, "As to religion, I hold it to be the indispensable duty of all government to protect all conscientious professors thereof, and I know of no other business which government hath to do therewith."

Thomas Jefferson, in his *Notes on Virginia* (1782), emphasized that the government has no authority over the natural right of conscience. "The legitimate powers of government extend only to such acts as are injurious to others. But it does me no injury for my neighbor to say there are twenty gods, or no God. It neither picks my pocket nor breaks my leg."

Jefferson also derided the notion that uniformity of belief should be considered either desirable or attainable in a free society: "Millions of innocent men, women, and children, since the introduction of Christianity, have been burnt, tortured, fined, imprisoned; yet we have not advanced one inch toward uniformity. What has been the effect of coercion? To make one half the world fools, and the other half hypocrites. To support roguery and error all over the earth."

Meanwhile, James Madison, fighting to end all religious assessments on the taxpayers of Virginia, wrote in his *Memorial and Remonstrance* (1785), "Who does not see that the same authority which can establish Christianity, in exclusion of all other religions, may establish, with the same ease, any particular sect of Christians, in exclusion of all other sects?"

The Virginia Assessment Bill was defeated, and in 1786 Madison persuaded the Virginia legislature to pass Thomas Jefferson's historic *Virginia Act for Establishing Religious Freedom.* It separated church from state, freeing all citizens from any obligation to support any religion, leaving each citizen to profess any belief he chose. Or none.

By the next year, the Constitution of the United States was being drafted without any references to God. There was not to be, said James Madison, "a shadow of right in the government to meddle with religion." To further secure that principle, Article VI of the Constitution provides that "no religious Test shall ever be required as a Qualification to any Office or public Trust under the United States."

To make the division between church and state even clearer, the First Amendment added the prohibition: "Congress shall make no law respecting an establishment of religion, or prohibiting the free exercise thereof."

At that point in history, no other country in the world had established total freedom of worship by erecting what Jefferson called "a wall of separation between church and state." As historian Irving Brant has said, Madison, Jefferson, and their colleagues "knew what they were doing. English history had demonstrated to them that without complete religious liberty, without freedom of conscience, and separation of church and state, there could be no freedom of speech, or of the press, or the right of assembly."

As clear as the wording of the First Amendment appears to be in regard to religion, generations of Americans have argued over its meaning. One of the more renowned Supreme Court decisions about how to build a wall between church and state was *McCollum v. Board of Education* (1948). Vashti McCollum was protesting the fact that in her fourth-grade child's public school in Champaign, Illinois, religious teachers, employed by private religious groups, were allowed to come into school once a week and give religious instruction (thirty minutes for the lower grades, forty-five minutes for junior high school students). Pupils who chose not to participate in the religious instruction had to leave their classrooms and work on secular studies elsewhere in the building.

Delivering the 8 to 1 opinion of the Court, Justice Black declared this procedure to be unconstitutional. "Not only are the State's tax-supported public school buildings used for the dissemination of religious doctrines," said Black, but "the State also affords sectarian groups an invaluable aid in that it helps to provide pupils for their religious classes through use of the State's compulsory public school machinery. This is not separation of Church and State."

As Justice Felix Frankfurter said in a concurring opinion, "Separation means separation, not something less."

On the other hand, in *Zorach v. Clauson* (1952), separation did seem, to some of the Justices, to mean something less. The Supreme Court held, 6 to 3, that it was proper to allow students, on written request of their parents, to leave the New York public school system, on a regular schedule, to attend religious classes in religious centers outside of school. The other students remained in their classrooms.

Justice Douglas, writing for the Court, explained that this released-time system was constitutional because the religious instruction did not take place in public school classrooms and did not involve the expenditure of any public funds. It was essentially the same, Douglas said, as permitting a Jewish student to be absent from school to attend synagogue on Yom Kippur or allowing a Catholic student to take time out to go to mass on a Holy Day of Obligation. "In each case," he noted, "the teacher requires parental consent in writing. In each case, the teacher, in order to make sure the student is not a truant, goes further and requires a report from the priest, the rabbi, or the minister. The teacher, in other words, cooperates in a religious program to the extent of making it possible for her students to participate in it. Whether she does it occasionally for a few students, regularly for one, or pursuant to a systematized program designed to further the religious needs of all the students, does not alter the character of the act."

What about the *McCollum* decision? "In the *McCollum* case," Douglas said, "the classrooms were used for religious instruction and the force of the public school was used to promote that instruction. Here, as we have said, the public schools do no more than accommodate their schedules to a program of outside religious instruction. We follow the *McCollum* case. But we cannot expand it to cover the present released time program unless separation of Church and State means that public institutions can make no adjustments of their schedules to accommodate the religious needs of the people. We cannot read into the Bill of Rights such a philosophy of hostility to religion."

Although Douglas and Black were usually on the same side in First Amendment cases, they split in this one. In dissent, Black maintained that even though the religious instruction was taking place outside of school, the state was nonetheless aiding religion through this released-time arrangement by using its "compulsory education laws to help religious sects get attendants presumably too unenthusiastic to go unless moved to do so by the pressure of this state machinery. . . . This is not separation but combination of Church and State."

The state must be completely neutral, Black insisted, and the majority of the Court has in *Zorach* abandoned neutrality by supporting a program which, it says, "*merely* 'encourages religious instruction or cooperates with religious authorities.' . . . Government should not be allowed, under cover of the soft euphemism of 'co-operation,' to steal into the sacred area of religious choice."

Justice Robert H. Jackson, in his dissent, also stressed the presence here of the coercive power of the state. By contrast with students *voluntarily* attending religious classes *after* school hours, under the released-time system a truant officer is involved, and "if the youngster fails to go to the Church school, the truant officer dogs him back to the public schoolroom."

Meanwhile, as certain students go off to religious classes during school hours, the schooling of those who remain is "more or less suspended" in order that the nonreligious pupils "will not forge ahead of the churchgoing absentees." Accordingly, during that time, the public school "serves as a temporary jail for a pupil who will not go to Church. It takes more subtlety of mind than I possess to deny that this is governmental constraint in support of religion. It is as unconstitutional, in my view, when exerted by indirection as when exercised forthrightly. . . . We start down a rough road when we begin to mix compulsory education with compulsory godliness."

Jackson noted that since he sent his own children to privately supported church schools, he was able to "challenge the Court's suggestion that opposition to this plan can only be irreligious, atheistic, or agnostic. My evangelist brethren [on the Court] confuse an objection to compulsion with an objection to religion. It is possible to hold a faith with enough confidence to believe that what should be rendered to God does not need to be decided and collected by Caesar.

"The day that this country ceases to be free for irreligion it will cease to be free for religion—except for the sect that can win political power."

In 1968 the Supreme Court was confronted with another question concerning the slippery wall between church and state: Is it unconstitutional to pass a law requiring local public school authorities to lend textbooks, without charge, to all students in grades seven through twelve—*including* students attending private schools, both secular and religious? New York State had passed such a law, and it was challenged, eventually reaching the Supreme Court in the 1968 case *Board of Education v. Allen*.

Justice Byron R. White, speaking for the majority of

the Court (6–3) held the law *not* to be unconstitutional because it met a test set by the Court in the earlier *Abingdon Township v. Schempp.* (In that case, eight Justices had held that a law does not breach the wall between church and state if its purpose is secular [nonreligious] and if its primary effect "neither advances nor inhibits religion.")

The lending of textbooks to parochial schools meets this test, said Justice White in *Allen,* because individual students—not the parochial schools directly—ask for the books. No state funds go to the parochial schools. ("The financial benefit is to parents and children.") Furthermore, ownership of the books remains "at least technically" with the state; no *religious* books are loaned; and each book loaned has to be approved by public school authorities.

There is nothing in the record, the majority of the Court said, to support the proposition that "all textbooks, whether they deal with mathematics, physics, foreign languages, history or literature, are used by the parochial schools to teach religion." Therefore, it is constitutional for the state to lend nonreligious books to religious schools.

The argument may at first seem unassailable. Not so, said three dissenting members of the Court (Hugo Black, Abe Fortas, and William O. Douglas). Lending books paid for by tax funds to parochial schools, they said, might well serve to support religious purposes.

The notion, said Douglas, that the pupil himself or herself selects the book is not based on reality. Actually, the books to be lent will be those asked for by the parochial school attended by the student. "Can there be the slightest doubt," Douglas asked, "that the head of the parochial school will select the book or books that best promote its sectarian creed?

"And the textbook," Douglas continued, "goes to the heart of education in a parochial school. It is the chief, although not solitary, instrumentality for propagating a particular religious creed or faith. How can we possibly approve such state aid to a religion?" Furthermore, Douglas reemphasized, since it will be the parochial school which actually asks for the books to be lent at public expense, the school will select those books which most support its particular religious viewpoint. Even though the books are "secular," they can vary widely in their perspectives, whether in history or economics or embryology.

For example, Douglas pointed out, one history text (*Land of the Free*, by Caughey, Franklin, and May, 1965) lamented the slaughter of the Aztecs by Cortés for its destruction of a New World culture; another (*America Yesterday*, by Furlong, Sharkey, and Sharkey, 1963) justified the slaughter of the Aztecs on the grounds that the Spaniards "carried the true Faith" to a barbaric people practicing human sacrifice. Note the term "true Faith." Which book would a parochial school choose? And should the state provide that book? The majority of the Court, however, saw no First Amendment problem in the state lending textbooks to *all* students, without charge.

Three years after *Allen* the Court seemed to change direction somewhat by reinforcing the wall of separation between church and state. In *Earley v. DiCenso* the Court ruled that the state of Rhode Island could not constitutionally pay a 15 percent salary supplement to teachers in those *nonpublic* schools in which less money was being spent to educate each pupil than the average expenditure in the public schools. (The intent of the law was to provide equal educational opportunity, insofar as funds for teachers were concerned, for *every* student in the state.)

According to that Rhode Island law, the nonpublic school teachers receiving public money to supplement their salaries were required to teach only courses that were also offered in the public schools; to work only with materials which were also used in the public schools; and to agree not to teach courses in religion. (At the time the case was brought, all the nonpublic school beneficiaries under the bill taught at Roman Catholic schools.) By setting these "secular" conditions for parochial school teachers getting the extra pay, Rhode Island legislators believed there would be no basic violation of the separation between church and state.

Chief Justice Warren E. Burger, speaking for a majority of the Court, disagreed. Textbooks were the issue in the *Allen* case, Burger recalled, but "teachers have a substantially different ideological character than books. In terms of potential for involving some aspect of faith or morals in secular subjects, a textbook's content is ascertainable, but a *teacher's* handling of a subject is not. We cannot ignore the dangers that a teacher under religious control and discipline poses to the separation of the religious from the purely secular aspects of precollege education. The conflict of functions inheres in the situation. . . .

"We need not and do not assume that teachers in parochial schools will be guilty of bad faith or any conscious design to evade the limitations imposed by the [Rhode Island] statute and the First Amendment. We simply recognize that a dedicated religious person, teaching in a school affiliated with his or her faith and operated to inculcate its tenets, will inevitably experience great difficulty in remaining religiously neutral. Doctrine and faith are not inculcated or advanced by neutrals. With the best of intentions such a teacher would find it hard to make a total separation between secular teaching and religious doctrine."

In the years since *Earley v. DiCenso* the Supreme Court has had continuing difficulty in defining and adhering to a clear standard of what kind of public aid to religious schools is constitutional. In 1977, for instance, the Court, in a broadly split decision, upheld an action of the Ohio legislature providing certain tax-supported services to parochial school students—hearing, speech, and psychological diagnoses; and remedial counseling and training—provided that all these services take place at "neutral" sites off the school premises. Also approved were state-supplied standardized tests. However, the Court held it would be impermissible for the state to lend such instructional material as maps or audiovisual aids to students in nonpublic schools. Nor could the state pay for such educational activities by religious schools as field trips.

The diagnostic and other services were allowed, said Justice Harry A. Blackmun, because they "are not closely associated with the educational mission of the non-public school [and] will not create an impermissible risk of the fostering of ideological views." (That is, public tax money could be used to help remedy a parochial school student's hearing defect but not to support his religious education.)

Yet, if lending textbooks without charge to parochial schools is constitutional under the *Allen* decision, why not maps? Or should the state avoid *all* kinds of support to religious schools? The guidelines used by the Supreme Court in deciding what kind of state tax aid to parochial schools is constitutional—and what kind is not—are essentially these:

1. If the purpose of state aid is secular—as in speech therapy, for instance—then the Establishment Clause of the First Amendment has not been violated. As for textbooks, the majority of the Court decided in the *Allen* case that since no religious books were being lent by the state, the intent of that form of state aid was secular.

2. Public tax funds must not be used to advance religion.

3. The state, in providing aid, must not become entangled in religious affairs. For example, certain public funds targeted for nonreligious use in religious schools may nonetheless require continual monitoring by the state to make sure the schools are not using the money for religious purposes. This kind of continual surveillance, the Court has said, would lead to "excessive entanglement" by the state in religion.

In the Rhode Island case, *Earley v. DiCenso*, for example, Chief Justice Burger noted that parochial school teachers receiving a salary supplement from the state were forbidden to teach any course in religion and also had to teach "only those courses that are offered in the public schools and use only those texts and materials that are found in the public schools."

But how would it be possible to make sure that those teachers were obeying the law? "A comprehensive . . . and continuing state surveillance," said Burger, "will inevitably be required to ensure that these restrictions are obeyed and the First Amendment [separation of church and state] otherwise respected. Unlike a book, a teacher cannot be inspected once so as to determine the extent and intent of his or her personal beliefs and subjective acceptance of the limitations imposed by the First Amendment." Accordingly, these continual inspections would "involve excessive and enduring entanglement between state and church."

The Court appears to make yet another distinction between constitutional and unconstitutional state aid to church-related schools. Most forms of aid to religious colleges and universities are allowed, by contrast with the considerable restrictions on state assistance to elementary and secondary parochial schools. The explanation, as Gene Maeroff of *The New York Times* points out, is that the Court feels that "the wall separating church and state should be higher and stronger for elementary and secondary schools than for colleges and universities because young children are more susceptible to religious teachings."

In any case, the history so far of High Court decisions on state aid to religious schools has not given total comfort either to those who oppose any state help whatsoever or to those who feel that the wall of separation is far too high. The end result, however, has been that the American public school system remains unaligned with any religion—a condition that the First Amendment clearly mandates.

XVIII

*It is bitterly ironical that a free government should
inflict a penalty for refusal to salute a symbol of freedom.*

The preceding chapter explored the Establishment Clause of the First Amendment: There shall be no law respecting an establishment of religion. The First Amendment then goes on to forbid any law "prohibiting the free exercise" of religion.

Does this mean that it would be unconstitutional, by way of example, for a public school to expel children of Jehovah's Witnesses for disobeying a state law that required all public school students to salute the American flag?

In *Minersville School District v. Gobitis* the Supreme Court heard a case in which two such children had refused to salute the flag on the ground that doing so would violate their religious beliefs. To freely exercise their religion, the students and their parents said, they must be allowed to reject the flag salute because they considered the flag "an image" within the meaning of God's command in the Old Testament: "Thou shalt not make unto thee any graven image . . . thou shalt not bow down thyself to them, nor serve them."

Lillian Gobitis, twelve, and her brother William, ten,

were expelled from the public schools of Minersville, Pennsylvania, for their refusal to salute the national flag as part of a daily school exercise for teachers and students. By an 8 to 1 vote the High Court declared that the Gobitis children *could* constitutionally be expelled.

In delivering the opinion of the Court, Justice Felix Frankfurter maintained that there are certain laws that a legislature considers essential to secure "that orderly, tranquil, and free society without which religious toleration itself is unattainable." The Pennsylvania flag salute law is such a statute, he maintained, for it recognizes that "the ultimate foundation of a free society is the binding tie of cohesive sentiment. . . . We live by symbols. The flag is the symbol of our national unity, transcending all internal differences, however large, within the framework of the Constitution."

It may be, Frankfurter conceded, that a compulsory flag salute is not the best way of "training children in patriotic impulses." Perhaps the deepest patriotism is engendered by giving all beliefs "unfettered scope" and leaving their adherents free to salute the flag or not. But this is a matter of educational policy, and it is not proper for the courts to decide educational policy.

The High Court's decision had an immediate effect, as Leo Pfeffer pointed out in *God, Caesar, and the Constitution:*

> The Court's decision was announced on June 3, 1940. Between June 12 and June 20, hundreds of physical attacks upon the Jehovah's Witnesses were reported in the United States Department of Justice. At Kennebunk, Maine, their Kingdom Hall was burned. At Rockville, Maryland, the police assisted a mob in dispersing a

Jehovah's Witnesses Bible meeting. At Litchfield, Illinois, practically the entire town mobbed a company of some sixty Witnesses who were canvassing it. At Connersville, Indiana, several Witnesses were charged with riotous conspiracy, their attorney beaten, and all driven out of town. At Jackson, Mississippi, members of a veterans' organization forcibly removed a number of Witnesses and their trailer homes from the town. In Nebraska, a Witness was lured from his house, abducted, and castrated. In Richwood, West Virginia, the chief of police and deputy sheriff forced a group of Witnesses to drink large doses of castor oil, and paraded the victims through the streets, tied together with police department rope. In the two years following the *Gobitis* decision there was an uninterrupted record of violence and persecution of the Witnesses. Almost without exception, the flag and flag salute were the causes.

A quite different reaction to the *Gobitis* decision was expressed by *The Christian Century*: "It is bitterly ironical that a free government should inflict a penalty for refusal to salute a symbol of freedom."

Three years after *Gobitis* the Court reversed itself. The case, *West Virginia State Board of Education v. Barnette*, also involving Jehovah's Witnesses, resulted from a ruling by the West Virginia Board of Education—after the *Gobitis* decision—that all teachers and pupils be required to salute the flag. A refusal would be "regarded as an Act of insubordination, and . . . dealt with accordingly." That meant expulsion from school with no readmittance until the student had yielded and saluted the flag. Meanwhile, the student would be listed as "unlawfully absent" and could be proceeded against as a delinquent. In addition, his parents or guardians were liable to prosecution.

In his opinion for the Court (which divided 6 to 3), Justice Robert H. Jackson said that Jehovah's Witnesses' children "have been expelled from school and are threatened with exclusion for no other cause [than refusing to salute the flag]. Officials threaten to send them to reformatories maintained for criminally inclined juveniles. Parents of such children have been prosecuted and are threatened with prosecutions for causing delinquency."

Jackson recalled that in the *Gobitis* case one basis on which the Court had justified the expulsion of children refusing to salute the flag was its view that it did not have the competence to interfere with school boards and legislators in matters of educational policy. (If the Court were to act otherwise, Justice Frankfurter had said in *Gobitis*, it would become "the school board for the country.") Jackson, speaking for a new majority, rejected that argument. He emphasized that each citizen is protected by the Bill of Rights against the state itself and all of its creatures, "Boards of Education not excepted." Furthermore, the fact that boards of education *"are educating the young for citizenship is reason for scrupulous protection of Constitutional freedoms of the individual, if we are not to strangle the free mind at its source and teach youth to discount principles of our government as mere platitudes"* (emphasis added).

In the same decision Jackson made another point that is fundamental to a full understanding not only of the First Amendment but of everything else in the Bill of Rights: "The very purpose of a Bill of Rights was to withdraw certain subjects from the vicissitudes of political controversy, to place them beyond the reach of majorities and officials and to establish them as legal principles to be applied by the courts. *One's right to life, liberty, and*

*property, to free speech, a free press, freedom of worship
and assembly, and other fundamental rights may not be
submitted to vote; they depend on the outcome of no
elections"* (emphasis added).

Jackson went on to what he considered "the very heart"
of the *Gobitis* decision, which the Court was now over-
turning. In that previous ruling the Court had held that
"national unity is the basis of national security" and that
the authorities therefore have "the right to select appropriate compulsory means for its attainment."

Does the state have the right to go beyond persuasion
and example in its desire to attain national unity? Does
the state have the right to try to achieve national unity by
such means as *compulsory* flag salutes?

No, said Jackson: "Those who begin coercive elimina-
tion of dissent soon find themselves exterminating dissenters. Compulsory unification of opinion achieves only
the unanimity of the graveyard."

In this country, on the other hand, "the First Amendment to our Constitution was designed to avoid these ends
by avoiding these beginnings. . . . We set up government
by the consent of the governed, and the Bill of Rights
denies those in power any legal opportunity to coerce that
consent. Authority here is to be controlled by public opinion, not public opinion by authority."

A free society means the freedom to differ, and that
"freedom to differ is not limited to things that do not
matter much. That would be a mere shadow of freedom.
The test of its substance is the right to differ as to things
that touch the heart of the existing order."

Justice Jackson then distilled the essence of true Amer-
icanism: "If there is any fixed star in our constitutional
constellation, it is that no official, high or petty, can pre-

scribe what shall be orthodox politics, nationalism, religion, or other matters of opinion or *force citizens to confess by word or act their faith therein*" (emphasis added).

Accordingly, the West Virginia State Board of Education had acted unconstitutionally in compelling the flag salute because it thereby invaded "the sphere of intellect and spirit which it is the purpose of the First Amendment to our Constitution to reserve from all official control."

Since the *West Virginia State Board of Education v. Barnette* decision, lower courts have used it to support rulings that schools cannot force students to stand during the Pledge of Allegiance because refusing to stand is an expression of political or religious belief and therefore protected by the First Amendment.

In one New York case, a student who did not want to participate in the flag salute on political grounds was ordered by school authorities to leave the room if she refused to stand during the salute; the court said she did not have to stand *or* leave the room. In Arizona, when school officials insisted that students stand during the singing of the national anthem—even when certain pupils claimed that doing so would violate their religious beliefs—the court ruled the order unconstitutional because it interfered with the protesting students' "free exercise" of religion.

The New York case cited above was *Frain v. Barron* (1969). Mary Frain, a student at Jamaica High School, had refused to recite the Pledge of Allegiance because she said that to do so would indicate her approval of the government's policies, and she disagreed with some of them. Moreover, for her to stand during the Pledge would imply that she agreed with the words "liberty and justice for all," and she did not agree that all Americans had equal justice. Then why did she not at least leave the room, as ordered, during the Pledge? Because being sent from the classroom was a way of punishing students and stigmatizing them as troublemakers, and she did not believe she should be punished for following her conscience.

The Federal District Court agreed with Mary Frain, ruling that a student cannot be stigmatized for obeying her conscience rather than obeying school authorities. Accordingly, Mary Frain was allowed to remain seated in the classroom during the Pledge of Allegiance.

In 1977 Deborah Lipp, a sixteen-year-old sophomore at Mountain Lakes High School in New Jersey, became a figure of fierce controversy because of her attitude toward the Pledge of Allegiance. In all other respects, Deborah Lipp was a model student, receiving straight A's and working part-time as a teacher's aide helping eight- and ten-year-olds with perceptual problems.

One day in May, however, a teacher, noticing that Deborah was not standing for the Pledge, told her that she must stand and show respect if she wanted to remain at Mountain Lakes High School. The principal backed up the teacher, threatening Deborah with expulsion. New Jersey State law supported the principal and the teacher. The law stated that students with "conscientious scruples" against saluting the flag or making the Pledge of Allegiance would not have to do either but were required to stand at attention while the Pledge is given "to show full respect to the flag."

Deborah Lipp refused to be intimidated, believing the requirement that she stand was an "absolutely absurd" denial of the "liberty" promised to everyone by the Pledge of Allegiance. And she quoted Supreme Court Justice

William O. Douglas: "The right to dissent is the only thing that makes life tolerable. . . . The affairs of government could not be conducted by democratic standards without it."

With the help of the American Civil Liberties Union, Deborah Lipp went into Federal District Court to challenge the New Jersey law requiring every student to stand during the Pledge. Her lawyer, Constance Hepburn, cited, during her argument, a 1973 Federal Court of Appeals decision in a similar case which held that "the act of standing is itself part of the pledge" and therefore could not be commanded by the state if a student had conscientious objections to reciting the Pledge itself. Said that 1973 court: "Standing in silence is an act that cannot be compelled."

Meanwhile, editorials sharply criticizing Deborah appeared in the local newspapers along with hostile letters to the editor about her and her case. Deborah herself received some supportive mail and phone calls but also many abusive letters and calls that abounded in foul language. There were also bomb threats. Many of these ferocious critics, Deborah noted, "describe themselves as patriots and call me un-American, Communist, and other names. Do they consider harassment and threats of violence more American than lawful use of the U.S. judicial system? I suggest these people reassess their values.

"I've been told I should go to Russia," Deborah wrote in an article for the New York *Daily News*. "Perhaps the people who feel this way—people who don't like to hear different opinions expressed—would feel more at home there. Certainly in Russia I wouldn't have the right to do what I've done here. I have no intention of leaving my country."

But why did she keep refusing to at least stand at attention during the flag salute and Pledge of Allegiance? "The Pledge," wrote Deborah, "states that I am standing for a country of liberty and justice for all.' I don't believe that that country exists. I look around me and see every day that blacks, poor people, women, American Indians, atheists, and countless other minorities do not have equal rights under the law. I can't bring myself to believe that my standing [during the Pledge] will change the injustice that exists, nor can I close my eyes to that injustice and salute a 'dream' and not do anything to further that dream, as so many people would have me do." Furthermore, she said, forcing her to stand during the Pledge would be an unconstitutional denial of her freedom of expression.

At home, her father, a management official of a computer company, criticized her stand. "He tries to tell me about patriotism," Deborah said. "I don't know how to define that word. If it means love of the Constitution, then I'm patriotic. But if it means love for the country for what it is today—with the ugliness, the poverty, and the government corruption—then I'm not patriotic. But I do love the freedom I have in this country to do what I'm doing right now. I love the freedom to fight a law I don't like. In other countries, I'd have to keep my mouth shut."

In August 1977 a federal judge in Newark overturned the "compulsory standing" New Jersey law because, he said, it compelled Deborah Lipp—and any other student who refused to make the Pledge—to commit an act of "symbolic speech." That is, since the act of standing is itself part of the Pledge, the state, by forcing Deborah to stand, was making her affirm a belief she did not in fact hold. (Among the cases the judge cited was *West Virginia*

State Board of Education v. Barnette.) From now on, New Jersey students opposed to the Pledge of Allegiance could remain seated while their classmates recited it and saluted the flag—so long as the seated dissidents did not "whistle, drum, tap dance or otherwise be disruptive."

Deborah was delighted that her faith in the Constitution, "a marvelous, magnificent document," had been redeemed. Looking back at the furor that had attended her exercising her First Amendment rights, Deborah recalled the bumper stickers—SEND THE LIPPS BACK TO SIBERIA—that had appeared around the state. "Well," she said, "I am standing up for my personal beliefs. If I can't do that in New Jersey, then this state isn't as good as Siberia."

The Constitutional Powers of the Free Press

"The First Amendment is couched in absolute terms—freedom of speech shall not be abridged . . . Free speech, free press, free exercise of religion are placed separate and apart; they are above and beyond the police power . . ."—William O. Douglas (Wide World photo)

XIX

*The Government's power to censor the press was
abolished so that the press would remain forever free
to censure the government.*

All the First Amendment says about the press is that
Congress shall make no law abridging its freedom. (By
means of the Fourteenth Amendment, that prohibition
was later applied to the individual states.)

Yet—especially in this century—there have been many
court battles over the precise meanings of those few
words. One of the more crucial was *Near v. Minnesota*
(1931).

There had been no doubt when the First Amendment
was adopted in 1791 that it clearly outlawed any form of
government censorship of the press—prior restraint—such
as existed for so long in England, where the government
had the power to license publications. Nonetheless, it
was not until this case that the Supreme Court ruled
directly on the issue of press censorship.

At the core of *Near v. Minnesota* was the so-called
1925 Minnesota Gag Law, which allowed the state to
temporarily or permanently shut down a publication held
to be "a public nuisance." The law was directed against
anyone "engaged in the business" of regularly disseminat-

ing an "obscene, lewd and lascivious" or a "malicious, scandalous and defamatory" publication. Not only could a county attorney bring suit to shut down such a blight, but any "reputable citizen" might start an action if the county attorney failed to act.

Jay M. Near was one of the publishers of *The Saturday Press*, a Minneapolis weekly which, in a series of articles, had been charging that Jewish gangsters controlled gambling, racketeering, and bootlegging in that city. (From one of the articles: "Practically every vendor of vile hooch, every owner of a moonshine still, every snake-faced gangster and embryonic egg in the Twin Cities is a JEW. . . . It is Jew, Jew, Jew, as long as one cares to comb over the records.")

The Saturday Press also accused local law-enforcement officials of being in cahoots with the Jewish cabal. Moreover, according to First Amendment historian Fred Friendly, copublishers Jay M. Near and Howard Guilford "were self-admitted scandalmongers and occasional blackmailers." Could such people be permitted to publish scandal with impunity?

A county attorney who had been criticized by the paper approached that question by getting a judge to issue a temporary restraining order under the Minnesota Gag Law. The district court ordered Near and Guilford not "to produce, edit, publish . . . sell or give away any publication whatsoever which is a malicious, scandalous or defamatory newspaper, as defined by the law." Nor could they operate "said nuisance" under "the name and title of *The Saturday Press* or any other name or title." The case was appealed, and the highest court in the state affirmed that the paper was indeed a public nuisance and so must be permanently shut down.

The decision was appealed to the Supreme Court. In oral arguments before that body, Justice Louis Brandeis, himself a Jew—the first Jew to sit on the Court and the object of no little anti-Semitism in the long debate before he was confirmed—was clearly disturbed by the Minnesota Gag Law. "It is difficult to see," Brandeis said, "how one is to have a free press . . . without the [First Amendment] privilege this Minnesota Act seems to limit." After all, Brandeis noted, the paper is trying to expose collusion between criminals and public officials. "You are dealing here with a scandal that ought to be a matter of prime interest to every citizen."

"Assuming it to be true," answered the attorney arguing for the state of Minnesota.

"No," Brandeis said firmly. "A newspaper cannot always wait until it gets the judgment of a court. These men set out on a campaign to rid the city of certain evils."

"So they say," said the attorney for Minnesota.

"Yes, of course, so they say." Justice Louis D. Brandeis was becoming impatient. "They acted with courage. They invited suit for criminal libel [after publication] if what they said was not true. . . . Now if that campaign was not privileged [under the First Amendment], if that is not one of the things for which the press exists, then for what does it exist?"

In his decision for the 5 to 4 majority of the Court, Chief Justice Charles E. Hughes recalled the eventually successful struggle in England against the censoring power of the state and quoted a famous line by the eighteenth-century English jurist Sir William Blackstone: "The liberty of the press is indeed essential to the nature of a free state; but this consists in laying no *previous* restraints upon publications, and not in freedom from censure for criminal matter when published."

That is, there is to be no censorship of any material *before* publication. But there is the possibility of punishment *after* publication if it can be proved in court that, for example, a paper has violated the law of libel. So too in this case, said Justice Hughes. If Near and Guilford have indeed libeled anyone, they can be sued after publication.

Can the state *never* engage in *prior* restraint of the press?

"Only in exceptional cases," said the Chief Justice. In time of war, "no one would question that a government might prevent actual obstruction to its recruiting service or the publication of the sailing dates of transports or the number and location of troops." None of these exceptions, Hughes continued, apply to the case at hand.

What about such abuses of freedom of the press as are charged here, the scandalmongering and apparent anti-Semitism? Hughes quoted James Madison, whom he described as "the leading spirit in the preparation of the First Amendment":

> Some degree of abuse is inseparable from the proper use of everything, and in no instance is this more true than in that of the press. . . . It is better to leave a few of its noxious branches to their luxuriant growth, than, by pruning them away, to injure the vigour of those yielding the proper fruits. And can the wisdom of this policy be doubted by any who reflect that to the press alone, chequered as it is with abuses, the world is indebted for all the triumphs which have been gained by reason and humanity over error and oppression; who reflect that to the same beneficent source the United

States owe much of the lights which conducted them to the ranks of a free and independent nation?"

Therefore, said the Chief Justice, the First Amendment protects *all* the press, including "miscreant purveyors of scandal," from censorship.

As United States Court of Appeals Judge Cuthbert Pound once said, "The rights of the best of men are secure only as the rights of the vilest and most abhorrent are protected." This, of course, is true not only of the First Amendment but of all rights and liberties guaranteed by the Constitution.

Near v. Minnesota struck down a *state* law violating freedom of the press. Forty years later, in the most dramatic confrontation between newspapers and the federal government in American history, the Supreme Court prevented the President and the Justice Department from censoring the press. It was the first time the executive branch had tried, through the courts, to prevent the publication of material that it claimed would irreparably injure national security. Under attack was not a minor scandal sheet but two of the most prestigious newspapers in the country, *The New York Times* and *The Washington Post.*

The case of the Pentagon Papers began on June 13, 1971, when the *Times* published the first of a series of articles based on a secret Defense Department history of America's involvement in the Vietnamese War. It was later learned that these documents had been given to the *Times,* and later to other newspapers, by Daniel Ellsberg, a former Defense Department and Rand Corporation official who became an opponent of the war. While still engaged in government work, Ellsberg had covertly copied these classified papers.

The Pentagon Papers showed that for years vital decisions about the Vietnamese War—involving the lives of many thousands of Americans and Vietnamese—had been made at the highest levels of the government in ways that deliberately deceived the American people. During the 1964 presidential campaign, for instance, while Lyndon Johnson portrayed his opponent, Barry Goldwater, as a dangerous hawk who wanted to escalate the war, Johnson and his advisers, according to the Pentagon Papers, were secretly planning to do just that: to expand the war.

There were many other instances recorded in the Pentagon Papers of the White House and leaders of the State and Defense departments saying one thing publicly (that victory was in sight, for instance) while knowing the opposite. And in the process the nation—ignorant of this hidden decision-making and therefore of its consequences —was drawn ever more deeply, and destructively, into the war.

It was essential, said the *Times* on deciding to print the Pentagon Papers, that the public be informed of what had really been going on both because it was entitled to know the facts of a war that had cost the country so much and also so that it would be on guard against any future attempts by government to deceive the citizenry.

The government, on the other hand, strenuously maintained that publishing these secret documents would greatly endanger national security and could result in the death of American prisoners in Vietnam. Also, having them spread out in the newspapers would seriously weaken future American conduct of foreign policy, it maintained, because other nations would no longer trust the ability of this country's leaders to maintain the total confidentiality that is often essential in diplomatic dealings. If the press were now allowed to publish the secret Pentagon Papers, what protection could there be for secret international negotiations and consultations in the years ahead?

Furthermore, the government emphasized, under the Constitution the President is empowered to conduct foreign affairs, and this gives him the right and responsibility to protect the nation against disclosure of materials that endanger national security. The Pentagon Papers were just such material.

On June 15, 1971, two days after the *Times* had started to print the Pentagon Papers, an assistant United States attorney in New York asked in court that a temporary restraining order be issued barring the *Times* from going on with the series. Federal District Judge Murray Gurfein granted the order, the first time in American history that a federal judge had prohibited a newspaper from publishing a specific article or series of articles.

Four days later Judge Gurfein decided the *Times* should be permitted to go ahead and publish, but the articles did not appear because the case was now before the United States Court of Appeals. In a 5 to 3 decision that court ruled that the *Times* could resume publication only if it omitted any materials which the government decided were a threat to national security. The *Times* refused to go on with the series on that basis. To do so, the newspaper said, would be to submit to government censorship. The Pentagon Papers case was on its way to the United States Supreme Court.

Meanwhile, *The Washington Post* had obtained its own set of Pentagon Papers from Daniel Ellsberg. That paper too was stopped from publishing the series by the majority of a three-judge appellate court until a full hearing was held. Dissenting Judge J. Skelly Wright argued: "As if the long and sordid war in Southeast Asia had not already done enough harm to our people, it now is used to cut the heart out of our free institutions and system of government." But the majority of that court had declared: "Freedom of the press, as important as it is, is not boundless."

Although the full Court of Appeals for the District of Columbia soon decided that the *Post* should be able to go ahead and print, the final decision was up to the Supreme Court. Until it made up its mind, neither the *Post* nor the *Times* could continue publication of the Pentagon Papers.

On June 30, 1971—only fifteen days after the government had first moved to censor the *Times*—the High Court delivered its decision. (The extraordinary speed was due to the extraordinary importance of the constitutional issue: prior restraint of the press. Actual censorship had already been exercised. Was it to be allowed to continue?)

By a 6 to 3 vote, in *The New York Times Company v. United States*, the Supreme Court told the *Times* and the *Post* to go ahead and print the rest of the material. The decision, said the American Civil Liberties Union, "was a great event in American history in general and in constitutional history in particular."

Among the majority, Justice Hugo Black, with Justice William O. Douglas concurring, reminded his brethren that in the First Amendment "the Government's power to censor the press was abolished so that the press would remain forever free to censure the Government. The press was protected so that it could bare the secrets of Government and inform the people."

Black then focused on the nature of these particular documents which the government wanted kept secret. "Paramount among the responsibilities of a free press," he said, "is the duty to prevent any part of the Government from deceiving the people and sending them off to distant lands to die of foreign fevers and foreign shot and shell. In my view, far from deserving condemnation for their courageous reporting, *The New York Times, The Washington Post,* and other newspapers should be commended for serving the purpose that the Founding Fathers saw so clearly. In revealing the workings of Government that led to the Vietnam war, the newspapers nobly did precisely that which the Founders hoped and trusted they would do."

As for the government's argument that the President—through his constitutional power over the conduct of foreign affairs and his authority as Commander in Chief—must protect national security against publication of material that would endanger it, Black pointed out: "To find that the President has 'inherent power' to halt the publication of news by resort to the courts would wipe out the First Amendment and destroy the fundamental liberty and security of the very people the Government hopes to make 'secure.' No one can read the history of the adoption of the First Amendment without being convinced beyond any doubt that it was injunctions like those sought here that Madison and his collaborators intended to outlaw in this Nation for all time. . . . The guarding of military and diplomatic secrets at the expense of informed representative government provides no real security for our Republic."

Mr. Justice Douglas, citing *Near v. Minnesota* as having forbidden prior restraint of the press, said, "The dominant purpose of the First Amendment was to prohibit the widespread practice of governmental suppression of embarrassing information. . . . A debate of large proportions goes on in the Nation over our posture in Vietnam. That debate antedated the disclosure of the contents of the present documents. The latter are highly relevant to the debate in progress. Secrecy in government is fundamentally antidemocratic, perpetuating bureaucratic errors. Open debate and discussion of public issues are vital to our national health."

More cautious, among those in the majority, was Justice William J. Brennan. He agreed that in this specific case the First Amendment "stands as an absolute bar" against imposing prior restraint. But not in all cases. Remember, Brennan said, in *Near v. Minnesota* the Court declared that in time of war the government might censor the press if a newspaper were about to publish "the sailing dates of transports or the number and location of troops."

In this case, however, said Brennan, the government had not even alleged that publishing the Pentagon Papers will "inevitably, directly, and immediately" do anything like imperiling "the safety of a transport."

A somewhat similar approach was taken by Justice Potter Stewart. While agreeing with the executive branch of the government that it was not "in the national interest" for some of the material in the Pentagon Papers to be published, Stewart nonetheless had to let the First Amendment take precedence because he saw no evidence that disclosure of any of these documents "will surely result in direct, immediate and irreparable damage to our Nation and its people."

The three dissenters, supporting the government's position, were Chief Justice Warren E. Burger and Justices John Marshall Harlan and Harry A. Blackmun. The harshest dissenter was Blackmun.

After complaining of this "hurried decision of profound constitutional issues" without sufficiently careful deliberation, Blackmun noted that "the First Amendment, after all, is only one part of an entire Constitution. Article II of the great document vests in the Executive Branch primary power over the conduct of foreign affairs and places in that branch the responsibility for the Nation's safety. Each provision of the Constitution is important, and I cannot subscribe to a doctrine of unlimited absolutism for the First Amendment at the cost of downgrading other provisions."

Blackmun went on to echo the fears of Judge Malcolm Wilkey (a lower court judge who deliberated on the case) concerning the possible results of the majority decision. "I hope," Blackmun said, "that damage has not already been done. If, however, damage has been done, and if, with the Court's action today, these newspapers proceed to publish the critical documents and there results therefrom 'the death of soldiers, the destruction of alliances, the greatly increased difficulty of negotiation with our enemies, the inability of our diplomats to negotiate,' to which list I might add the factors of prolongation of the war and further delay in the freeing of United States prisoners, then the Nation's people will know where the responsibility for these sad consequences rests."

Seldom if ever in the nation's history had a Supreme Court Justice threatened the press with becoming a pariah to the nation by exercising its freedom to publish.

Blackmun's anger notwithstanding, *The New York Times Company v. United States* expanded the meaning of the First Amendment in a significant way. As the *Times* said in an editorial following the verdict, the case goes beyond an affirmation of the press's right to be free of prior restraint by government. "Its more profound significance," said the *Times*, "lies in the implicit but inescapable conclusion that the American people have a presumptive right to be informed of the political decisions of their Government and that when the Government has been devious with the people, it will find no constitutional sanction for its efforts to enforce concealment by censorship."

Although there was much rejoicing among members of the press and the public on the day the Pentagon Papers case was decided, it came to be more fully recognized that among the nine Justices only two, Black and Douglas, had upheld the press's right to publish without any possibility at all of prior restraint by the government. The rest had held, in various ways, that under certain circumstances—such as providing vital information to the enemy in time of war—the government might have the power to censor the press.

Yet, in a later case, *Nebraska Press Association v. Stuart*, the Court appeared to almost entirely rule out the possibility that government can tell the press what *not* to print. That case did not concern the conflict between the First Amendment and "national security." This time another chronic dilemma was at issue: the conflict between the First Amendment rights of the press and a defendant's right to a fair trial under the Sixth Amendment, which states in part:

In all criminal prosecutions, the accused shall enjoy the right to a speedy and public trial, by an *impartial* jury of the State and district wherein the crime shall have been committed. [Emphasis added]

XX

*. . . The press may be arrogant, tyrannical, abusive,
and sensationalist, just as it may be incisive, probing,
and informative. But at least in the context of prior
restraints on publication, the decision of what, when,
and how to publish is for editors, not judges.*

A labor leader was on trial in New York City in the early
1970s. The charge: using his position of considerable
power at an airport—where many of his members worked
—to get more than nine thousand dollars' worth of airline
tickets free.

Early in the trial a reporter for the New York *Daily
News* wrote that the labor leader had long been "a target
of local and federal law-enforcement authorities" and had
also "figured prominently in an award-winning series in
the *News* exposing the incursions by organized crime at
John F. Kennedy airport."

The defendant's lawyer angrily protested that the story
had prejudiced his client's Sixth Amendment rights to a
fair trial "by an impartial jury." This *Daily News* story,
he claimed, contained decidedly prejudicial material about
his client that would not be admissible in court but
could so influence a juror reading it that he would not be
impartial. (Jurors are instructed not to read press accounts of a trial in which they are serving, but unless they
are sequestered—kept from going home until the trial is

over—there is no way of making sure they obey the judge on this score.)

Agreeing with the defense attorney was the federal judge conducting the labor official's trial. He ordered the reporter from the *Daily News* not to print anything "that does not happen in this courtroom with respect to this case." (Such a restriction by a judge of what the press can print is called a gag order.)

When two other New York newspapers, the *Times* and the *Post*, also printed details of the defendant's unsavory past, they too were ordered by the judge to print nothing during the trial except what actually occurred in the courtroom. The *New York Post* said it would voluntarily comply with the judge's instructions. The other papers refused. A lawyer for the *Times* told the court that it was necessary for reporters to print background information because such material "tells the public what the public significance of the case is." The lawyer for the *Daily News* argued that no judge had the right to tell the press what to print or what not to print.

Furious, the judge accused the *Times* and the *Daily News* of engaging in a "blatant, flagrant attempt" to prevent the defendant from getting a fair trial. The press had its First Amendment rights, the judge said, but the defendant has constitutional rights too. Finally, however, the judge grudgingly yielded to the press. He removed the gag order, probably because he feared being overruled by a higher court.

As has happened throughout American history, here was a direct conflict between the public's First Amendment "right to know" and the defendant's Sixth Amendment right to a fair trial. It is a dilemma that one federal appeals court has called a "civil libertarian's nightmare."

The press says it cannot be censored, but many defense attorneys claim that unless the press is somehow prevented from publishing certain material before or during the trial (or both), their clients cannot be assured the impartial jury guaranteed them by the Sixth Amendment.

The first gag order on record was handed down by a California judge in 1893. He ordered a newspaper not to report on a divorce case which, he said, was of "a filthy nature." That order was overturned by the California Supreme Court. On the other hand, without imposing gag orders on the press, courts have from time to time set aside convictions obtained in an atmosphere made grossly prejudicial to the defendant by the press.

In 1961 the Supreme Court itself for the first time overturned a conviction on the basis of prejudicial press coverage. The case, *Irvin v. Dowd*, involved a murder trial, and the High Court unanimously declared: "It is not required . . . that the jurors be totally ignorant of the facts. . . . It is sufficient if the juror can lay aside his impression or opinion and render a verdict based on the evidence presented in court." But in the *Dowd* case, the Court went on, the press had so inflamed public opinion that a fair trial was impossible. "With his life at stake," the decision said, "it is not requiring too much that the petitioner be tried in an atmosphere undisturbed by so huge a wave of public passion and by a jury other than one in which two-thirds of the members admit, before hearing any testimony, to possessing a belief in his guilt."

In 1963 the Supreme Court heard the case of *Rideau v. Louisiana*. Two months *before* the trial of this alleged robber-kidnapper-murderer, a local television station showed—three times in two days—a twenty-minute interview with the defendant. As the sheriff and two state troopers stood beside him, the defendant gave a detailed confession of the robbery, the kidnapping, and the murder.

Rideau's lawyer, claiming that this television film was highly prejudicial pretrial publicity, asked the lower court for a change of venue. (That is, he urged that the trial be held in a part of the state where the television film had not been shown.) His request was denied, and on the basis of that denial the Supreme Court reversed Rideau's conviction.

Justice Potter Stewart, speaking for the majority, said that "to the tens of thousands of people who saw and heard it," that television film "in a very real sense, *was* Rideau's trial—at which he pleaded guilty to murder. Any subsequent proceedings in a community so pervasively exposed to such a spectacle could be but a hollow formality. . . . We do not hesitate to hold . . . that due process of law in this case required a trial before a jury drawn from a community of people who had not seen and heard Rideau's television 'interview.' "

One of the more notorious illustrations of the damage the press can do to a defendant's right to a fair trial is the case of Dr. Samuel Sheppard, an osteopath, who had been accused in 1954 of bludgeoning his wife to death in their home in a suburb of Cleveland. During the weeks before Sheppard's trial, not only was there pervasive press and broadcast coverage of the case, but much of it seemed deliberately prejudicial. As Supreme Court Justice Tom Clark said years later, "throughout this period the newspapers emphasized evidence that tended to incriminate Sheppard and pointed out discrepancies in his statements to authorities."

A characteristic story in the *Cleveland Press* said that

"the police have virtually completed their investigations of the July 4 murder of Mrs. Marilyn Rees Sheppard. Their conclusion is that they have convincing evidence to prove Dr. Sam Sheppard . . . was the killer."

Furthermore, what was the effect on a purportedly "impartial jury" when, ten days before the trial began, the *Cleveland Press* ran on its front page the results of a public opinion poll which revealed that an overwhelming majority of those asked thought Sheppard would be found guilty?

The trial itself was later described by Supreme Court Justice Tom Clark as "bedlam." In journalist-historian Alan Barth's description, "The trial took place in a tiny courtroom so overcrowded by newspaper and wire service representatives, telegraphic and broadcasting equipment, spectators and witnesses that the defendant and his law-yers had scarcely any means of private communication." Furthermore, as Mr. Justice Clark was to add, "In the corridors outside the courtroom, there was a host of pho-tographers and television personnel with flash cameras, portable lights and motion picture cameras." Inside the courtroom, "the jurors themselves were constantly ex-posed to the news media."

Convicted by those jurors in 1954, Sheppard was sent to prison. In 1961 a new lawyer for Sheppard, F. Lee Bailey, appealed the conviction on the ground that the defendant had been deprived of a fair trial by a prejudi-cial press. Three years later, after he had been in prison for ten years, Sheppard was released on a writ of habeas corpus, and in 1966 the Supreme Court agreed that he had not had a fair trial. Later, at a new trial, Sheppard was acquitted.

In the 8 to 1 Supreme Court decision in 1966, Justice

Clark, speaking for the majority, noted that there has been a traditional "Anglo-American distrust for secret trials." Over several centuries, he said, the press has guarded "against the miscarriage of justice by subjecting the police, prosecutors, and judicial processes to extensive public scrutiny and criticism." That is why the High Court has been "unwilling to place any direct limitations on the freedoms traditionally exercised by the news media, for 'what transpires in the courtroom is public property.' "

But what about defendant Sam Sheppard's Sixth Amendment protections against the "Roman holiday" atmosphere of the trial, largely created by the press? There are steps, said Justice Clark, that the trial judge could have taken. He could have limited the number of reporters in the courtroom at the first sign that "their presence would disrupt the trial." He could and should have insulated the witnesses from the press. He could have ordered police officers, witnesses, and lawyers for both sides not to give certain leads, gossip, and other prejudicial information to the press (for instance, the information given to the press by police and the coroner that in the earlier stages of the case Sheppard had refused to take a lie detector test). If the press did not have that kind of prejudicial information, it would have had to report only what actually took place in the courtroom.

Clark also pointed out that throughout the country "unfair and prejudicial news comment on pending trials" had increased, and he suggested ways to deal with this serious hindrance to justice. If, for instance, a trial judge believed that the pretrial atmosphere created by the press would indeed prevent a fair trial, he could delay the trial until the impact of the stories in the press had become weaker. He could transfer the case to another venue (in this case, another county), where the newspapers and broadcast stations had not been focusing on the case so intensively. He could sequester the jury so that it would not have access to newspaper, radio, or television reports on the story. And in any case, where "publicity during the proceedings threatens the fairness of the trial, a new trial should be ordered."

At base, however, said Justice Clark, "the cure lies in those remedial measures that will prevent the prejudice at its inception. The courts must take such steps by rule and regulation that will protect their processes from prejudicial outside interferences. Neither prosecutors, counsel for defense, accused, witnesses, court staff nor enforcement officers coming under the jurisdiction of the court should be permitted to frustrate its function." Thus, under certain circumstances, these sources of information should be forbidden to speak to the press about matters that may prejudice the jury until the trial is over.

With these sources cut off, according to this theory, the press will be able to report only what takes place in open court and will not be able to circulate "inaccurate information, rumors and accusations" that make up "inflammatory publicity." As an example, Clark observed that in the *Sheppard* case, "the prosecution repeatedly made evidence available to the media which was never offered in the trial. Much of the 'evidence' disseminated in this fashion was clearly inadmissible" in the courtroom. But, "the exclusion of such evidence in court is rendered meaningless" when the press "makes it available to the public."

Seven years after delivering that decision, Tom Clark, having left the Supreme Court, took pains to point out in an interview with *The Christian Science Monitor* that no-

where in his ruling on the *Sheppard* trial had he intended
to justify any court orders *directly controlling the press
itself*. His aim was to silence, under extraordinary circumstances, certain of the press's prejudicial *sources*.

In the period since the Supreme Court's reversal of Dr.
Sheppard's conviction, however, there have been attempts
by courts to directly prohibit the press from printing particular kinds of information about a case. These gag orders have usually been overturned on First Amendment
grounds. In a confrontation between a judge and a reporter in New York, for example, the judge ordered that
details of the prior convictions of five defendants not be
published until the trial was over. A reporter for *The New
York Times* violated that order, and the Appellate Division of the New York Supreme Court supported the journalist, ruling that the judge did not have the power to
abrogate the reporter's First Amendment rights. But the
issue of judicial gag orders has so far been most fully and
decisively considered by the Supreme Court in *Nebraska
Press Association v. Stuart* (1976).

On the night of October 18, 1975, in the small town of
Sutherland, Nebraska, a ten-year-old girl was raped and
then shot to death. Also killed, as they came into the
house, were five members of her family. The suspect was
thirty-year-old Erwin Charles Simants, who was arrested
the morning following the murders. Soon after the killings
Simants had briefly confessed to a member of his family,
and his confession was widely reported in the newspapers
and on radio and television throughout the area. In Nebraska, just five years before the Simants trial, a panel of
journalists, judges, and lawyers had agreed on a set of
voluntary guidelines to help insure fair trials. Among the
guidelines was a pledge by the press that it would publish

no matters "likely to interfere with a fair trial": it would not disclose confessions by *suspects*, it would offer no views as to their guilt or their character, and it would publish no statements predicting or influencing the outcome of a trial.

Under the competitive pressures involved in hot pursuit of the gory story, however, the Nebraska press overlooked the guidelines to which it had agreed. A sense of the press's zeal was provided by chief prosecutor Milton Larson, who recalled shouting on the night of the murders, "There's a TV helicopter overhead, and we haven't even gotten the six bodies out."

By six the next morning an array of murder details had been carried on the Associated Press wire, including the report that Simants had confessed to a member of his family. Later that morning, after Simants had been arrested and booked, the sheriff held a news conference at which he strongly indicated that he considered Simants to be the killer. The sheriff was quoted to that effect on both the Associated Press and United Press–International wires. Meanwhile, an NBC-TV reporter from Denver had flown in and reported on the network—including the local NBC station reaching prospective jurors—that "Simants reportedly confessed."

Prejudicial reporting continued in the newspapers. Nearly the whole front page of the *North Platte Telegraph* was devoted to a story in which Simants's father was quoted as saying, "My son killed five or six people here."

The next procedure for Simants was a preliminary hearing. (The purpose of such a hearing is to determine whether a crime has been committed and whether there is probable cause to believe that it was committed by the suspect.) As he later revealed, the county judge scheduled to preside over that hearing was greatly distressed by press coverage of the case, and he kept thinking of what the Supreme Court had said in *Sheppard v. Maxwell* about the dangers to justice of pretrial publicity. At the same time, both the prosecution and the county defender had asked him to place a gag order on all journalists and to bar the press from the preliminary hearing. The county judge refused to close the hearing, but he did order that no one present, including the press, release "any testimony given" or "evidence adduced" during the preliminary hearing.

The judge, Donald Ruff, later explained why he had imposed the gag rule. Not only had one girl been raped before her murder but another, even younger girl had been sexually molested. "I felt," said the judge, "that if I had to sit on the jury, and I had that type of information going into the trial, it would be extremely difficult for me to give a fair trial to Simants. Furthermore, in this community, we have a panel of maybe five or six thousand jurors we can draw from, and I had a great concern that we wouldn't be able to get any one of them to give Simants a fair trial if this type of information came out."

The press obeyed the gag rule but appealed the ruling to District Court Judge Hugh Stuart. He ended the county judge's restrictions on the press, but substituted some of his own. As Fred Friendly reported for *The New York Times*, Stuart prohibited newspaper, radio, or television from reporting before the trial "any confession or admission of guilt by Simants; the results of the pathologist's report; the identity of the victims who had been sexually assaulted; and the description of those crimes." He also ordered the press not to print the specifics of the very gag order he had just imposed on it.

Judge Stuart justified the gag order by saying that "because of the nature of the crimes [charged in the complaint] there is a clear and present danger that pre-trial publicity could impinge upon the defendants' right to a fair trial." Accordingly, "an order setting forth the limitations of pre-trial publicity is appropriate."

Why not move the trial to another location? Then there wouldn't even be a theoretical need for a gag order. That couldn't be done in Nebraska, where state law mandates that a trial cannot be moved except to an adjacent county. The adjacent counties had been blanketed by the same prejudicial press and television information that had pervaded the county in which the crime had taken place.

Immediately on Judge Stuart's imposing of the gag order, the Nebraska Press Association—aided by a national group of journalists (the Reporters Committee for Freedom of the Press)—appealed, and that appeal eventually reached the Supreme Court. On July 30, 1976, the Court handed down its decision on the first case ever to have come before it dealing directly with a judge's right to censor the press in the interest of a fair trial.

Unanimously, the Court held all elements of the Nebraska gag order, in the Simants case, to be unconstitutional. Said Chief Justice Warren E. Burger, delivering the opinion of the Court: "Prior restraints on speech and publication are the most serious and least tolerable infringements on the First Amendment."

The Chief Justice implied, however, that even though the gag order had now been ruled unconstitutional, it is conceivable that in the future, under highly exceptional circumstances, another gag order might be permitted by the Court. "We reaffirm," said Burger, "that the guarantees of freedom of expression are *not* an absolute prohibition under all circumstances, but the *barriers to prior restraint remain high and the presumption against its use continues intact"* (emphasis added).

In fact, only three of the nine Justices (William J. Brennan, Potter Stewart, Thurgood Marshall) declared gag orders to be absolutely unconstitutional. A fourth, Justice Byron R. White, came very close to that position, but did not go all the way. A majority of the Court agreed with the Chief Justice that in the future the Court might still be open to arguments in favor of gag rules on the press in the interests of a fair trial but that those arguments would have to be extraordinarily persuasive with regard to the particular trial at issue.

A majority of the Court also indicated that it might look favorably, in certain circumstances, on a trial judge's barring the press from certain *pretrial* proceedings. It also appeared that a majority would approve, in certain circumstances, a trial judge limiting statements to the press by attorneys in a case, witnesses, court and police officers, and other participants in the proceedings.

Mr. Justice Brennan, for example, suggested in his concurring opinion that "judges may stem much of the flow of prejudicial publicity at its source, before it is obtained by representatives of the press." In other words, although reporters should not be silenced, sources officially connected with the case could be ordered not to talk to them. (However, suggests the American Civil Liberties Union, *defense* attorneys and *defendants* should not be gagged, because the weight of public opinion is usually on the side of the prosecution and since it is the defendant's Sixth Amendment right to a fair trial that is at issue, his public statements are hardly intended to prejudice his own case.)

Of all the Justices, Brennan was the most explicit in stating that the press itself must remain free of *any* prior restraint by the courts. The press, Brennan said, can publish anything "pertaining to pending judicial proceedings or the operation of the criminal justice system, no matter how shabby the means by which the information is obtained." He pointed out that if judges were to feel able to censor the press in order to avoid prejudicial publicity, the result would be particularly destructive to those smaller newspapers and radio and television stations around the country which lack adequate financial means to contest such restrictions. To make his point, Brennan cited a letter from the editor and publisher of a small Alabama paper, the *Anniston Star*:

> Small town dailies would be the unknown, unseen and friendless victims if the Supreme Court upholds the [gag] order of Judge Stuart. If the already irresistible powers of the judiciary are swollen by absorbing an additional function, that of government censor, the chilling effect upon vigorous public debate would be deepest in the thousands of small towns where independent, locally owned, daily and weekly newspapers are published.
>
> Our papers are not read in the White House, the Congress, the Supreme Court or by network news executives. The causes for which we contend and the problems we face are invisible to the world of power and intellect. We have no in-house legal staff. We retain no great national law firms. We do not have spacious profits with which to defend ourselves and our principles, all the way to the Supreme Court, each and every time we feel them to be under attack.
>
> Our only alternative is obedient silence. You hear us

when we speak now. Who will notice if we are silenced? The small town press will be the unknown soldier of a war between the First and Sixth Amendments, a war that should have never been declared, and can still be avoided.

Only by associating ourselves . . . with our stronger brothers are we able to raise our voices on this issue at all, but I am confident that the Court will listen to us because we represent the most defenseless among the petitioners.

On the basic question of censoring the press, Brennan included in his opinion a statement that has since been widely quoted: "The press may be arrogant, tyrannical, abusive, and sensationalist, just as it may be incisive, probing, and informative. But at least in the context of prior restraints on publication, *the decision of what, when, and how to publish is for editors, not judges*" (emphasis added).

Less than three years after the Supreme Court's decision in *Nebraska Press Association v. Stuart*, another case involving prior restraint of the press began to move through the federal courts. Clearly, the issue had not been settled by Justice William Brennan's declaration that editors, not judges, are to decide "what, when, and how to publish." There might still be exceptions. This time, the conflict was not free press versus fair trial, but free press versus national security, as in the Pentagon Papers Case.

In March 1979, the Department of Justice moved to prevent *The Progressive*—a Wisconsin-based monthly magazine—from publishing an article, "The H-Bomb Secret: How We Got It, Why We're Telling It." The government claimed that this description of how a hydrogen bomb is designed and functions would enable other countries to produce H-bombs of their own much more swiftly, with the result that "modern civilization will be one step closer to its potential destruction in a nuclear holocaust."

The Progressive, on the other hand, insisted that there were no secrets in the article and that its author, Howard Morland, had obtained his information by reading publicly available literature, interviewing scientists, and going on government-directed tours of nuclear plants. The whole point of the article, explained Erwin Knoll, editor of The Progressive, was "to show how much unnecessary secrecy is being maintained in the name of national security, with the result that Americans are deprived of information they very much need concerning such issues as the environmental hazards of nuclear materials, along with their occupational health and safety risks." In addition, Knoll said, the public is kept from knowing enough about nuclear matters to have a sound basis for judgment on such crucial affairs as disarmament negotiations and federal spending priorities on nuclear weaponry and energy. Therefore, if The Progressive could prove, by this article, that "the greatest secret of them all, the H-bomb," is really no secret at all, Americans might be awakened to demand that the government release more information that directly and literally affects their lives.

While some nuclear scientists agreed with the government that the article had to be censored on grounds of national security, others supported the magazine's contention that Morland's work contained no information that was not already common knowledge among many scientists, including those who do not have access to classified information. Said Edward Teller, "father" of the H-bomb, "What is known to a million people is not a secret."

On March 9, Federal District Judge Robert Warren of

Wisconsin imposed a temporary restraining order on *The Progressive*, barring publication of the acutely controversial article. He hardened his ruling into a preliminary injunction on March 26, saying: "What is involved here is information dealing with the most destructive weapon in the history of mankind, information of sufficient destructive potential to nullify the right to free speech and to endanger the right to life itself." This was the first preliminary injunction against press publication in the nation's history. (The 1971 action against *The New York Times* in the Pentagon Papers case was a brief, temporary restraining order.)

The judge did suggest to *The Progressive* that it negotiate a settlement with the government, omitting the more "sensitive" parts of the article. Erwin Knoll refused: "I don't believe that the First Amendment is negotiable. If the founders had intended it to be negotiable, they would have written a mediation process into the Constitution."

What made this case, *The United States v. The Progressive*, different from the battle over the Pentagon Papers is that, as several Supreme Court Justices pointed out in 1971, the government—in trying to censor the Pentagon Papers—could not point to a specific law by which Congress had authorized the silencing of the press for national security reasons. In the 1979 case, which has to do with nuclear matters, there *is* such a law—the Atomic Energy Act of 1954. It clearly empowers the attorney general to try to get preliminary injunctions, and other restraints on publication, when he believes the Atomic Energy Act has been violated to the endangerment of national security.

Until now untested in the courts, this law, the government claimed, provides that *all* data—including lawfully obtained information—on the design, manufacture, or utilization of nuclear weapons and certain nuclear materials are "restricted." Included is "the use of special nuclear material in the production of energy." It does not matter whether the information is in the government's files or not. *Anything* to do with these nuclear matters is "classified at birth."

Subject to the penalties of the Atomic Energy Act (which forbids communication of "restricted data") were the reporting of a journalist like Howard Morland, a private scientist's research on nuclear energy, or a university professor's original work based on deductive reasoning. All this data is restricted until the government declassifies it, but the government is under no legal obligation to let anyone know when it *has* declassified any information. Indeed, the declassification guidelines are themselves classified. No one working in this field, therefore, can ever be sure that he is not harboring "restricted data," even if his research paper or newspaper story is based entirely on material in the public domain. The Government alone knows what is declassified and what is unlawful to communicate. Said *The Progressive*: "We can imagine no more chilling restraint on the free interchange of ideas, free speech, and freedom of press."

The Atomic Energy Act does say, however, that there will be no prosecution of those communicating "restricted data" unless the possessor of that information has "reason to believe" it will be used to harm the United States or give advantage to a foreign nation.

Howard Morland and the editor of *The Progressive* claimed that they never did have any such "reason to believe." In rebuttal, the government pointed out that officials of the Departments of Justice and Energy came to them on March 2, 1979—before court action was taken—and told them that if the article were printed, it "will work to the advantage of other nations." But what if, as indeed was the case, *The Progressive* did not believe these agents of the government? Under the First Amendment, is a citizen guilty of criminal behavior because he does not trust what his government tells him and thereby refuses to be censored?

As Nathan Lewin, a Washington constitutional lawyer, pointed out in *The New Republic*, what this part of the Atomic Energy Act actually comes down to is that "the Government's warning is a self-fulfilling prophecy: lawful and innocent conduct becomes illegal because government agents tell [someone] that they think his conduct will have bad consequences."

In addition, these provisions of the Atomic Energy Act, as interpreted by the government, raise the possibility of the Act being used as a system of licensing the press—a practice which the framers of the First Amendment intended to abolish forever because of grievous licensing abuses of press freedom in England and in the colonies. If this section of the Atomic Energy Act were ever to be ruled constitutional, a government agent could appear in the office of a newspaper, magazine, book publisher, scholar, or free-lance writer and demand that a scheduled article be destroyed because it has been denied what is, in effect, a license to print under the Atomic Energy Act.

The American Civil Liberties Union, defending *The Progressive*'s editor and managing editor, attacked the constitutionality of these sections of the Atomic Energy Act on grounds of vagueness and overbreadth.

A law is unconstitutional if it can be shown that its language is so vague, so unspecific, that citizens trying to exercise their First Amendment rights—as well as officials trying to enforce the law—have no definite guidelines as to what is actually prohibited.

"Overbreadth" means that a statute is unconstitutional if its regulatory powers are so broad that it covers, for example, areas of expression that are protected by the First Amendment.

The *vagueness* of the Atomic Energy Act's censorship provisions, said the American Civil Liberties Union, comes from the law's mandate that everything concerning certain nuclear matters is "classified at birth" until declassified by the government. Since the government does not have to disclose what it has declassified—or when—a possible violator of the law has no way of knowing what he is forbidden to say or write.

Moreover, as attorneys for *The Progressive* argued in court papers, this censorship by government—and the further self-censorship it leads to—"may go on so long as the secret alleged by the government is in existence. Thus, there is no end until the government decides to publish the information."

With regard to the Atomic Energy Act's *overbreadth*, the American Civil Liberties Union maintained that this law's definition of "restricted data" is "grossly overbroad on its face." For example, "encyclopedia articles on nuclear weaponry, newspaper articles on Einstein's life and work, historical accounts of the Manhattan Project and the bombs dropped at Hiroshima and Nagasaki, press reports on the deployment of nuclear weapons, debate over limitation on nuclear weapons—all these fall well within the definition." So do certain kinds of reporting on the workings of nuclear energy for domestic purposes.

Soon after the March 28, 1979 accident at the Three

Mile Island nuclear plant near Harrisburg, Pennsylvania, a pregnant twenty-four-year-old woman was asked by a *New York Times* reporter how she felt about the risks of radiation from the nuclear power station. "I've never thought about it," she said. "We don't really know that much about it. You just have to take the Government's word that it's safe."

In its battle to assert its First Amendment right not to be censored by the government, *The Progressive* continually maintained that if it were to lose, the citizens of the nation would have to take the government's word about many matters of nuclear life and death. By way of further illustration from recent history, there was the Navy's plan to store some 1,200 nuclear weapons in forty-eight earth-and-concrete "igloos" two miles from Honolulu International Airport. The traffic there is intense, with an unusually high mix of different kinds of airplanes, creating the possibility of midair collisions. And indeed, there have been quite a few one-plane crashes.

Catholic Action Hawaii and various environmental and peace groups brought the Navy to court, asking that the government be compelled to prepare an environmental-impact statement to go with their plans for stockpiling those H-bombs so near the airport. In federal court, an information-classification specialist from the Department of Energy said that the Navy could not even discuss the environmental impact of nuclear-weapons storage. The release of such information, he explained, would be a violation of the Atomic Energy Act's secrecy provisions because, by necessity, the disclosures would include restricted data about how those nuclear weapons are designed. Could he at least say whether an airplane crash near the "igloos" (housing the H-bombs) might lead to a scattering of radioactive material? No, under the Atomic Energy Act, the public is not allowed access to that information.

In addition to arguing that the Atomic Energy Act's vagueness and overbreadth violate the First Amendment, *The Progressive* also contended that to successfully censor the magazine, the government had to meet the stringent standards established by the Supreme Court in the Pentagon Papers case. As the American Civil Liberties Union emphasized, the Court then had ruled that there could be no prior restraint of a publication on the grounds of national security unless the government could prove beyond any doubt that the publication would "surely" result "directly and immediately" in "grave and irreparable" damage to the nation. But, said the ACLU, the government, in *The Progressive* case, had only alleged that publication of the Morland article "could possibly" result in "serious" harm at some time in the indefinite future. This, the ACLU argued, is clearly insufficient basis on which to suppress the First Amendment rights of the magazine; for, as the Supreme Court said in *Near v. Minnesota*: "[I]t has been generally, if not universally, considered that it is the chief purpose of the [First Amendment's] guaranty to prevent previous restraints upon publication."

Meanwhile, as the case moved through the courts, *The Progressive*—forbidden since March 9, 1979 from publishing Howard Morland's article on the H-Bomb and on the unnecessary secrecy with which the government enshrouded it—had been subject to by far the longest period of government censorship in the nation's history. Attempts were made to expedite the court action because of the vital First Amendment issues involved, but this time—unlike the swift resolution of the Pentagon Papers —the courts would not be hurried.

There were those at *The Progressive* who wondered whether this lack of urgency in a case which so threatened the First Amendment was due to the fact that this was a small Wisconsin monthly—by contrast with the mighty *New York Times* and *Washington Post*. However the case was eventually decided, the fact could not be erased that the magazine had been silenced for so long. "It is an unfortunate precedent," said Floyd Abrams, a leading First Amendment lawyer. "Should the government again try to censor a publication which then moves, on First Amendment grounds, to get a swift decision, the courts may well refer back to what happened to *The Progressive* and say, 'What's the hurry?' " And if the article at issue is especially timely, the government, even if it eventually loses, may have suppressed that article long enough for it to be ineffective when it finally appears.

During the earlier stages of *The Progressive*'s fight to publish, there were editorials in a number of the more prominent American newspapers urging the magazine to surrender and publish a government-edited version of Howard Morland's article. Instead of joining *The Progressive*'s campaign to quickly move the case through the courts, these journalists were fearful that because nuclear secrecy is so emotional and fearful an issue, the magazine would lose and thereby greatly weaken all newspapers' and magazines' protections against prior restraint. Said Erwin Knoll, editor of *The Progressive*: "As for this notion that we should voluntarily surrender our freedom so that theirs won't be imperiled, the answer is very clear. Rights exist only when they can be exercised. If there is no First Amendment for *The Progressive*, there is no

First Amendment for anyone." (Or, as some journalists might have said in 1735: "We beg you, John Peter Zenger, not to defend yourself against these charges of seditious libel. This is not the right time. The Royal Governor, the courts, are all against you. Later. Next generation, next century, when the climate improves, then it will be time to fight for a free press.")

Eventually, most of the press did come to the support of *The Progressive*, and the case moved on to the Seventh Circuit Court of Appeals. On September 17, 1979, however, the government announced that it was abandoning its efforts to prevent the magazine from publishing Howard Morland's article on the H-bomb. Why the change of mind after the prior restraint had been in existence for more than six months? Because some newspapers had begun to print material that was similar to much of the information in Howard Morland's article. Furthermore, a researcher for the American Civil Liberties Union had found the same kind of information on the public shelves of the government's atomic energy library in Los Alamos, New Mexico.

And finally, on September 16, the Madison, Wisconsin, *Press Connection* published a detailed letter from an independent researcher into nuclear weapons that also contained the "secrets" in the censored Morland article. (The letter's author, Charles R. Hansen, claimed, as had Morland, that all his data had come from unclassified sources.)

With the "secrets" out, the Justice Department decided it was pointless to continue the prior restraint on *The Progressive*. However, the government made it clear that the section on violating national security secrets in the 1954 Atomic Energy Act will continue to be enforced in the future. Said a Justice Department spokesman: "In this particular effort we have been thwarted, but we intend to keep on trying to stop the spread of such information."

The question of the constitutionality of the Atomic Energy Act as a vague, overbroad, and dangerous infringement of the First Amendment is not likely to be resolved soon. Nor is a new argument by the government (put forth in the course of *The Progressive's* court battles) that while the First Amendment protects political speech, it does *not* protect such "technical speech" as information about nuclear weapons. As *The New York Times* said, until these constitutional issues are ruled on, the government's doctrines in these matters will lie around "like loaded pistols."

Loaded pistols aimed at the First Amendment.

XXI

As a reporter, I could not give even the appearance of cooperating with the government, of becoming an agent for the government.

The press has a nearly total right to publish whatever news it is able to gather. There can be no prior restraint, no government censorship, except perhaps in such extreme cases of national emergency as the printing of vital military information in time of war or—depending on the outcome of a future *Progressive*-like case—the disclosure of "restricted data" on nuclear weapons and materials at any time. But *gathering* the news is not as firmly protected by the First Amendment as the *publication* of what has finally been assembled.

The press does not have complete access to information. Grand jury sessions, for instance, are closed to reporters. The press is usually barred from family courts (dealing with juveniles) and their equivalents. Nor do journalists have an unrestricted right to enter and report from prisons.

Furthermore, on June 2, 1979, the Supreme Court made it possible for lower court judges to greatly limit the press's access to pretrial hearings and to trials themselves—an issue, as detailed in the previous chapter, that has long placed the First Amendment rights of reporters and readers in conflict with defendants' Sixth Amendment rights to trial by an "impartial jury."

In *Gannett Co., Inc. v. De Pasquale,* Justice Potter Stewart, speaking for a 5 to 4 majority, ruled that the public *and* the press could be barred from pretrial hearings—and even, it was implied, from trials themselves—whenever a judge finds a "reasonable probability" that the publicity resulting from an open courtroom would be harmful to the defendant. This need not be done on a "last resort" basis. The judge can take protective measures, said Mr. Justice Stewart, "even when they are not strictly and inescapably necessary."

But does not the Sixth Amendment guarantee a defendant "the right to a speedy and public trial"?

This guarantee, said Potter Stewart, is "personal to the accused." If he chooses to waive the guarantee, and the judge agrees, the courtroom can be closed, for the press and the public have no constitutional right of access to a criminal proceeding. Nor, said Stewart, does this decision have anything to do with the kinds of "gag orders" that the Supreme Court struck down in *Nebraska Press Association v. Stuart.* That case had to do with attempts to directly forbid the press from publishing certain pretrial information "irrespective of its source." Here the press may be denied access, at the judge's discretion, to "one, albeit an important source": what goes on at a pretrial hearing or a trial. But this *Gannett* decision, Stewart emphasized, "does not in any way tell the press what it may and may not publish." Denying access is not the same, he said, as prior restraint. Many journalists disagree, saying the effect is similar.

In dissent, Justice Harry Blackmun insisted that, with

limited exceptions, courtrooms should be presumed to be open to the public and press because "it has been said that publicity 'is the soul of justice.' And in many ways it is: open judicial processes, especially in the criminal field, protect against judicial, prosecutorial, and police abuse; provide a means for citizens to obtain information about the criminal justice system and the performance of public officials; and safeguard the integrity of the courts." A pretrial hearing or a trial should be closed, said Blackmun, only when the defendant shows that he would be harmed if the proceedings were open, that less drastic alternatives than barring the press and public would not sufficiently protect him, and that "there is a substantial probability that closure will be effective in protecting against the perceived harm." The majority of the Court had gone much too far, said Blackmun, and made it too easy for courtrooms to be closed. This is an especially unfortunate development, he added, since some ninety percent of criminal cases are disposed of before trial—leaving pretrial proceedings, on which the *Gannett* case was based, "the only opportunity the public has to learn about police and prosecutorial conduct, and about allegations that those responsible to the public for the enforcement of laws are themselves breaking them."

Nonetheless, in the *Gannett* case, the majority of the Court significantly limited the press's access potential to the courtroom—for the time being.

Another issue central to the gathering of news is the protection of confidential sources. There are many times when a story can be developed only with the help of a source of information who will not tell what he knows unless his identity is kept secret. A national survey of newspaper editors in 1973 underlined the pervasive value of confidential sources, and the situation has not changed. Said the managing editor of the *San Francisco Chronicle*: "An absolutely staggering number of news stories, political and non-political, arise from information received in confidence." In addition, reporters from *The New York Times, The Wall Street Journal, Newsweek*, ABC, and CBS said, responding to the survey, that much of the information they work with every day comes from sources insisting on anonymity.

A source may be a member of a city, state, or federal agency who is outraged at corruption going on around him but who feels he must remain anonymous or he'll be fired for blowing the whistle. A source may work for a private corporation and demand confidentiality for the same reason, or he may be a member of a tightly knit political group, outside the mainstream of society, that is suspicious of all strangers. This last kind of source will talk only to a reporter he trusts, and the first basis of trust is a promise by the reporter not to reveal where he obtained his information. Without such an agreement there is hardly any way by which the public can learn what the members of that political group are thinking and where that thinking may lead it.

Clearly, without confidential sources fewer instances of public and private wrongdoing would be disclosed. Accordingly, the press maintains that the right of a journalist to refuse to reveal the identity of a confidential source is an integral part of its First Amendment protection and, more basically, of the public's First Amendment "right to know."

In 1972, however, the Supreme Court, focusing directly on this issue for the first time, decided in *Branzburg v.*

Hayes, by a 5 to 4 vote, that reporters do not have a constitutional right to protect the confidentiality of their sources. Three separate cases were involved in the *Branzburg* decision, but the one most closely watched by members of the nation's press concerned Earl Caldwell, a reporter for *The New York Times.* In 1969 the *Times* had assigned Caldwell to cover the Black Panther party at its headquarters in the San Francisco Bay area. At the time the Panthers were one of the more voluble and seemingly influential black revolutionary groups.

White reporters for the *Times* had been unable to handle the assignment because the Panthers did not trust white journalists. Caldwell, who is black and had a history of working with various black community organizations, established a relationship of trust with the Panthers. "I was able," he said later, "to look closely into their operation, talk with anyone I wanted to, examine all their programs—without restrictions."

For a year, Caldwell's dispatches on the Black Panther party were the most comprehensive filed by any journalist. Then, in February 1970, as part of a federal investigation of the Panthers, Caldwell was subpoenaed to appear before a grand jury in San Francisco with all his tape recordings, documents, and notebooks. It was clear to Caldwell from previous interviews with FBI agents that he would be asked to name the sources for some of his stories and that the government would try to link those names with criminal charges against the Panthers.

Caldwell refused even to appear before the grand jury, claiming that if he went behind those closed doors—even if he refused to answer all questions once he was inside— he would lose the trust of his sources in the Black Panther party. "As a reporter, I could not give even the appearance of cooperating with the government, of becoming an agent for the government," Caldwell explained. "If I told the Panthers afterward that I had said nothing, how would they have known that to be true? The grand jury proceedings are secret, and the mere fact that I went into the room would make the Panthers suspicious of my intentions. ('If you're not saying anything, why are you going at all?') Also, it was my contention that the Government was interfering with my First Amendment rights by trying to compel me to answer those questions. After all, a reporter has the right to do his work without government harassment and without the government trying to press him into its service as a spy."

Caldwell asked the Federal District Court to quash the subpoena on the ground that its inevitable effect "will be to suppress vital First Amendment freedoms of [myself], of *The New York Times*, of the news media, and of militant political action groups by driving a wedge of distrust and silence between the news media and the militants."

Among the journalists who filed affidavits in support of Caldwell's First Amendment position was Mike Wallace of CBS: "If I were now forced to reveal such confidential information [from sources insisting that their identities not be revealed], I could never again count on the cooperation of those people or anyone else in developing similar material in the future. In my opinion the public would be the loser in the long run."

The District Court denied Caldwell's motion that he be freed of the subpoena, but it did order that the questioning of Caldwell be so limited that his ability to continue gathering news about the Panthers would not be damaged. Therefore, the court ordered that he not be required to reveal confidential sources.

Nonetheless, Earl Caldwell continued to refuse to appear before the grand jury because, he said, his mere appearance would erode the trust in which he was held by the Black Panthers. The United States Court of Appeals agreed with the lower court that Caldwell should not be forced to disclose confidential sources because "the First Amendment requires this qualified privilege" for a reporter. The case finally came before the United States Supreme Court, and for the first time in the history of the republic that body was to decide whether a reporter has a constitutional right to protect his sources, even if subpoenaed by a grand jury.

Walter Cronkite of CBS addressed the issue in an affidavit he had submitted backing Caldwell in the Federal District Court:

> On the basis of . . . my experience as a news correspondent, it is my opinion that compelling news correspondents to testify before grand juries with respect to matters learned in the course of their work would largely destroy their utility as gatherers and analysts of news. Furthermore, once it is established and believed that news correspondents are to be utilized in grand jury investigations, they will be of precious little value to such investigations because they will no longer have access to the information that grand juries might want.

The Supreme Court disagreed with Earl Caldwell and the journalists who supported him. All four of the Justices who had been appointed by President Richard Nixon voted against Caldwell's claim to First Amendment protection of sources' confidentiality (Chief Justice Warren E. Burger, Justices William E. Rehnquist, Harry A. Blackmun, Lewis F. Powell, Jr.). The swing vote was that of Byron R. White, who wrote the majority opinion:

The sole issue before us is the obligation of reporters to respond to grand jury subpoenas as other citizens do and to answer questions relevant to an investigation into the commission of a crime. Citizens generally are not constitutionally immune from grand jury subpoenas; and neither the First Amendment nor any other constitutional provision protects the average citizen from disclosing to a grand jury information he has received in confidence.

A reporter, White continued, is not entitled to a special testimonial privilege (the right not to testify) that "other citizens do not enjoy." When journalists are asked to "respond to relevant questions put to them in the course of a valid grand jury investigation," they must fulfill that responsibility just like every other citizen.

Justice William O. Douglas led the forces of dissent: "A newsman has an absolute right not to appear before a grand jury." As for the argument that the First Amendment must be balanced against the need of government for efficient law enforcement, Douglas thundered: "My belief is that all of the 'balancing' was done by those who wrote the Bill of Rights. By casting the First Amendment in absolute terms, they repudiated the timid, watered-down, emasculated version of the First Amendment" which the government had advanced in this case.

"Today's decision," Douglas continued, "will impede the wide-open and robust dissemination of ideas and counterthought which a free press both fosters and protects and which is essential to the success of intelligent self-government." In fact, "there is no higher function [than that of the press] performed under our constitutional regime." The majority decision now undercuts that function because "a reporter is no better than his source of information. Unless he has a privilege to withhold the identity of his source, he will be the victim of governmental intrigue or aggression. If he can be summoned to testify in secret before a grand jury, his sources will dry up and the attempted exposure, the effort to enlighten the public, will be ended. If what the Court sanctions today becomes settled law, then the reporter's main function in American society will be to pass on to the public the press releases which the various departments of government issue."

Also dissenting were Justices Potter Stewart, William J. Brennan, Jr., and Thurgood Marshall. Said Stewart: "The Court's crabbed view of the First Amendment reflects a disturbing insensitivity to the critical role of an independent press in our society." By declaring that a reporter, when called before a grand jury, has no First Amendment right to protect his sources, the Court "invites state and federal authorities to undermine the historic independence of the press by attempting to annex the journalistic profession as an investigative arm of government."

Unlike Douglas, however, Stewart did not take an absolutist position on a journalist's First Amendment right to protect the identity of his sources. There may be, Stewart said, occasions when a reporter must appear before a grand jury and reveal confidences. But for that to happen, he wrote, "the government must (1) show that there is probable cause to believe that the newsman has information that is clearly relevant to a specific probable violation of law; (2) demonstrate that the information sought cannot be obtained by alternative means less destructive of First Amendment rights; and (3) demonstrate a compelling and overriding interest in the information." There should be no "fishing expeditions" (hauling in a reporter to testify on the mere chance that he may know something of use).

Similarly, a member of the majority, Justice Lewis F. Powell, indicated his belief that under particular circumstances journalists have a qualified (not an absolute) privilege to refuse to testify rather than reveal sources. Powell was not as specific as Stewart in describing what those circumstances might be, but he thought that a reporter could withhold "information bearing only a remote and tenuous relationship to the subject of the investigation." Nor would a reporter be stripped of protection if ordered to give up the names of confidential sources "without a legitimate need of law enforcement" for those names. Essentially, said Powell, this balancing of reporters' rights, on the one hand, and law-enforcement needs, on the other, should be decided on a case-by-case basis.

Since *Branzburg*, many lower courts have used the Stewart-Powell approach as a guideline in determining whether or not to force a reporter to testify before grand juries or at trials. Also since *Branzburg*, legislatures in twenty-six states have acted on a suggestion made by Justice White in his majority decision. He pointed out that although reporters have no *constitutional* (First Amendment) right to refuse to testify in order to protect confidential sources, the individual states and Congress could, by passing laws, "recognize a newsman's privilege, either qualified or absolute," to withhold testimony. The twenty-six state statutes now recognizing such a privilege—called shield laws—differ in the degree of protection they give journalists. Some are absolute, saying that a journalist need never testify before any state legislative or judicial body if it means giving up his sources and that he need never supply any of his unpublished notes, whether or not they disclose sources. Other shield laws are less rigid, allowing for situations when reporters must testify or turn over their notes.

The problem with these state shields, however, is that no law, no matter how absolute its language, is immune to constitutional challenge. As reporters keep discovering, there are judges who rule that a defendant's Sixth Amendment right to information in his favor at a trial can pierce even the strongest press shield law.

As an illustration, there is the case of John Hammarley, who, while a reporter for the *Sacramento Union*, wrote a series of articles about a murder case. The reports were based on interviews with Edward Carlos Gonzales, an alleged former member of the "Mexican Mafia," and an eyewitness to the murder of Ellen Delia in February 1977. Gonzales became a pivotal prosecution witness and named four men as having been involved in the murder. One of them was Juan Hernandez.

Hernandez's attorney, the public defender in Sacramento, felt that the printed interviews with Gonzales that had implicated Hernandez could lead to his client's conviction. He therefore asked the court to compel John Hammarley to turn over the tapes of those interviews, as well as notes on his conversations with Gonzales. The defense attorney believed that if he were able to compare what was printed with Hammarley's tapes and notes, he might be able to find inconsistencies in Gonzales's story that could free his client.

A Sacramento Superior Court judge ordered Hammarley to turn over the material, emphasizing that in this clash between the right to a fair trial and the reporter's First Amendment rights the latter must give way, since the defense was asking for information "essential" to a fair trial for Juan Hernandez.

But California has a strong reporters' shield law protecting reporters from having to hand over notes and tapes. Nonetheless, said the judge, the shield law is a statute, and no legislature can "deprive a defendant of his [constitutional] right to due process and a fair trial."

Journalist Hammarley, supported by much of the press, defied the court order, saying, "Once I surrender the tapes and notes in my possession, I will lose total control over them. And once that happens I would lose . . . the confidence I've built up in my news sources. I understand there are often times when a constitutional conflict exists between the rights to a fair trial and to a free and open press. But I feel morally bound to stand up for my profession and my rights."

Juan Hernandez insisted, with at least equal fervor, that he had the right to get as much information as he could to prevent his being convicted of murder. California's Third District Court of Appeals agreed with Hernandez, upholding the lower court's order that Hammarley turn over his notes and tapes. Said the appellate court: "The state may not abridge a defendant's constitutional right to a fair trial by denying the accused access to all evidence that can throw light on issues in the case . . . At stake here is the defendant's right meaningfully to confront and cross-examine his primary accuser with the benefit of all evidence reasonably available to challenge his credibility." Since there is no way for the defendant to get accuser Gonzales's unpublished statements except from the reporter, Hammarley, the California press shield law must yield to the defendant's Sixth Amendment rights. Subsequently, the State Supreme Court—California's highest tribunal—also ruled for the defendant and against the reporter.

There will be many more such cases. Since *Branzburg*, journalists are increasingly being subpoenaed—by prosecution or defense—and ordered to produce notes, outtakes (television film not used during a broadcast), and other unpublished material. Some have gone to jail rather than comply. Others have convinced the court that their material was not central to the case or could be obtained from people other than the reporter.

It is hard to tell, meanwhile, whether the growing use of subpoenas against journalists has led to a significant drying up of sources. There certainly appears to be no lessening of investigative reporting, almost always based in large part on informants. But here and there a reporter does tell of people who will no longer supply information for fear that their identities will be revealed once the journalist is faced with jail if he remains silent.

Seeking stronger protection than state shields, many journalists are pressing for a federal shield law—"an unthwartable" national statute, as one of them puts it, which would insure that no reporter would be forced to turn over his notes, including the names of confidential sources.

Aside from the fact that no law is absolutely "unthwartable" if it is found to violate someone's constitutional rights, the federal shield approach creates graver problems for the press than those it is intended to solve. If Congress were to decide to protect journalists from testifying, it would then be in the position of determining who was a legitimate reporter and who was not.

In the 1972 *Branzburg* decision, Justice White spoke to the thorny question of defining those journalists who might be protected by shield laws. "What about the traditional doctrine," he said, "that liberty of the press is the right of the lonely pamphleteer who uses carbon paper or a mimeograph just as much [as it is the right] of the large metropolitan publisher who utilizes the latest photo-composition methods?"

Is, therefore, the unaffiliated one-man-shop muckraker, who may publish very irregularly, to be covered by a law which protects the press's confidential sources? Is the high school and college press to be protected? What about a group of angry tenants who decide to put out a paper attacking their landlord? Are only those reporters with official press cards to be shielded?

After all, White emphasized, freedom of the press is a fundamental *personal* right and is not limited to news-papers and periodicals. It includes, for instance, writers of and researchers for books. "The press in its historic con-notation," White quoted from a previous Supreme Court decision, "comprehends every sort of publication which affords a vehicle of information and opinion." Not only the "organized press," he emphasized, informs the popu-lace. There are "lecturers, political pollsters, novelists, academic researchers, and dramatists. Almost any author may quite accurately assert that he is contributing to the flow of information to the public, that he relies on confi-dential sources of information, and that these sources will be silenced if he is forced to make disclosures."

But Congress would hardly pass a law shielding "al-most any author." The number of people exempt from testifying would be too large. Therefore, to get a federal shield law, stiff lines will have to be drawn between the "official" and the "unofficial" press, and it will be the government that is given the power to draw the lines. In order to protect itself from having to reveal its sources, the press will have agreed to an equivalent of licensing, although one of the primary reasons for the adoption of the First Amendment was to prevent the American state from ever having any licensing hold on the press, as had been the brutal case in England for centuries and in the colonies for an embittered period.

Furthermore, what the government gives it can take away. A particular political party controlling Congress can amend the federal shield law and remove certain kinds of journalists that greatly offend it. Reporters for the established press are not likely to be affected, but splinter muckrakers may be—if they ever get included in the first place.

Instead of a federal shield law, the Powell-Stewart approach formulated in *Branzburg* may continue to prevail. A claim by a reporter that he should not have to turn over his notes or testify for fear of disclosing a confidential source will have to be decided case by case, based on whether the information in question is central to the case and cannot be obtained from another source. There is no easy, general solution in this embattled area of First Amendment law.

The Outer Limits of Protected Speech—and Beyond

Frank Collin, national director of the National Socialist Party of America, and his Nazi colleagues. Their attempt to march in Skokie, Illinois, sorely tested Justice Oliver Wendell Holmes's insistence that, under the First Amendment, there must be freedom not only "for those who agree with us, but freedom for the thought we hate." (UPI photo)

XXII

The First Amendment requires that we protect some falsehood in order to protect speech that matters.

"Reporters tend to forget," an editor once said, "how much pain they can inflict when they print. Much of it is essential to accounts of wrongdoing, but some of it gets us into trouble." An example of this would be when a reader takes a newspaper to court on a charge that he has been defamed by a story.

Defamation, as the Student Press Law Center in Washington notes, "is generally defined as a false communication which injures an individual's reputation by lowering the community's regard for that person or by otherwise holding an individual up to hatred, contempt, or ridicule."

Libel is that form of defamation which is expressed through printing and writing, as in newspapers, books, magazines, letters, petitions, and circulars, or through signs and pictures, as in cartoons, drawings, photographs, and symbols. Slander is defamation through spoken words. What about radio and television? There, Joel Gora says in *The Rights of Reporters: An American Civil Liberties Union Handbook*, "defamatory remarks based upon a prepared script are treated as libel, while defamatory words uttered extemporaneously are treated as slander."

Most court actions for defamation are based on charges of libel, and the compensation sought by the allegedly abused party is money damages, sometimes in quite large amounts. The claim usually is that as a result of the libel and the consequent injury to reputation, the plaintiff has suffered economic losses, long-term lowering of prestige in the community, and such damage to his feelings that it can lead sometimes to prolonged mental distress.

The area of libel law is, as Professor Thomas Emerson says, "among the most complex and troublesome in the whole field of First Amendment doctrine." A landmark case in the law of libel was *The New York Times Company v. Sullivan.*

On March 29, 1960, as the civil rights movement began to gather momentum in the South, a full-page advertisement appeared in *The New York Times* signed by sixty-four people, many of whom were renowned figures in public affairs, trade union work, the arts, and religion. Among them were a number of Southern black clergymen.

The advertisement charged that thousands of black Southern students then engaging in nonviolent demonstrations to obtain their constitutional rights had to face "an unprecedented wave of terror by those who would deny and negate that document [the Constitution] which the whole world looks upon as setting the pattern for modern freedom."

The advertisement continued with a series of paragraphs which claimed to give illustrations of that "wave of terror." It ended with a plea for funds to support the student nonviolent movement, to aid in the struggle for the right to vote, and to help the legal defense of Dr. Martin Luther King, Jr., who was fighting a perjury indictment then pending in Montgomery, Alabama.

Two "wave of terror" paragraphs made certain claims about the police of Montgomery that were later admitted to be errors of fact; for instance, that the police had padlocked the dining hall of the Alabama State College campus in Montgomery in order to starve the students into submission and that they had arrested Dr. King seven times (he had been arrested four times.) As for a claim that the police once assaulted King, that charge had never been proved in court.

On seeing this full-page ad in *The New York Times,* L. B. Sullivan, then commissioner of public affairs in Montgomery, Alabama, filed a libel suit against the New York Times Company and against four black Alabama clergymen who had signed the ad. (Sullivan's duties as public affairs commissioner included the supervision of the Montgomery police, and he claimed that the false charges against the police in *The New York Times* advertisement defamed him as the head of the police department.)

A jury in the Circuit Court of Montgomery County awarded Sullivan the full amount of the damages he had claimed, five hundred thousand dollars. All the defendants were found guilty. This judgment was affirmed by the Supreme Court of Alabama.

When the case was decided by Supreme Court of the United States, the very first sentence of Justice William J. Brennan Jr.'s opinion for the Court emphasized the historical importance of what was about to come: "We are required in this case to determine for the first time the extent to which the constitutional protections for speech and press limit a State's power to award damages in a libel action brought by a public official against critics of his official conduct." In other words, should it be more difficult, under law, for a public official to win a libel suit than it is for a private citizen?

The Supreme Court declared unanimously in *Times v. Sullivan* that from then on it would indeed be more difficult for public officials to win libel suits. It would not be impossible for a public official to win such a suit, but it would be harder for him than for a private citizen.

With regard to Public Affairs Commissioner L. B. Sullivan's claims, Brennan noted that there had indeed been errors of fact in *The New York Times* advertisement and that, moreover, no one at the *Times* had tried to check the accuracy of the statements in the ad.

Nonetheless, Brennan continued, "We consider this case against a background of a profound national commitment to the principle that debate on political issues should be uninhibited, robust, and wide-open, and that it may well include vehement, caustic, and sometimes unpleasantly sharp attacks on government and public officials. . . . The present advertisement, as an expression of grievance and protest on one of the major public issues of our time, would seem clearly to qualify for the constitutional protection."

But there *were* factual errors in the advertisement, errors that, according to L. B. Sullivan, defamed him. Can critics of public officials simply go around spreading untruths? Said Brennan: "Erroneous statement is inevitable in free debate, and . . . it must be protected if the freedoms of expression are to have the 'breathing space' that they 'need to survive.'"

Furthermore, Brennan said, if it were necessary for a defendant in this kind of libel case to prove that *every-*

thing he had written was true, the result would be that people wanting to criticize public officials might well decide to censor themselves because of doubts about whether, if they were brought to court, they could prove the accuracy of every single point of their criticism. Fear of the expenses of having to go to court to defend themselves against charges of inaccuracy would be an additional deterrent. This state of affairs cannot be allowed, said Brennan, because "it dampens the vigor and limits the variety of public debate."

There was still the claim by Sullivan that his reputation had been harmed by the advertisement in *The New York Times*. Brennan's answer: "Injury to official reputation affords no more warrant for repressing speech that would otherwise be free than does factual error." Criticism of the conduct of public officials "does not lose its constitutional protection because it is effective criticism and hence diminishes their official reputations."

Are there any circumstances, then, under which a public official, claiming that he has been defamed, can get satisfaction in court? Brennan's reply set a new rule for libel cases brought by people in public office. A public official is prohibited from "recovering damages for a defamatory falsehood relating to his official conduct *unless he proves that the statement was made with 'actual malice'—that is, with knowledge that it was false or with reckless disregard of whether it was false or not"* (emphasis added).

It is not enough for a public official to prove inaccuracies in what has been said or written about him. He or she has to show, and this is often difficult to do, that the alleged libeler *knowingly* disseminated a falsehood or just

245

went ahead recklessly, without caring about whether his statements were true or not.

(In a later case, *St. Amant v. Thompson* [1968], Justice Byron R. White further defined the meaning of "reckless disregard": "There must be sufficient evidence to permit the conclusion that the defendant in fact entertained serious doubts as to the truth of his publication." However, the defendant cannot simply *say* he had no serious doubts. It has to be shown, says White, that the statements were published "in good faith." What does that mean?

As White explained, "Professions of good faith will be unlikely to prove persuasive, for example, where a story is fabricated by the defendant, is the product of his imagination, or is based wholly on an unverified anonymous telephone call. Nor will they be likely to prevail when the publisher's allegations are so inherently improbable that only a reckless man would have put them in circulation. Likewise, recklessness may be found where there are obvious reasons to doubt the veracity of the informant or the accuracy of his reports." However, a publication's "failure to investigate" the accuracy of a reporter's work, "does not in itself establish bad faith.")

The landmark decision in *Times v. Sullivan* made it unmistakably clear, in any case, that, as Justice Brennan put it, the law of libel "must be measured by standards that satisfy the First Amendment."

In a concurring decision, Justice Hugo Black, joined by Justice William O. Douglas, said that the Court had not gone nearly far enough. Under the First and Fourteenth Amendments, said Black, the state is completely prohibited from awarding damages to public officials against "critics of their official conduct" because "an unconditional right to say what one pleases about public affairs is what I consider to be the minimum guarantee of the First Amendment." How can a country live in freedom, Black asked, if "its people can be made to suffer physically or financially for criticizing their government, its actions or its officials?" Accordingly, Black and Douglas would have done away with the loophole allowing public officials a victory in a libel case if they can prove "actual malice" on the part of the defendant.

"Malice, even as defined by the Court," Justice Black wrote, "is an elusive, abstract concept, hard to prove and hard to disprove. The requirement that malice be proved provides at best an evanescent protection for the right critically to discuss public affairs and certainly does not measure up to the sturdy safeguard embodied in the First Amendment."

In another concurring opinion, Justice Arthur J. Goldberg agreed with Black and Douglas that "the First and Fourteenth Amendments to the Constitution afford to the citizen and to the press an absolute, unconditional privilege to criticize official conduct *despite the harm which may flow from excesses and abuses*" (emphasis added).

Goldberg too was greatly disturbed by the elusiveness of the charge "actual malice," because it could lead to damages being imposed "upon a jury's evaluation of a *speaker's state of mind*" (emphasis added).

"If individual citizens," Goldberg added, "may be held liable in damages for strong words, which a jury finds false and maliciously motivated, there can be little doubt that public debate and advocacy will be constrained."

Goldberg then went on to the specific subject in this case, a newspaper advertisement. There are times when dissenting views can get into a publication only by means of a paid advertisement—if the publication agrees to accept it. Under the "actual malice" doctrine, said Goldberg, "if newspapers, publishing advertisements dealing with public issues, thereby risk liability, there can also be little doubt that the ability of minority groups to secure publication of their views on public affairs and to seek support for their causes will be greatly diminished." Rather than risk being sued for libel, publishers may well accept fewer such advertisements.

In addition to setting much stiffer standards by which public officials could win libel cases, even with the "actual malice" loophole, *Times v. Sullivan* was historic in another sense. After 166 years, the Supreme Court addressed itself to the constitutionality of the Alien and Sedition Acts of 1798 (passed by the Federalist government to punish criticism of the President and other officials by the opposition).

Said Justice Brennan: "Although the Sedition Act was never tested in this Court, the attack upon its validity has carried the day in the court of history. Fines levied in its prosecution were repaid by an Act of Congress on the ground that it was unconstitutional. . . . Jefferson, as President, pardoned those who had been convicted and sentenced under the Act and remitted their fines, stating: 'I discharged every person under punishment or prosecution under the sedition law, because I considered, and now consider, that law to be nullity, as absolute and as palpable as if Congress had ordered us to fall down and worship a golden image.' The invalidity of the Act has also been assumed by Justices of this Court. These views reflect a broad consensus that the Act, *because of the restraint it imposed upon criticism of government and public officials,* was inconsistent with the First Amendment" (emphasis added).

Brennan also recalled James Madison's declaration that in this new nation, "the censorial power is in the people over the Government, and not in the Government over the people." Accordingly, Brennan continued, "the right of free public discussion of the stewardship of public officials was thus, in Madison's view, a fundamental principle of the American form of government." This fundamental principle was underlined by the Supreme Court in *Times v. Sullivan.*

In subsequent years, the Court, having made it more difficult for public officials to win libel suits, decided to include "public figures," as well as public officials, in the category covered by *Times v. Sullivan.* Public figures too would have to prove "actual malice" (that the alleged libel was made with knowledge that it was false or with reckless disregard of whether it was false or not).

Who is a public figure? "That designation," Justice Lewis F. Powell has said, "may rest on either of two alternative bases. In some instances, an individual may achieve such pervasive fame or notoriety that he becomes a public figure for all purposes and in all contexts. More commonly, an individual voluntarily injects himself or is drawn into a particular public controversy and thereby becomes a public figure for a limited range of issues. In either case, such persons assume special prominence in the resolution of public questions" (*Gertz v. Robert Welch,* 1974).

Why should it be made harder for a public figure to win a libel suit than it would be for an ordinary citizen? Because, according to Powell, public figures, like public officials, "usually enjoy significantly greater access to the channels of effective communication and hence have a more realistic opportunity to counteract false statements than private individuals normally do."

A public figure, for instance, has easier and wider access to the press, including television, than other citizens. If he feels he has been defamed, he can use those channels of communication to state his side of the story. That being the case, robust public debate on public issues is encouraged by making it difficult for a public figure to intimidate his critics through the use of libel suits.

In *Gertz v. Robert Welch*, the Court tried to clarify further the difference between a public figure and someone not well enough known to fit that designation. Six years before, a Chicago policeman, Nuccio, shot and killed a young man. The latter's family hired Elmer Gertz, an attorney, to represent them in a civil suit for damages against Nuccio. The March 1969 issue of *American Opinion*, a monthly publication of the John Birch Society, carried an article charging that a "frame-up" was underway against Nuccio, who was also on trial for murder. This frame-up, the article went on to assert, was part of a Communist plot to discredit local law-enforcement agencies.

Elmer Gertz had nothing to do with Nuccio's murder trial. He had been retained to handle only the civil suit for damages against the policeman. Nonetheless, *American Opinion* named Gertz as an architect of the frame-up. It also listed a number of Gertz's alleged left-wing affiliations and called him a "Leninist" and a "Communist-fronter." In addition, the magazine claimed that the police had a file on Gertz so big that it took "a big, Irish cop to lift" it.

In truth, the Supreme Court later noted, Gertz had no criminal record; he had not belonged to some of the organizations *American Opinion* had accused him of being involved with, nor was there any evidence that he was a "Leninist" or a "Communist-fronter."

Elmer Gertz sued *American Opinion* for libel. In its response the publication claimed that Gertz was a public figure and that the article about him concerned an issue of public interest. Therefore, it maintained, under the doctrine of *Times v. Sullivan* and its successors, the article criticizing Gertz was protected by the First Amendment unless "actual malice" could be proved.

At first the Federal District Court in Chicago ruled that Gertz was *not* a public figure, and the jury awarded him fifty thousand dollars in damages. On reflection, however, the trial judge overruled the jury and ruled in favor of *American Opinion.* The judge explained that although Gertz was neither a public official nor a public figure, a *public issue* was definitely involved in *American Opinion*'s article involving him; in order to win damages, therefore, he would have had to prove "actual malice" and had not been able to do so.

The Court of Appeals agreed with the trial judge, but the Supreme Court reversed both decisions and ruled in favor of Gertz. In delivering the opinion of the Court, Justice Powell made a number of basic points about the First Amendment: "Under the First Amendment, there is no such thing as a false *idea*. However pernicious an opinion may seem, we depend for its correction not on the consciences of judges and juries but on the competition of other ideas" (emphasis added).

However, Powell added immediately, "there is no constitutional value in false statements of *fact*. Neither the intentional lie nor the careless error materially advances society's interest in 'uninhibited, robust, and wide-open' debate on public issues" (emphasis added).

Powell thereby seemed to imply that factual errors made in wide-open debate are not protected by the First Amendment. But he went on to emphasize that the issue is more complicated than that. "Although the erroneous statement of fact is not worthy of constitutional protection," Powell continued, "it is nevertheless inevitable in free debate. . . . And punishment of error runs the risk of inducing a cautious and restrictive exercise of the constitutionally guaranteed freedoms of speech and press. Our decisions recognize that a rule of strict liability that compels a publisher or a broadcaster to guarantee the accuracy of his factual assertions may lead to intolerable self-censorship. . . . *The First Amendment requires that we protect some falsehood in order to protect speech that matters*" (emphasis added).

That does not mean, Powell warned, that the law of libel is dead. If someone has been defamed, the state still has the power to see to it that his "wrongful injury" is redressed. But if that someone is a public official or a public figure, he can recover damages for injury to his reputation "only on clear and convincing proof that the defamatory falsehood was made with knowledge of its falsity or with reckless disregard for the truth [that is, 'actual malice']."

After all, Powell said, "public officials and public figures have voluntarily exposed themselves to increased risk of injury from defamatory falsehoods concerning them. No such assumption is justified with respect to a private individual. . . . Thus, private individuals are not only more vulnerable to injury than public officials and public figures; they are also more deserving of recovery."

But what of Elmer Gertz? Is he or is he not a public figure? The fact, said the Court, that Gertz had been active in community and professional affairs, and had written several books and articles on legal subjects, does *not* make him a public figure. Yes, he was "well-known in some circles," but "he had achieved no general fame or notoriety in the community." As for the murder trial of the Chicago policeman, which led *American Opinion* to attack Gertz, the lawyer "plainly did not thrust himself into the vortex of this public issue, nor did he engage the public's attention in an attempt to influence its outcome."

Accordingly, a majority of the Supreme Court decided that Elmer Gertz did not have to meet the stiff standards required of a public figure or public official in order to win a libel suit.

Justice Douglas dissented because of his conviction that the First Amendment protects all public discussion of public issues. This approach cuts through the question of whether or not the person claiming to be defamed is in the public or private category. So long as public affairs are being discussed, all such speech should be free of actions for libel. And by "public affairs," Douglas emphasized, he meant more than just political affairs. "Science, economics, business, art, literature, etc., are all matters of interest to the general public. Indeed, any matter of sufficient general interest to prompt media coverage may be said to be a public affair."

It was the intent of the First Amendment, said Douglas, to encourage open discussion of all these public matters, but the threat of libel action makes such speech perilous rather than free. All the more so when it is a jury that ultimately decides whether speech is to be punished or not. "Discussion of public matters," Douglas pointed out, "is often marked by highly charged emotions, and jurymen, not unlike us all, are subject to those emotions."

Even in the most neutral circumstances, Douglas said, a jury's verdict is unpredictable; but in a libel action involving "those who venture to discuss heated issues," the emotional atmosphere may be such that "a virtual roll of the dice" will leave some defendants liable "for often massive claims of damage." That is why *all* public discussion of public affairs should be protected from juries and all other agents of the state. Since the issue in the *Gertz* case was of public interest, Douglas maintained, *American Opinion* had been protected by the First Amendment for what it had said about Elmer Gertz.

One Supreme Court Justice, Hugo Black, believed there should be no libel laws, that all speech, whether or not concerned with public issues, should be free of damage suits. In a 1962 interview at New York University Law School, Black said, "I believe with Jefferson that it is time enough for government to step in to regulate people when they *do* something, not when they *say* something, and I do not believe myself that there is *any* halfway ground if you enforce the protections of the First Amendment."

One of the nation's leading First Amendment lawyers, who has often argued before the Supreme Court, unexpectedly met the chief officer of a business corporation a few years ago. They had first met in the late 1960s when the lawyer defended a magazine against a libel suit brought against it by that corporation. The libel action had failed.

This time the corporate officer was much more amiable than the lawyer had expected in view of their brief but dissonant common history. "Oh, I'm not that upset about having lost the case," the executive said. "You see, the effect of the suit was that your client did not publish an article about us for a year and a half after the case was over." He smiled at the lawyer. "You're very expensive."

That the fear of libel suits can chill, and sometimes freeze, expression is common knowledge in journalism and book publishing. In 1976 a prestigious firm published a book by a reputable investigative reporter. It claimed that in a celebrated murder case a woman had been imprisoned after her due process rights were grievously abused by the district attorney and a detective on his staff. When a libel action asking for huge damages was begun by the public officials named in the book, several other muckraking projects in the publishing house, still in manuscript, were ordered watered down considerably.

As another illustration of the possible domino effect of libel suits, in October 1976 McDonnell Douglas Corporation sued *The New York Times* and writer Robert Sherrill for twenty-five million dollars in defamation damages because of a book review Sherrill had written for that paper. Two books were involved, and each dealt with the 1974 crash of a Turkish Airlines DC-10 outside Paris in which 346 persons were killed. The writers assessed the degree to which the blame for the crash could be fixed on a number of American regulatory agencies and on McDonnell Douglas Corporation, the manufacturer of the plane.

Sherrill, the *Times* reviewer, agreed with the authors of

the books that the greatest risk in flying is not bad weather but rather "the airplane manufacturer who chooses higher profits over safer equipment and who is permitted to do so by a Federal Aviation Agency that is intellectually lethargic and politically motivated." The headline on the review in the *Times* was THE CHEAP DOOR THAT COST 346 LIVES.

Some months after the filing of the libel action by Mc-Donnell Douglas, a lawyer for the *Times* checked to see how many reviews of the book had appeared in other publications after the announcement had been made of the libel action. He found very few reviews. "I think it's rather obvious why McDonnell Douglas brought that action against us," the lawyer said. "They never really expected to win, but they've accomplished their main purpose. They've put the fear of a libel suit in editors around the country, and the result has been self-censorship."

The libel action against the *Times* never went to trial.

Toward the end of its 1978–79 term, the Supreme Court handed down two decisions that may significantly increase the number of libel suits filed against the press.

The first, *Herbert v. Lando*, held that in libel suits brought by public figures, journalists can be compelled to reveal their "state of mind" as they were researching and writing (or broadcasting) a story. As we have seen, fifteen years before, in *New York Times Co. v. Sullivan*, the Court had ruled that public officials (and in later decisions, public figures) could not win a libel suit unless they proved "actual malice": that the newspaper or broadcasting station had gone ahead, knowing the material was false or with reckless disregard as to whether it was false.

In the *Herbert* case, Mr. Justice White, delivering the majority opinion for a Court split 6 to 3, emphasized that in order to try to prove "actual malice," public figures must be able to get "direct evidence through inquiry into the thoughts, opinions and conclusions" of journalists. From now on, defendants in this kind of libel suit would have to reveal what they had been thinking about the credibility of the material they were working with at all stages of a story's preparation. Accordingly, the person who had allegedly been defamed would be able to probe into the very thought processes of reporters and editors. It is true that in the past, some journalists had volunteered to offer "state-of-mind" testimony in their defense against libel actions, but this marked the first time that *all* journalists in "public figure" libel suits would henceforth be commanded by the state to disclose their thoughts.

The suit had been brought by Colonel Anthony Herbert against CBS producer Barry Lando, Mike Wallace, and CBS, Inc., as well as against *The Atlantic Monthly* (for which Lando had written an article on Herbert and the television show at issue). A section of CBS's *60 Minutes* had concentrated on Colonel Herbert; his lawyers claimed that "the broadcast was a deliberately selective presentation directed at creating but a single impression—that Herbert was a liar, an opportunist, and a brutal person."

Until that national television exposure, Herbert, it was claimed, had become widely known as an honorable soldier who, driven by conscience, had accused certain fellow officers of having covered up American war crimes in Vietnam. But as a result of the broadcast, his lawyers charged, "Herbert's reputation and good name were destroyed and he sustained severe financial losses."

During pretrial discovery procedures (whereby combatants in a lawsuit can be questioned as to relevant facts in the case by opposing lawyers), Colonel Herbert claimed that he had the right to ask the kinds of questions that would reveal the defendants' state of mind throughout the whole process of researching and putting together "The Selling of Colonel Herbert," as that segment of 60 Minutes had been called.

Barry Lando was willing to answer all kinds of other questions. Indeed, he was interrogated for 26 days and his answers filled 2903 pages of transcript. But Lando refused to respond to such "state-of-mind" probes as:

> What was the basis for his decision to interview one soldier three times and not to interview another soldier at all?

> What was his motivation for including a statement by one individual, and not another, concerning Herbert's treatment of the Vietnamese?

> Why was certain other material left out of the program?

> What was the nature of conversations between him and his CBS colleagues, including Mike Wallace, with regard to material that was included or excluded from the broadcast?

That last area of questioning involves the normal decision-making process that goes on in every newsroom in the country, and until *Herbert v. Lando*, it is unlikely that any journalist had ever expected he might be asked to reveal in a court of law what was said in such conversations.

The federal district judge agreed with Colonel Herbert as to his right to ask "state-of-mind" questions, but stayed the pretrial discovery procedure until his ruling was appealed. In a 2–1 decision, the Second Circuit Court of Appeals reversed the decision of the lower court, declaring that to allow questions on how a journalist "formulated his judgments on what to print or what not to print" would be condoning judicial review of editorial thought processes. After all, it had seemed to be well established that the state (including the judiciary) was forbidden by the First Amendment to interfere with how a newspaper or broadcasting station came to decide what to print or broadcast. In 1974 Justice Byron White had said: "We have learned, and continue to learn, from what we view as the unhappy experiences of other nations where government has been allowed to meddle in the internal editorial affairs of newspapers."

Furthermore, said the Second Circuit Court of Appeals, to allow Colonel Herbert to ask "state-of-mind" questions would bring about an "inquiry, which on its face would be virtually boundless, endangering a constitutionally protected realm." Moreover, such probing into journalists' thoughts "unquestionably puts a freeze on the free interchange of ideas within the newsroom. . . . A reporter or editor, aware that his thoughts might have to be justified in a court of law, would often be discouraged from the creative verbal testing, probing, and discussion of hypotheses and alternatives which are the *sine qua non* of responsible journalism."

Nonetheless, in April 1979, the Supreme Court reversed the Second Circuit Court of Appeals and found in favor of Colonel Herbert's right to probe the thoughts of the reporters he claimed had defamed him. Justice

Byron White said, for the majority of the Court, that in a libel case involving a public figure, "the thoughts and editorial processes of the alleged defamer" must be "open to examination." How else will the public figure be able to prove, if he can, that the journalist knew that what he printed or broadcast was false—or that he recklessly didn't care?"

Said Walter Cronkite: "The day after the decision came down, I was listening to our editorial conference at CBS News in a way I've never listened before. There's a chilling effect right there. And I realized that if those conversations were ever taped and played back in a libel suit, we'd have no defense."

At CBS, just as at practically every other newsroom in broadcast stations and newspapers, it is not uncommon for a reporter, returning from an interview, to be asked something like "Is that yo-yo still lying?" It's what the editor thinks at the time. Later facts can change his mind. But before a jury, that line could be devastating to the defense.

Floyd Abrams, who argued the defendants' case before the Supreme Court, said of the decision: "This is not so much a terrible libel opinion as it is a terrible First Amendment opinion. We made objections to these 'state of mind' questions not because this was a libel case but because we thought the First Amendment should protect the press against *any* inquiries of this nature. In other words, this is fundamentally an interrogation case which raises the question as to what types of inquiry may be put to journalists with the imprimatur of the government" (the courts being an arm of the government).

"As of now," Abrams continued, "the Supreme Court's ruling deals only with libel cases, but so much First

Amendment law involves fighting off future dangers, not only present risks." With state-of-mind questions now established in libel cases, Abrams warns, this interrogatory tool may also be extended to congressional investigations, presidential inquiries, and judicial probes. A future Senator Joseph McCarthy, searching for "subversives" in the press, might be able to force journalists to say why they used one person and not another as a source, what they thought of the trustworthiness of the source, why certain material was left out of a story, what was said in conversations between reporter and editor about the subject of the story.

Sticking to the future of libel cases alone, however, Abrams says: "I was in court when Spiro Agnew, while Richard Nixon's vice-president, subpoenaed large numbers of Washington reporters for interrogation during his charges that there had been prosecutorial misconduct against him. Similarly, I was present when CREEP (the Committee to Re-elect the President [Nixon]) subpoenaed Woodward and Bernstein of *The Washington Post*, Nick Gage of *The New York Times* and others to testify as witnesses in its libel countersuit against the Democratic National Committee. CREEP was demanding all the reporters' notes, drafts, and the like. The question raised by the *Herbert* decision is: What if CREEP had gotten the idea not just to sue the Democrats but to also sue the *press* for libel? Or suppose Spiro Agnew had decided to sue the press for libel?

"Can it be," says Abrams, "that from now on, a sitting vice-president, let us say, can force the press to answer questions like those at issue in the *Herbert* case? Questions like: 'Why did you print this negative material about me and not this other favorable material?' 'What did your editor say to you about me?' 'Your paper has always been out to get me, right?'

"What it comes down to," Abrams emphasizes, "is that letting the state get so intrusively into the mind of the journalist is putting the press in a situation where it is simply not the kind of autonomous entity that it ought to be in this country."

But what of Mr. Justice White's insistence, in his majority opinion in *Herbert*, that it is only basic fairness to allow a public figure—who has the heavy burden of proving actual malice—to probe the state of mind of those he claims have defamed him?

In his dissent in *Herbert*, Mr. Justice Stewart pointed out that "actual malice" (as first used in *Times v. Sullivan*) "has nothing to do with hostility or ill will." It has only to do with whether the alleged libeler knew that something was false or recklessly disregarded whether it was false. "Why" questions—"Why did you print this and not that?"—are irrelevant. This kind of case, says Stewart, concerns only "that which was in fact published. What was *not* published has nothing to do with the case. And liability ultimately depends upon the publisher's state of knowledge of the falsity of what he has published, not at all upon his motivation in publishing it—not at all, in other words, upon actual malice as those words are ordinarily understood."

And *this* means, Stewart added, that since "a publisher's [or reporter's] motivation in a case such as this is irrelevant, there is clearly no occasion to inquire" into his thought processes from the moment he started to work on the story. The only relevant issues are whether the defendant knew, at the end, that what he was publishing was untrue, entertained serious doubts as to its truth, or recklessly ignored whether it was true or not.

But how can the person who claims to have been defamed get the answers to those questions without drilling into the defendant's mind? Says Floyd Abrams: "If a jury hears that ten people have told a journalist that something is not true, and yet he goes ahead and prints it, the jury quite properly may find that he published with serious doubts as to the truth of the story." Similarly, as Mr. Justice White himself wrote in *St. Amant v. Thompson* (1968), there are other non-state-of-mind ways of winning this kind of libel suit, such as showing, through objective evidence, that the defendant has fabricated a story or has based it entirely on an unverified telephone call.

There is yet another possible peril to the press in the *Herbert v. Lando* decision. Pretrial discovery—including the interrogations of the parties to the suit—is already alarmingly lengthy and costly. (Barry Lando, for instance, was questioned for twenty-eight days, even without state-of-mind questions.) In their opinions on the case, several of the High Court Justices deplored this grim fact of legal life, suggesting that trial court judges do something to curb discovery procedures. But the suggestions were only that, and in libel cases, now that journalists can be forced to answer all kinds of state-of-mind questions, the discovery process can become even more expensive. It was already close to a question of survival when small publications had to defend particularly onerous libel suits; yet after *Herbert v. Lando*, with discovery wide open in these actions, it is not unlikely that some stories may simply not be printed—for fear of libel actions—by economically marginal publications.

There is also the extensive amount of time that has to be taken away from editorial work to defend these suits, further adding to the cost.

"How many weeks of pretrial discovery," Floyd Abrams has asked, "could *The Nation* afford? Or *Commonweal?* Or many other small newspapers, magazines, and broadcast stations?"

On June 26, 1979, the Supreme Court handed down another decision, *Wolston v. Reader's Digest Association, Inc.*, which the Reporters Committee for Freedom of the Press vehemently criticized, claiming that it would greatly "encourage harassing libel suits and will discourage publishing news about public events."

In 1957–58, there had been a grand jury investigation of Soviet espionage agents in the United States. During its course, Ilya Wolston was summoned to appear before that grand jury, but on one occasion he did not show up. Eventually Wolston pleaded guilty to a charge of criminal contempt of court and received a suspended sentence. He was never, however, indicted for espionage.

In 1974, the Reader's Digest Association published a book, *KGB: The Secret Work of Soviet Secret Agents,* by John Barron. The only reference to Wolston in the book was his inclusion in a list of "Soviet agents identified in the United States." That list was based on an erroneous FBI document published in 1960.

Wolston sued for libel and lost twice in the lower courts, which held that he was a "public figure" because, by failing to appear before the grand jury and making himself liable to a contempt citation, he "became involved in a controversy of a decidedly public nature in a way that invited attention and comment, and thereby created in the public an interest in knowing about his connection with espionage." And, indeed, there had been considerable press attention to Wolston at the time.

The lower courts, having decided that Wolston was a public figure, said that he had no case. As we have seen, to win a libel suit, a public figure has to prove "actual malice." In this instance, Wolston would have had to show that the author of the book had known the erroneous FBI report was false or had recklessly disregarded truth or falsehood in printing what he did. But, said the lower courts, there was no evidence of "actual malice" in this case.

On the other hand, if the Supreme Court were to declare that Wolston was *not* a public figure, he might well, at a subsequent trial, win defamation damages by showing that the author had acted carelessly or negligently—though not with actual malice—with resultant harm to Wolston's reputation, economic potential, and mental state.

The High Court reversed the lower tribunals and held that Wolston is not a public figure. Yes, there had been much press coverage of Ilya Wolston in 1958 but—Justice William Rehnquist said for the 8 to 1 majority—Wolston did not "voluntarily thrust" himself into the news. Yes, Wolston's refusal to appear before the grand jury had been news. But, "a private individual is not automatically transformed into a public figure just by becoming involved in . . . a matter that attracts public attention. . . . A libel defendant must show more than mere newsworthiness to justify application of the demanding burden [of the 'actual malice' standard]."

But what about Wolston's conviction for contempt of court? Didn't that in itself make him a public figure? In refuting that argument, Justice Rehnquist denied that "any person who engages in criminal conduct automatically becomes a public figure for purposes of comment on a limited range of issues relating to his conviction."

In a concurring opinion, Mr. Justice Blackmun, joined by Mr. Justice Marshall, lamented so restrictive a definition of "public figure." The Court, Blackmun said, seems to hold "that a person becomes a limited-issue public figure only if he literally or figuratively 'mounts a rostrum' to advocate a particular view." Then why did Blackmun join the majority? Because, he said, the lapse of sixteen years between the public attention Wolston received then and his present private status no longer made him a "public figure" at the time the book was published.

The lone dissenter, Mr. Justice Brennan, said briefly though vehemently that Ilya Wolston was a "public figure" both in 1958 and in 1974. And he quoted the opinion, in the case, of the Court of Appeals: "The issue of Soviet espionage in 1958 and of Wolston's involvement in that operation continues to be a legitimate topic of debate today, for that matter concerns the security of the United States."

As many in the press saw it, the *Wolston* decision could lead to a significant rise in libel suits because if a "public figure" is only someone who "voluntarily thrusts" himself into the news, all kinds of *involuntary* subjects of news stories who feel aggrieved at their treatment by the press would henceforth be encouraged to retaliate through libel suits because they would not have to prove "actual malice."

Commenting on the decision, Floyd Abrams said: "One wonders about Mafia coverage, about coverage of others in organized or unorganized crimes." They do not "voluntarily thrust" themselves into the news. But, asks Abrams, "can it be that they are not public figures?"

The language of the Court in *Wolston* will be tested —on this and other points—in future cases brought before it. It appears, however, that for some time to come—as *Time* magazine has noted—"The media now knows that they must be more cautious, and readers and listeners will almost surely receive less detail about people they thought were in the news." Less detail will be printed in fear of possible libel suits.

Back in 1971, in *Rosenbloom v. Metromedia*, Mr. Justice Brennan, speaking for a plurality—but not the majority—of the Court, tried to show a way through the brambles of libel law that would strengthen the press's First Amendment right to publish news without undue fear of penalty: "If a matter is a subject of public or general interest, it cannot suddenly become less so merely because a private individual is involved, or because in some sense the individual did not 'voluntarily' choose to become involved. The public's primary interest is in the event . . . We honor the commitment to robust debate on public issues . . . by extending constitutional protection to all discussion and communication involving matters of public or general concern, without regard to whether the persons involved are famous or anonymous."

In the years since, the High Court has abandoned that perspective, reaching in *Wolston* the most restrictive definition yet of those public figures who must prove "actual malice" to win a libel suit against the press. As a result, there will be an increase in the power of lawyers at newspapers, broadcast stations, magazines, and book firms. Even the most fearless muckraking editors, after all, have to listen hard to the advice of attorneys trying to avoid libel actions against the paper or broadcast station. An editor who overrules a libel lawyer, with the result that the paper suffers a substantial imposition of damages in a law suit, is not likely to keep his job. And the further danger is that reporters, sensitive to a chill in the air, may come to censor themselves before they file anything for the editor to see.

Somehow this state of affairs does not seem to be what the framers of the First Amendment had in mind.

XXIII

The Fairness Doctrine has no place in our First Amendment regime. It puts the head of the camel inside the tent and enables administration after administration to toy with TV or radio in order to serve its sordid or its benevolent ends.

When a libel action is brought against a newspaper, magazine, book publisher, or broadcasting station, the government, as represented by the court, is thereby involved in examining, and perhaps punishing, the press. But can the government go farther and tell the press *what* to publish, in the interest of "fair," "responsible," and "balanced" journalism?

So far as the print media is concerned, that question was answered conclusively in *Miami Herald Publishing Company v. Tornillo* (1974). Pat Tornillo, head of the Dade County Classroom Teachers' Association, was running for the Democratic nomination for the Florida House of Representatives in 1972. In an editorial, the *Miami Herald*, Florida's largest newspaper, characterized Tornillo as a "czar" and a lawbreaker involved in "illegal acts against the public trust." In a second editorial, published five days before the election, the newspaper wrote scornfully, "Give him public office, says Pat, and he will no doubt live by the Golden Rule. Our translation reads that as more gold and more rule."

Tornillo did not sue for libel but instead brought court action against the *Miami Herald* on the basis of a 1913 Florida statute which said a newspaper had to give free "reply" space to any candidate for office whom the paper had attacked with regard to his personal character or his official record.

Having been assailed in the *Miami Herald*, Tornillo demanded the rebuttal space guaranteed him by Florida law. The newspaper refused, claiming that the law was unconstitutional in that it gave the state power to direct the content of the paper, a violation of the First Amendment. Agreeing with Tornillo, however, the Florida Supreme Court (6–1) said that the right-of-reply statute enhanced, rather than violated, First Amendment freedoms because it furthered the "broad societal interest in the free flow of information to the public." That is, by mandating that reply space be given, the law enabled a political candidate attacked by a paper to add *his* information to that free flow.

There was wide national interest in the case. Nearly all the major news organizations, broadcast as well as print, were supporting the *Miami Herald*; Tornillo's rooters included then President Richard M. Nixon and Senator John McClellan. (If Tornillo won the case, McClellan pledged to introduce a federal right-of-reply bill in the Senate.)

During oral arguments before the Supreme Court, it appeared that the Justices were not convinced that Tornillo did indeed have a First Amendment right of *access* to the press. Justice William H. Rehnquist, for example, asked Tornillo's lawyer, "Isn't the First Amendment there for only one reason . . . to protect the people from the government? . . . It wasn't intended to protect one citizen from the speech of another citizen, was it?"

In the *Tornillo* decision, the Supreme Court unanimously overturned the Florida Supreme Court. Chief Justice Warren E. Burger admitted that by contrast with the early years of the nation, when "there was relatively easy access to the channels of communication" and "entry into publishing was inexpensive," the present situation amounted to "concentration of control of media." It has become enormously costly to buy a radio or television station or a newspaper, and so, "it is claimed, the public has lost any ability to respond or to contribute in a meaningful way to the debate on issues."

Tornillo and his supporters, the Chief Justice continued, argue, therefore, that "enforced access" to the press is essential if more and more of the citizens are to be directly involved in the "robust and wide-open" debate on public issues that the Supreme Court has called for in previous decisions.

The fundamental flaw in that argument, said Burger, is that any approach to enforced access requires the government to do the forcing, and the First Amendment forbids government "intrusion into the function of editors. A newspaper is more than a passive receptacle or conduit for news, comment, and advertising. The choice of material to go into a newspaper, and the decisions made as to limitations on the size of the paper, and content, and treatment of public issues and public officials—whether fair or unfair—constitutes the exercise of editorial control and judgment. It has yet to be demonstrated how governmental regulation of this crucial process can be exercised consistent with First Amendment guarantees of a free press as they have evolved to this time."

In a concurring decision, Justice Bryon R. White noted: "We have learned, and continue to learn, from what we view as the unhappy experiences of other nations where government has been allowed to meddle in the internal affairs of newspapers. . . . Of course, the press is not always accurate, or even responsible, and may not present full and fair debate on important public issues. But the balance struck by the First Amendment with respect to the press is that society must take the risk that occasionally debate on vital matters will not be comprehensive and that all viewpoints may not be expressed. The press would be unlicensed because, in Jefferson's words, '[w]here the press is free, and every man able to read, all is safe.' Any other accommodation—any other system that would supplant private control of the press with the heavy hand of government intrusion—would make the government the censor of what the people may read and know."

Yet part of the press—broadcasting and television—is subject to a certain degree of government intrusion. The "Equal Time" law, for instance, requires that radio and television stations provide all candidates for a particular office equal opportunity to be heard if one of those candidates has already been heard on the station. There have been various exemptions, but the hand of government is very much present, as a station violating the equal time rules can be penalized by the Federal Communications Commission.

Government is also involved in regulating the content of broadcasting by means of the Fairness Doctrine. As defined by Les Brown, TV analyst for *The New York Times*, the Fairness Doctrine requires of the broadcaster:

"(1) that he devote a reasonable amount of time to the discussion of controversial issues of public importance, and (2) that he do so fairly, by affording reasonable opportunity for the opposing viewpoints to be heard." If a station is found in repeated violation of the Fairness Doctrine, it could have difficulty getting its license renewed.

No one can tell the print media what to publish in the interest of fairness; why should broadcasting have weaker First Amendment rights than print? Justice William O. Douglas consistently believed that the government had no more business interfering with the content of broadcast programs than with what newspapers printed. "I fail to see," Douglas said, "how constitutionally we can treat TV and the radio differently than we treat newspapers. . . . The Fairness Doctrine has no place in our First Amendment regime. It puts the head of the camel inside the tent and enables administration after administration to toy with TV or radio in order to serve its sordid or its benevolent ends."

The majority of the Supreme Court, however, has continued to make a distinction, in terms of First Amendment protections, between the print and broadcast press. The basic justification, as distilled in Dorsen, Bender, and Neuborne's *Political and Civil Rights in the United States*, is "that the spectrum of broadcast frequencies is a public resource subject to an inherent physical limitation [only so many available channels] which prevents all those who possess the financial resources and the desire to communicate through the air waves to be satisfactorily accommodated." By contrast, there is no inherent physical limitation to the number of newspapers or other publications that can be printed simultaneously.

This is the "scarcity theory." As the Supreme Court

said in 1943 (*National Broadcasting Company v. United States*): "Unlike other modes of expression, radio is not available to all. That is its unique characteristic, and that is why, unlike other modes of expression, it is subject to governmental regulation."

In 1969 (*Red Lion Broadcasting Company v. Federal Communications Commission*), the High Court, by a 7 to 0 vote, underscored the distinction between broadcasting stations and newspapers in terms of government regulation of speech. (William O. Douglas, not having heard the oral arguments, did not participate in the case, and because of the recent resignation of Justice Abe Fortas the ninth seat was empty.)

At issue was the Fairness Doctrine. Fred Cook, a journalist, had been attacked by a commentator on Pennsylvania radio station WGCB (operated by the Red Lion Broadcasting Company). Cook demanded free reply time, and the station refused.

Said Mr. Justice White for the Court: Although broadcasters claim that the Fairness Doctrine abridges "their freedom of speech and press," the characteristics of broadcasting "justify differences in the First Amendment standards" applied to broadcasters. White continued:

> Because of the scarcity of radio frequencies, the Government is permitted to put restraints on licensees in favor of others whose views should be expressed on the unique medium. But the people as a whole retain their interest in free speech by radio and their collective right to have the medium function consistently with the ends and purposes of the First Amendment. *It is the right of the viewers and listeners, not the right of the broadcasters, which is paramount.* . . . It is the purpose of the First Amendment to preserve an uninhibited market-

THE FIRST FREEDOM

place of ideas in which truth will ultimately prevail, rather than to countenance monopolization of that market, whether it be by the Government itself or a private licensee.

The First Amendment confers no right on broadcast licensees to prevent others from broadcasting on "their" frequencies and no right to an unconditional monopoly of a scarce resource which the Government has denied others the right to use. [If there were no such regulations as the Fairness Doctrine,] station owners and a few networks would have unfettered power to make time available only to the highest bidders, to communicate only their own views on public issues, people and candidates, and to permit on the air only those with whom they agreed. There is no sanctuary in the First Amendment for unlimited private censorship operating in a medium not open to all. . . . In view of the scarcity of broadcast frequencies, the Government's role in allocating those frequencies, and the legitimate claims of those unable without governmental assistance to gain access to those frequencies for expression of their views, we hold the regulation and ruling at issue here are both authorized by statute and constitutional. [Emphasis added]

However, the debate over broadcasters' First Amendment rights continued. In 1972 David Bazelon, then chief judge of the United States Court of Appeals for the District of Columbia Circuit, raised a series of provocative arguments *against* the Fairness Doctrine. The case was *Brandywine–Main Line Radio, Inc. v. Federal Communications Commission.* A radio station, WXUR, had been under the control of Rev. Carl McIntire, a fundamentalist preacher of aggressively right-wing political views. The FCC had revoked the station's license because it had failed to adhere to the Fairness Doctrine.

In his dissenting opinion, Judge Bazelon pointed out that the FCC, by forcing WXUR off the air, had deprived its listeners of *that* station's ideas, "however unpopular or disruptive we might judge these ideas to be." (As Justice Douglas had pointed out in another television case, "Under our Bill of Rights, people are entitled to have extreme ideas, silly ideas, partisan ideas.")

As to the FCC's charge that WXUR had failed to share its channel with those holding opposing ideas, Bazelon noted that it is very difficult for a station such as WXUR to be held firmly and continually to the Fairness Doctrine, since "the monitoring procedures which the FCC requires for identification of controversial issues are beyond the capacity of a small staff, or a shoestring operation."

The paperwork can be extensive and expensive, particularly on a station such as WXUR, which airs a great deal of controversial programming. Said Bazelon: "The ratio of 'reply time' required for every issue discussed would have forced WXUR"—if the FCC had allowed the station to continue broadcasting but only in strict conformity with the Fairness Doctrine—"to censor its views. To decrease the intensity of its presentation." Otherwise, the station would have been swamped in FCC paperwork. "The ramifications of this chilling effect," said Bazelon, "will be felt by every broadcaster who simply has a lot to say."

The Fairness Doctrine also has a chilling effect on the networks, big and profitable as they are. Richard Salant, when president of CBS News, explained: "We get a letter from the FCC, notifying the network of a complaint of unfairness and everybody has to dig. The reporters, the producers of the show, everybody has to dig out stuff and try to reconstruct why they did what they did. . . . If nothing else, it takes you away from your work. And when it is the government, through the FCC, moving into areas of program content, the effect is *chilling*. We have more lawyers than we have reporters."

Accordingly, the Fairness Doctrine does much more than cause expensive inconvenience to broadcasters. It can also serve to inhibit rather than encourage the free play of ideas that the First Amendment exists to protect. As Judge Bazelon put it, "In the context of broadcasting today, our democratic reliance on a truly informed American public is threatened if the overall effect of the Fairness Doctrine is the very censorship of controversy which it was promulgated to overcome."

An illustration: Louis Seltzer, president of WCOJ, a five-thousand-watt radio station in West Chester, Pennsylvania, wrote the American Civil Liberties Union in 1973 in an attempt to persuade it to stop supporting the Fairness Doctrine:

> The Fairness Doctrine is *un*fair. As a practical matter, I know that it has served to muzzle this station for 25 years. An example: We aired only one or two [shows] of a well-produced series put out by the Anti-Defamation League of the B'nai B'rith on "The radical Right." Why? Simply because airing these programs would open the floodgates to a paranoid response from the "nut" groups. . . . True, we could refuse to run the reply programs on the basis of their patent untruth, but this would cost us a $10,000 lawsuit up to the Supreme Court of the United States, and even then there would be a possibility of losing. . . . This station is not small,

but it is not that large. We have neither the time nor the money to devote to such Joan-of-Arcian causes.

An obvious response to Mr. Seltzer's complaint is that the First Amendment exists for the benefit of "nut" groups too, but the point is that because of fear of *governmental* interference with what he chose to put on the air, Seltzer did censor himself.

The power of the federal government to insist that broadcasting have "balance" has led to this analogy by Richard Salant:

> Suppose the English governor had told Tom Paine that he could go ahead and publish all he liked—but *only* if at the back of his pamphlets, he also printed the Royal Governor's views. That command, far from being an implementation of free speech, would have been just the opposite. It's a restriction on speech if, in order to be allowed to express your own views, you also have to present those of someone arguing on the other side.

Salant, like others in broadcasting, emphasizes that the *publicized* examples of station and network self-censorship may be only a small percentage of such management decisions: "When one's very survival in one's business—broadcasting—depends on licensing by the government . . . does anybody think for a moment that there are not those who have said, 'Let's skip this one, let's not make waves, let's stay out of trouble'?"

Even in his own CBS organization, Salant, who was consistently supportive of his investigative reporters, had a "constant fear that somebody down the line—reporters or producers or somebody—will think, 'Gee, we've caused such headaches to management, or to ourselves, in having to dig out all this stuff, I'll play it easy for a while.'" Salant even sent a memorandum to his news staff in the early 1970s telling them he considered self-censorship a "high crime."

Soon after that memorandum was circulated, a news official at WCBS-TV, New York, admitted, "Sure, I let some stories pass because they're too controversial. There are enough pressures in this business; who needs trouble from the FCC?"

Broadcast news reporters and producers speak with some passion about the constraints under which they have to work, by contrast with their colleagues in the printed press. One of them, Bill Monroe of *Meet The Press*, who used to be Washington editor of NBC's *Today* show, emphasizes:

> It is thoroughly understood in the industry that the most likely outcome of bold journalism is trouble with the FCC: a penalty, amounting to harassment, in the form of an official request for justification, in 10 or 20 days after a program has been aired, that the program is in compliance with the Fairness Doctrine. Any newsman who has seen the effort that a broadcast executive and his staff must make to prepare an answer to such an official request can only assume that his boss, as a human being, would have a desire to minimize such official challenges in the future.

In agreement is J. Edward Murray, associate editor of the *Detroit Free Press* and a past president of the American Society of Newspaper Editors. Like William O. Douglas, Murray believes that broadcast journalists should have the same full First Amendment freedoms that he, a newspaper editor, can exercise. Let us suppose there

279

was a Fairness Doctrine for newspapers, says Murray: "We investigate and expose policemen who are on the 'take' in the dope rackets. If an equivalent weight of time must be given to policemen who are not on the 'take,' the whole campaign becomes so unwieldy and pointless as to be useless. Must the good cops get equivalent space with the bad cops?"

What about the scarcity argument? Is the limited number of channels a justification for government supervision of the fairness of those operating the channels? Judge David Bazelon, in his dissenting opinion in the WXUR case, noted that as of September 1972 there were 7,458 commercial broadcasting stations on the air but only 1,749 daily newspapers in circulation. (As of 1979, the ratio is still roughly the same.)

"Nearly every American city," Bazelon wrote, "receives a number of different television and radio signals. Radio licensees represent diverse ownership; UHF, local and public [television] offer contrast to the three competing networks; neither broadcasting spectrum is completely filled. But of 1,400 newspaper cities, there are only 15 left with face-to-face [daily] competition."

If this was not enough to torpedo the notion that broadcasting's First Amendment rights must be less because of the scarcity of broadcasting channels, Bazelon went on to note that as technology keeps advancing, it will be possible "to provide to the television viewer 400 channels. . . . Even now we possess the know-how necessary to do away with technical scarcity through CATV [cable television]."

The Supreme Court, still adhering to the scarcity theory, has so far refused to extend to broadcasters the full spectrum of First Amendment rights available to the print media. In one of his recurring protests on this matter, Justice William O. Douglas said flatly:

My conclusion is that TV and radio stand in the same protected position under the First Amendment as do newspapers and magazines. The philosophy of the First Amendment requires that result. . . . The fear that Madison and Jefferson had of government intrusion . . . was founded not only on the spectre of a lawless government but [on the spectre] of government under the control of a faction that desired to foist its views of the common good on the people. . . . The sturdy people who fashioned the First Amendment would be shocked at the intrusion of government into a field which in this Nation has been reserved for individuals. . . .

The prospect of putting government in a position of control . . . is to me an appalling one, even to the extent of the Fairness Doctrine. The struggle for liberty has been a struggle against government. The essential scheme of our Constitution and Bill of Rights was to take government off the backs of people. Separation of powers was one device. An independent judiciary was another device. The Bill of Rights was still another. And it is anathema to the First Amendment to allow government any role of censorship over newspapers, magazines, books, art, music, TV, radio, or any other aspect of the press.

There is another argument, however, in favor of government intrusion into the content of television and radio. The airwaves, it is claimed, are a public resource; therefore, unlike print publishers, those who own a broadcast channel are caretakers of that resource for the public at large.

Justice Douglas's answer: "It is said . . . that govern-

ment can control the broadcasters because their channels
are in the public domain in the sense that they use the
airspace that is the common heritage of all the people.
But parks are also in the public domain. Yet people who
speak there do not come under government censorship."

One of the strongest attacks on government constric-
tion of broadcasters' First Amendment rights came during
Judge David Bazelon's dissenting opinion in the case concerning the revocation of the license of WXUR, the radio
station that gave much room to right-wing views and did
not much "balance" those views with contesting perspectives:

> In this case I am faced with a prima facie violation of
> the First Amendment. The Federal Communications
> Commission has subjected Brandywine [WXUR's
> owner] to the supreme penalty: it may no longer oper-
> ate as a radio broadcast station. In silencing WXUR,
> the Commission has dealt a death blow to the licensee's
> freedom of speech and press. Furthermore, it has denied
> the listening public access to the expression of many
> controversial views. Yet the Commission would have us
> approve this action in the name of the Fairness Doc-
> trine, the constitutional validity of which is premised on
> the argument that its enforcement will *enhance* public
> access to a marketplace of ideas without serious infringe-
> ment of the First Amendment rights of individual broad-
> casters.

XXIV

There are as many different definitions of obscenity as there are men (and women), and they are as unique to the individual as his dreams.

If the Fairness Doctrine limits the First Amendment freedoms of broadcasters, there are other areas of speech which fall *outside* the protection of the First Amendment, whether for broadcasters, print journalists, or filmmakers. As discussed in previous chapters, defamation (libel and slander) is punishable under certain circumstances. Another such area is obscenity, which, the Supreme Court declared in 1957, is not sheltered by the First Amendment.

Yet there is no evidence that the framers of the Constitution intended to exclude obscenity from the First Amendment. Before the American Revolution, only Massachusetts had an obscenity statute, and it was primarily concerned with antireligious material. All the other colonies let sexual materials alone. Nor did obscenity figure in the deliberations leading up to the First Amendment.

Benjamin Franklin wrote and circulated erotic publications (among them, *Letter of Advice to Young Men on the Proper Choosing of a Mistress*); James Madison was known for his "Rabelaisian anecdotes"; and as Judge Jerome Frank has pointed out, the libraries of many Founding Fathers included flavorsome tales abounding in explicit sex. Thomas Jefferson, moreover, wrote in an 1814 letter: "I am really mortified that . . . the sale of a book can become a subject of inquiry, and of criminal inquiry too. . . . Are we to have a censor whose imprimatur shall say what books may be sold and what we may buy? . . . Whose foot is to be the measure to which ours are all to be cut or stretched?"

Later in the nineteenth century, however, censors did arise in the land, most notably Anthony Comstock, who worked successfully to get laws passed prohibiting obscene literature from being sent through the mails. He also "exposed" writers and painters whose work he judged to be obscene, and among the many honors he accumulated for his cleansing work was an appointment to President Woodrow Wilson's International Purity Congress.

"Comstockery" (as George Bernard Shaw called it) continued into the twentieth century, but the United States Supreme Court did not deal directly with the issue until *Roth v. United States* in 1957. Justice William J. Brennan, Jr., speaking for the majority, said flatly that "obscenity is not within the area of constitutionally protected speech or press."

But, as the Court came to find, it is ceaselessly difficult to define precisely—for constitutional purposes—just what obscenity is. It was Brennan who said wearily in 1973, "No other aspect of the First Amendment has, in recent years, demanded so substantial a commitment of [the Court's] time, generated such disharmony of views, and remained so resistant to the formulation of stable and manageable standards as obscenity."

At the start of its journey into the quicksand of obscenity in 1957 the Court thought it *had* reached some clear guidelines. Samuel Roth had been convicted in New York City of violating the federal obscenity statute by mailing obscene books, circulars, and advertising material. In affirming his conviction, Mr. Justice Brennan stated the difference between protected and unprotected expression in this area: "All ideas having even the slightest redeeming social importance—unorthodox ideas, controversial ideas, even ideas hateful to the prevailing climate of opinion" are protected. But obscenity is "utterly without redeeming social importance."

Brennan went on to underline that "sex and obscenity are not synonymous. . . . Sex, a great and mysterious motive force in human life, has indisputably been a subject of absorbing interest to mankind through the ages; it is one of the vital problems of human interest and public concern." What is the distinction, then, between sex and obscenity? "Obscene material," Brennan explained, "is material which deals with sex in a manner appealing to prurient interest"; that is, "material having a tendency to excite lustful thoughts."

How is one to decide, in a court of law, whether a work is indeed obscene and thereby punishable? A work is guilty of being obscene if, to the "average person, applying contemporary community standards, the dominant theme of the material taken *as a whole* appeals to prurient interest" (emphasis added). That is, a book or a movie or a play cannot be judged just on the basis of certain erotic words and scenes. If the work as a whole does not primarily excite lustful thoughts, it is protected by the First Amendment.

Justice Brennan recognized that in drawing a line between protected and unprotected expression, it was necessary to be most careful not to violate "the fundamental freedoms of speech and press. . . . Ceaseless vigilance is the watchword to prevent their erosion by Congress or by the States. The door barring federal and state intrusion into this area cannot be left ajar; it must be kept tightly closed and opened only the slightest crack necessary to prevent encroachment upon more important interests. It is therefore vital that the standards for judging obscenity safeguard the protection of speech and press for material which does not treat sex in a manner appealing to prurient interest."

Obscenity, then, represented that "slightest crack" in the door which otherwise barred state interference with free expression. And that was because obscenity is "utterly without redeeming social importance."

Justice William O. Douglas, joined by Justice Hugo Black, delivered a stinging dissent, a classic argument for the preferential place of the First Amendment in our system of values:

> When we sustain these convictions, we make the legality of a publication turn on the purity of thought which a book or tract instills in the mind of the reader. . . . Punishment is inflicted for thoughts provoked, not for overt acts nor antisocial conduct. This test cannot be squared with our decisions under the First Amendment. Even the ill-starred *Dennis* case [affirming the convictions of the leadership of the Communist party in 1951] conceded that speech to be punishable must have

some relation to action which could be penalized by government. . . .

The tests by which these convictions were obtained require only the arousing of sexual thoughts. Yet the arousing of sexual thoughts and desires happens every day in normal life in dozens of ways. . . .

The test of obscenity the Court endorses today gives the censor free range over a vast domain. To allow the State to step in and punish mere speech or publication that the judge or the jury thinks has an *undesirable* impact on thoughts but that is not shown to be a part of unlawful action is drastically to curtail the First Amendment.

Douglas noted that the trial judge in the *Roth* case charged the jury that "the federal obscenity statute outlaws literature dealing with sex which offends 'the common conscience of the community.' " Is that test permitted by the First Amendment? Said Douglas:

The standard of what offends "the common conscience of the community" conflicts, in my judgment, with the command of the First Amendment that "Congress shall make no law . . . abridging the freedom of speech, or of the press." Certainly that standard would not be an acceptable one if religion, economics, politics or philosophy were involved. How does it become a constitutional standard when literature treating with sex is concerned?

Any test that turns on what is offensive to the community's standards is too loose, too capricious, too destructive of freedom of expression to be squared with the First Amendment. Under that test, juries can censor, suppress, and punish what they don't like, provided the matter relates to "sexual impurity" or has a tendency "to excite lustful thoughts." This is community censorship in one of its worst forms.

If the First Amendment guarantee of freedom of speech and press is to mean anything in this field, it must allow protests even against the moral code that the standard of the day sets for the community.

Again Douglas underlined the difference between speech and conduct:

No one would suggest that the First Amendment permits nudity in public places, adultery and other phases of sexual misconduct in public places. . . . Government should be concerned with antisocial *conduct*, not with utterances. [Emphasis added]

The High Court continued to struggle with reconciling the First Amendment and the punishment of obscenity. In 1964, in *Jacobellis v. Ohio*, the Court reversed a state obscenity conviction of an exhibitor of *The Lovers*, a movie that had an explicit love scene in the last reel. According to Justices William J. Brennan, Jr., and Arthur J. Goldberg, no work could be judged obscene unless it had prurient appeal, was utterly without social importance, and went "substantially beyond the customary limits of candor in description or representation of [sexual matters]."

A key element of the Brennan-Goldberg judgment, in which three other Justices variously concurred, was that "the constitutional status of an allegedly obscene work must be determined on the basis of a national standard." That is, each local community could not decide, on the basis of *its* standards, whether or not a work was obscene. Said Brennan and Goldberg: "It is, after all, a national

Constitution we are expounding." That is, the First Amendment should have the same meaning throughout the land; otherwise the same work would be punishable in one city or town, would be protected in another, and would be perilously unsure of its status in a third.

"The Court," said Brennan and Goldberg, "has explicitly refused to tolerate a result whereby 'the constitutional limits of free expression in the Nation would vary with state lines.' . . . We see even less justification for allowing such limits to vary with town or county lines."

In his concurring opinion, Justice Black, joined by Justice Douglas, stated flatly that motion pictures are also included in the free press guarantees of the First Amendment and that the conviction of *anyone* exhibiting a motion picture is therefore a violation of the First Amendment.

The High Court kept having such difficulty with obscenity that its decisions continued to be split. *"Memoirs" v. Massachusetts* (1966) resulted in a three-part test to determine if a work fell outside the protection of the First Amendment. The case involved the eighteenth-century novel *Fanny Hill*. In clearing the book of criminality, three members of the Court (Chief Justice Earl Warren and Justices William J. Brennan, Jr., and Abe Fortas) declared that a form of expression is obscene only if (1) it is "utterly without redeeming social value"; (2) "the dominant theme appeals to a prurient interest in sex"; and (3) "the material is patently offensive because it affronts contemporary community standards relating to the description or representation of sexual matters."

Douglas and Black concurred in the decision because *Fanny Hill* had been found not to be obscene. But Douglas was still dissatisfied: "Publications and utterances were made immune from majoritarian control by the First Amendment, applicable to the States by reason of the Fourteenth. *No exceptions were made, not even for obscenity"* (emphasis added).

Douglas also noted, in passing:

> Every time an obscenity case is to be argued here, my office is flooded with letters and postal cards urging me to protect the community or the Nation by striking down the publication. The messages are often identical even down to commas and semicolons. The inference is irresistible that they were all copied down from a school or church blackboard. Dozens of postal cards often are mailed from the same precinct. Happily we do not bow to them. *I mention them only to emphasize the lack of popular understanding of our constitutional system.* [Emphasis added]

The three-part test which *Fanny Hill* passed remained the constitutional standard for determining obscenity until much of it was turned upside down in *Miller v. California* (1973). The defendant in the *Miller* case had been convicted of violating a state law by "knowingly distributing obscene matter," brochures advertising "adult" books.

By this time the Supreme Court included four appointees of Richard Nixon: Chief Justice Warren E. Burger and Associate Justices Harry A. Blackmun, Lewis F. Powell, Jr., and William H. Rehnquist. The Chief Justice strongly believed that obscenity was beyond the pale of the First Amendment. In the majority decision (5–4), Burger answered William O. Douglas and others who claimed that no form of expression, not even obscenity, could constitutionally be punished: "To equate the free and robust exchange of ideas and political debate with commercial exploitation of obscene material demeans the grand conception of the First Amendment and its high purposes in the historic struggle for freedom."

Douglas, in dissent, would not budge: "Since 'obscenity' is not mentioned in the Constitution or Bill of Rights," it cannot constitutionally be prohibited.

In *Miller* the majority of the Court threw out the previous standard by which a prosecutor had to prove that a work was "utterly without redeeming social value" before it could be condemned as obscene. The new test, said Chief Justice Burger, is that a work is obscene if it depicts or describes patently offensive sexual conduct specifically defined by the applicable state law and if, "taken as a whole," it does not have "serious literary, artistic, political, or scientific value."

The burden of proof is no longer on the prosecutor to show that the work is utterly without redeeming social value. Now the defense has to convince a judge or a jury that the indicted material has "serious literary, artistic, political, or scientific value."

What does "serious" mean? And to whom? Justice Brennan, in dissent, was appalled. Under the new test, he said, if a work has *some* social value, it can be censored because, "measured by some unspecified standard," it is not *serious* enough "to warrant constitutional protection." Defining obscenity so vaguely, Brennan continued angrily, "is nothing less than an invitation to widespread suppression of sexually oriented speech." Until this *Miller* decision, he pointed out, "the protections of the First Amendment have never been thought limited to expressions of *serious* literary or political value."

The First Amendment nowhere says that only "serious" speech is free in the United States.

Burger's majority decision made another major change in determining how obscenity cases were to be decided. No longer was there to be a national standard of obscenity. Burger, speaking for the three other Nixon appointees and Byron R. White, ruled that individual "community standards" would apply. Burger saw no reason why "the people of Maine or Mississippi" should "accept public depiction of conduct found tolerable in Las Vegas or New York City. . . . People in different States vary in their tastes and attitudes, and this diversity is not to be strangled by the absolutism of imposed uniformity."

The problem with that approach is that the United States Constitution is a national one. If the Sixth Amendment cannot mean one thing in Maine and another in Las Vegas, how can the First Amendment change by crossing state and county lines?

Since the *Miller* decision, with the differing local standards of thousands of communities being used to decide whether something is obscene or not, some national publishers and producers have had to go to considerable expense to defend themselves at various separate points around the country. The ultimate result, says Harvard Law professor Alan Dershowitz, can be that "some films will not even be made and some books will not even be published. If a filmmaker or a publisher knows that his product is legal in most cities and towns but is likely to be indicted and brought to costly trial in other places, he may well engage in self-censorship in order to avoid this kind of trouble, and not produce and distribute the work at all. And so, the most narrow, the most restrictive, local community standards will gradually determine what the rest of the country sees—and does not see."

The majority decision turned out to be dangerous on

another ground. In his dissent, Justice Brennan pointed out that from the *Roth* case on, the Supreme Court had "failed to formulate a standard that sharply distinguishes protected from unprotected speech." By this point, he declared, he seriously doubted that it was possible to reach a definition of obscenity that could be reconciled with the First Amendment.

Inherent in trying to separate "good speech" from "bad speech" in this area, Brennan said, is the problem of vagueness. The Court, said Brennan, has been using "such indefinite concepts as 'prurient interest,' 'patent offensiveness,' 'serious literary value,'" but "the meaning of these concepts necessarily varies with the experience, outlook, and even idiosyncracies of the person defining them."

As William O. Douglas had told his brethren in 1971: "Whatever obscenity is, it is immeasurable as a crime and delineable only as a sin. As a sin, it is present only in the minds of some and not in the minds of others. It is entirely too subjective for legal sanction. There are as many different definitions of obscenity as there are men; and they are as unique to the individual as his dreams."

One of the most revealing attempts by a Justice to define obscenity was that of Potter Stewart. In the 1964 *Jacobellis* case, Stewart, speaking for himself, not the majority of the Court, insisted that the only proper object of criminal obscenity laws is "hard-core pornography." But what *is* "hard-core pornography"? The Justice found himself unable to say: "I shall not today attempt further to define the kinds of material I understand to be embraced within that shorthand description; and perhaps I never could succeed in intelligibly doing so. But I know it when I see it, and the motion picture involved in this case is not that."

A Justice of the Supreme Court, however, is supposed to be more specific in his judgments than "I know it when I see it." But if Justice Douglas is correct, that there are "as many different definitions of obscenity as there are men," who, on or off the Court, could ever be precise in the matter of obscenity?

The result of this inherent vagueness led Douglas again to protest, in his 1973 *Miller* dissent, that the courts should have nothing whatever to do with obscenity prosecutions: "Obscenity—which even we cannot define with precision—is a hodge-podge. To send men to jail for violating standards they cannot understand, construe, and apply is a monstrous thing to do in a nation dedicated to fair trials and due process . . ."

After all, Douglas had also said with regard to obscenity: "There is no 'captive audience' problem. . . . No one is being compelled to look or to listen. Those who enter news stands or bookstalls may be offended by what they see. But they are not compelled by the State to frequent those places." (Nor are they compelled to frequent movie houses where certain films may offend them.)

Douglas himself practiced what he preached in this regard. "I am sure," he said in a 1973 dissent, "I would find offensive most of the books and movies charged with being obscene. But in a life that has not been short, I have yet to be trapped into seeing or reading something that would offend me. I never read or see the materials coming to the Court under charges of 'obscenity,' because I have thought the First Amendment made it unconstitutional for me to act as a censor."

What about children? Can something be punished as

obscene in terms of its effect on the young while remaining lawful if purchased or seen by adults? A majority of the Supreme Court reached this conclusion in *Ginsberg v. New York* (1968). It was held to be constitutional for a state to punish the owner of a stationery store and luncheonette for selling "girlie" magazines to a sixteen-year-old even though those magazines would not have been judged obscene if an adult had bought them. The reason, Justice Brennan said for the Court, is that a state does have the constitutional power to exercise its interest "in the well-being of its youth," and the New York State legislature had decided it would be "harmful to minors" if they were sold material that "predominantly appeals to the prurient, shameful or morbid interest of minors."

Justice Douglas disagreed: "It is one thing for parents and religious organizations to be active and involved" [in trying to protect children from allegedly "harmful" material], but "it is quite a different matter for the State to become implicated as a censor. As I read the First Amendment, it was designed to keep the State and the hands of all state officials off the printing presses of America. . . . Today this Court sits [once more] as the Nation's board of censors. With all respect, I do not know of any group in the country less qualified first, to know what obscenity is when they see it, and second, to have any considered judgment as to what the deleterious or beneficial impact of a particular publication may have *on minds either young or old*" (emphasis added).

Until he left the Supreme Court because of ill health in November 1975, Mr. Justice Douglas continued to warn against the dangerous vagueness of obscenity laws, making people subject to arrest for selling or distributing materials which they cannot know for certain are criminally obscene: "Every author, every bookseller, every movie exhibitor and perhaps every librarian is now at the mercy of the local police force's conception of what appeals to 'prurient interest' or is 'patently offensive.' The standards can vary from town to town and day to day in unpredictable fashion. . . . How can an author or bookseller or librarian know whether the community deems his books acceptable until after the jury renders its verdict?"

In certain cities or towns, therefore, booksellers, movie exhibitors, and librarians, fearful of somehow offending "community standards" and thereby being punished, may censor themselves and stock only those books and exhibit only those films which are not likely to offend anyone. (In the process, various elements of the community, who have not been consulted, will be limited as to what they can see or read. *Their* First Amendment rights will also have been abridged.)

A few years ago, Carole Grant, a soft-spoken, middle-aged woman, moved to Orem, Utah, with her husband, a former policeman, and their three children. Orem, with a population of thirty-five thousand, had no bookstores, and Carole Grant decided to open one.

Five months after the Book Rack, as she called it, had opened, Carole Grant was served with a criminal summons. She had been charged with violating the town's Ordinance 210, which established a Commission of Decency to ferret out obscene publications in Orem. For selling four books—*A Clockwork Orange, The Symbol, Last Tango in Paris,* and *The Idolators*—Carole Grant was accused of a crime. (Ordinance 210 also forbade teachers to assign any reading matter that contained explicit sexual material unless notarized approval had been obtained from parents.)

Criminal charges were also lodged against four Orem superstores, the kind that stock everything from groceries to furniture. Their crime had been selling such magazines as *Playboy*, *Penthouse*, and *Viva*.

As the censors made their moves, all the merchants in Orem who sold magazines and other publications held a meeting. One after another, each publicly swore to remove from their places of business all "obscene" or "doubtful" material. Acting as if they had become docile, fearful subjects of an authoritatian state, the merchants earnestly asked the allpowerful Commission of Decency to help them identify whatever obscene materials might still be in their stores.

As for the Book Rack, three large New York publishing houses—Random House, Dell, and Pocket Books—hired lawyers for the town's only bookseller. For several months negotiations were carried on to try to reach a settlement that would leave Carole Grant free of a criminal record. Meanwhile, she persisted in her conviction that she was a free citizen in a constitutional democracy. Carole Grant would make no pledges of future "good behavior" to the Commission of Decency. Instead, she pledged her allegiance to the First Amendment.

"I have very strong convictions on freedom to read and censorship," Carole Grant said. "I have sincerely tried to run a bookstore that I would be proud to go in and let my children go in. I love books, and believe people should be able to read whatever they want."

At last, all charges against Carole Grant were dropped. Seven days later, she closed the Book Rack. The pressures had been too much. As the National Ad Hoc Committee on Censorship said when it was all over, "As is often the case, there had been no need to prosecute; intimidation had finally sufficed."

Around the time that the blank face of censorship appeared in Orem, Utah, similar forces were at work in Burlington, Iowa. In order to drive a new "adult" moviehouse out of business, the city council passed an obscenity ordinance. Most residents of Burlington accepted the censorship law passively, but not the local paper, *Hawk Eye*, which ran an editorial entitled "Big Brother":

> [The new censorship bill] replaces individual freedom of choice, and personal tastes, with the police power of the state, employing a mythical "average person" and vague "contemporary community standards" to determine what citizens may or may not read or see. . . .
> Circumstances of this law's passage are a chilling commentary on the community's . . . sleepy disregard for individual freedom.
> The ordinance is the work of a group of clergymen and their followers who are notably inactive toward the real obscenities of racial discrimination, economic exploitation, social neglect, and private and public corruption; but who rush to make their prejudices into law at the first sign of individual tastes different from their own.
> But their success is due primarily to the embarrassed silence of those others who might have spoken out about the perils in any effort to limit the freedom of expression: the educators and lawyers and businessmen and union leaders who know better, but are afraid to say so.
> For the kind of repression directed here against certain cultural tastes is identical to the discrimination

voted in other times and other places against blacks, or union agitators, or Protestants, or Catholics, or snake worshippers, or anyone whose activities or life styles did not, at some point, conform to "contemporary community standards."

Despite the ferocity of the editorial, there was little reaction to it. The "sleepy disregard" of the townspeople extended even to attacks on them. No subscriptions were canceled. No ads were withheld. But the "adult" moviehouse did fight the obscenity ordinance in court, and it was struck down by Iowa's highest tribunal because the state legislature had already decreed that it alone could pass obscenity statutes. That is, no local government was empowered to deal with the issue. There already was a state obscenity law leaving adults free to read and see what they chose, though there were restrictions concerning children. Since this was a moviehouse for adults, the local ordinance was unconstitutional on that count too.

The *Hawk Eye* began to accept ads from the "adult" moviehouse, and there was hardly any public reaction to that either. "People here," said the editor, "don't say much when their rights are taken away or when their rights are given back."

XXV

*Despite my hatred of the Nazis' vicious doctrine, I—
as a Jew, and a refugee from Nazi Germany—realize
that it is in my interests to defend their right to
preach it.*

With libel and obscenity—difficult as they are to define
precisely—outside the protection of the First Amendment,
are there no other limits to speech? In 1942, the Supreme
Court (*Chaplinsky v. New Hampshire*) declared that
"fighting words"—offensive speech—were also *not* protected.

On a busy Saturday morning, Chaplinsky, a Jehovah's
Witness, had been distributing the literature of his sect
on the streets of Rochester, New Hampshire. As he
passed out his tracts, Chaplinsky was enthusiastically de-
nouncing all religion as a "racket" except, presumably,
the religious faith to which he himself adhered. Some
of the local citizens became quite irritated by Chaplinsky's
language; a disturbance took place, and a police officer
began to take the Jehovah's Witness to the station house.
On the way they met Rochester's city marshal, who was
accused by the decidedly unsubdued Chaplinsky of
being "a God damned racketeer and a damned Fascist."
Chaplinsky added that the entire government of Rochester was composed of fascists or agents of fascists.

Chaplinsky was convicted of violating a New Hampshire law: "No person shall address any offensive, derisive or annoying word to any other person who is lawfully in any street or other public place, nor call him by any offensive or derisive name, nor make any noise or exclamation in his presence and hearing with intent to deride, offend or annoy him, or to prevent him from pursuing his lawful business or occupation."

To some this law appeared to be a clear infringement of the First Amendment because it punished only speech. Chaplinsky had engaged in no action. He hadn't hit anybody. He had just been rude, derisive, and offensive. Nonetheless the Supreme Court unanimously affirmed Chaplinsky's conviction. The opinion was written by Justice Frank Murphy, whose record had indicated considerable sensitivity to First Amendment concerns:

> It is well understood that the right of free speech is not absolute at all times and under all circumstances. There are certain well-defined and narrowly limited classes of speech [which are not protected]. These include the lewd and obscene, the profane, the libelous, and the insulting or "fighting" words—those which by their very utterance inflict injury or tend to incite an immediate breach of the peace.

Chaplinsky, then, was guilty of having used "fighting words." As the state court had said, these were "words likely to cause" an average person at whom they were directed "to fight." Such utterances, Justice Murphy went on to say, "are no essential part of any exposition of ideas, and are of such slight social value as a step to truth that any benefit that may be derived from them is clearly outweighed by the social interest in order and morality."

The Court, however, has not always been of the same mind as to exactly what a "fighting word" is. Seven years later, the Justices were confronted with *Terminiello v. Chicago*. Father Arthur W. Terminiello, a Catholic priest who had been suspended by his bishop, gave a speech in Chicago attacking "atheist, communistic Zionist Jews, Negroes, the Roosevelt administration," and other targets in a decidedly inflammatory manner.

Inside the auditorium were some eight hundred people. Outside there had gathered fifteen hundred protestors fully as angry at Terminiello as he was at them. Police were present but proved unable to prevent a number of fierce clashes between his supporters and his detractors.

Justice Robert H. Jackson described the scene on the basis of the lower court record:

> The crowd constituted "a surging, howling mob hurling epithets at those who would enter and tried to tear their clothes off." One young woman's coat was torn off and she had to be assisted into the meeting by policemen. Those inside the hall could hear the loud noises and hear those on the outside yell, "Fascists, Hitlers!" and curse words like "damn Fascists." Bricks were thrown through the windowpanes before and during the speaking. About 28 windows were broken. The street was black with people on both sides for at least a block either way; bottles, stink bombs and brickbats were thrown. Police were unable to control the mob, which kept breaking the windows at the meeting hall, drowning out the speaker's voice at times and breaking in through the back door of the auditorium.

Jackson also told of reactions in the auditorium to Terminiello's speech:

. . . Another said that "Jews, niggers and Catholics would have to be gotten rid of." One response was, "Yes, the Jews are all killers, murderers. If we don't kill them first, they will kill us."

In a Chicago court Terminiello was found guilty of disorderly conduct. By a 5 to 4 vote, the Supreme Court reversed the conviction on the ground that the trial judge had misunderstood the First Amendment when he charged the jury that a "breach of the peace" could be committed by speech that "stirs the public to anger, invites dispute, brings about a condition of unrest, or creates a disturbance."

Speaking for the majority, Justice William O. Douglas said:

> A function of free speech under our system of government is *to invite dispute*. It may indeed best serve its high purposes when it induces a condition of unrest, creates dissatisfaction with conditions as they are, or *even stirs people to anger*. Speech is often provocative and challenging. It may strike at prejudices and preconceptions and have profound unsettling effects as it presses for acceptance of an idea.
>
> That is why freedom of speech, though not absolute (*Chaplinsky v. New Hampshire*) is nevertheless protected against censorship or punishment, unless shown likely to produce a clear and present danger of a serious substantive evil that rises far above public inconvenience, annoyance, or unrest. . . . There is no room under our Constitution for a more restrictive view. For the alternative would lead to standardization of ideas either by legislatures, courts, or dominant political or community groups. [Emphasis added]

What about "fighting words" as being outside First Amendment protections? Was Terminiello's language any less likely to incite people to physical retaliation than Chaplinsky's had been? There *had* been fights the night of his speech. Douglas said the majority of the Court had not addressed themselves to that question because the case had been decided on the preliminary issue of the error committed by the trial judge in the way he defined "breach of the peace" to the jury. Yet it did appear from Douglas's decision that he had come to the conclusion that Terminiello's words, as part of a public assembly and not an altercation between two people on the street, were protected free speech.

Among the dissenters in the *Terminiello* decision, Chief Justice Fred M. Vinson was convinced that the priest had used "fighting words" in the *Chaplinsky* sense and therefore his conviction should have been upheld. Justice Robert H. Jackson, joined by Justices Felix Frankfurter and Harold H. Burton, agreed with the lower court and jury that Terminiello's speech "was a provocation to immediate breach of the peace"—rioting and violence—and for that reason his conviction should stand. Jackson added:

> The Court has gone far toward accepting the doctrine that civil liberty means the removal of all restraints from these crowds and that all local attempts to maintain order are impairments of the liberty of the citizen. The choice is not between order and liberty. It is between liberty with order and anarchy without either. There is danger that, if the Court does not temper its doctrinaire logic with a little practical wisdom, it will convert the constitutional Bill of Rights into a suicide pact.

The Court has had to deal with other instances of highly provocative offensive speech, the central issue always being whether there is a point at which speech is *so* offensive that it loses First Amendment protection. And if there is such a point, how can it be determined?

Cohen v. California (1971) was a particularly intriguing and influential case involving "offensive speech," although at first it had the look of frivolity. As Justice John Marshall Harlan began his opinion for the Court: "This case may seem at first blush too inconsequential to find its way into our books, but the issue it presents is of no small constitutional significance."

Paul Robert Cohen had been convicted in Los Angeles for having violated that part of the California penal code which prohibits "maliciously and willfully disturb[ing] the peace and quiet of any neighborhood or person . . . by . . . offensive conduct." He was sentenced to thirty days in prison.

Cohen's offense, as described by Justice Harlan, was to have appeared in a corridor of the Los Angeles County Courthouse "wearing a jacket bearing the words 'Fuck the Draft,' which were plainly visible. There were women and children present in the corridor. The defendant was arrested. The defendant testified that he wore the jacket . . . as a means of informing the public of the depth of his feelings against the Vietnam war and the draft.

"The defendant," added Harlan, "did not engage in, nor threaten to engage in, nor did anyone, as the result of his conduct, commit or threaten to commit any act of violence. The defendant did not make any loud or unusual noise, nor was there any evidence that he uttered any sound prior to his arrest."

Yet Cohen was convicted. Affirming that conviction,

the California Court of Appeals ruled that "offensive conduct" is "behavior which has a tendency to provoke *others* to acts of violence." The state had proved that Cohen was guilty of violating the penal code because, said the Court of Appeals, "it was certainly forseeable that such conduct [as his wearing of that jacket] might cause others to rise up to commit a violent act against the person of the defendant or attempt to forceably remove his jacket."

By a 6 to 3 vote the Supreme Court reversed Cohen's conviction. The opinion, by Justice Harlan, has since been widely cited as a particularly lucid and forceful analysis of the First Amendment. Cohen, said Harlan, had been engaged in speech—the message on his jacket—not action. That is, "the only 'conduct' which the State sought to punish is the fact of communication."

Not *all* speech, however, is protected. Obscenity, for example, is punishable, but this is not such a case. "Obscene expression," said Harlan, "must be, in some significant way, erotic [tending to arouse sexual desire]. It cannot be plausibly maintained that this vulgar allusion to the Selective Service System would conjure up such psychic stimulation [toward sexual desire] in anyone likely to be confronted with Cohen's crudely defaced jacket."

What about the Court's doctrine of "fighting words" in *Chaplinsky v. New Hampshire?* It does not apply here, said Harlan. "While the four-letter word displayed by Cohen in relation to the draft is not uncommonly employed in a personally provocative fashion, in this instance it was clearly not 'directed to the person of the hearer.' No individual actually or likely to be present could reasonably have regarded the words on appellant's jacket *as a direct personal insult*" (emphasis added).

Harlan then came to the essence of *Cohen v. California*:

"The issue flushed by this case stands out in bold relief. It is whether California can excise, as 'offensive conduct,' one particular scurrilous epithet from the public discourse, either upon the theory of the court below that its use is inherently likely to cause violent reaction or upon a more general assertion that the states, acting as guardians of public morality, may properly remove this offensive word from the public vocabulary."

As for California's contention that the words on Cohen's jacket tended to provoke others to acts of violence, Harlan said that the government cannot constitutionally force dissidents "into avoiding particular forms of expression" just because of the state's "undifferentiated fear or apprehension of disturbance." Suppressing speech in this way would give censorship powers to "a hypothetical coterie of the violent and lawless," who might not like that form of speech. (It might also be added that should violence actually be attempted against a speaker—or in this case, the wearer of a jacket bearing vulgar words— the responsibility of the state, and its police, is to *protect* the person who is trying to communicate, not to *arrest* him).

What about the other claim, that Cohen's conviction was lawful because the states have a right "to maintain what they regard as a suitable level of discourse within the body politic" and that California therefore had the right to punish "public utterances of this unseemly expletive" on Cohen's jacket?

Justice Harlan responded: "The constitutional right of free expression is powerful medicine in a society as diverse and populous as ours. It is designed and intended to

307

remove governmental restraints from the area of public discussion, putting the decision as to what views shall be voiced largely into the hands of *each of us,* in the hope that use of such freedom will ultimately produce a more capable citizenry and more perfect polity and in the belief that no other approach would comport with the premise of individual dignity and choice upon which our political system rests" (emphasis added).

"To many," Harlan continued in the most compelling section of his opinion, "the immediate consequence of this freedom may often appear to be only verbal tumult, discord, and even offensive utterance. These are, however, within established limits . . . necessary side effects of the broader enduring values which the process of open debate permits us to achieve. That the air may at times seem filled with verbal cacophony is, in this sense, not a sign of weakness but of strength. We cannot lose sight of the fact that, in what otherwise might seem a trifling and annoying instance of individual distasteful abuse of a privilege, these fundamental societal values are truly implicated. That is why . . . 'futilities . . . come under the protection of free speech as fully as do Keats' poems or Donne's sermons.' "

Furthermore, if this particular word on Cohen's jacket is to be punished, what about other unacceptable words? "How is one to distinguish this from any other offensive word? Surely the State has no right to cleanse public debate to the point where it is grammatically palatable to the most squeamish among us."

But look at *that* word—on Cohen's jacket! Should it really be part of public debate? Well, said Harlan, "while the particular four-letter word being litigated here is perhaps more distasteful than most others of its genre, it is nevertheless often true that one man's vulgarity is another's lyric. Indeed, we think it is largely because governmental officials cannot make principled distinctions in this area that the Constitution leaves matters of taste and style so largely to the individual."

Harlan then made a particularly useful point about First Amendment protection of *emotional* speech, along with ideas:

> Much linguistic expression serves a dual communicative function: it conveys not only ideas capable of relatively precise, detached explication, but otherwise inexpressible emotions as well. In fact, words are often chosen as much for their emotive as their cognitive force. We cannot sanction the view that the Constitution, while solicitous of the cognitive content of individual speech, has little or no regard for that emotive function which, practically speaking, may often be the more important element of the overall message sought to be communicated. Indeed, as Mr. Justice Frankfurter has said, "one of the prerogatives of American citizenship is the right to criticize public men and measures—that means not only informed and responsible criticism but the freedom to speak foolishly and without moderation."

Harlan concluded his opinion by pointing out:

> We cannot indulge the facile assumption that one can forbid particular words without also running a substantial risk of suppressing ideas in the process. Indeed, governments might soon seize upon the censorship of particular words as a convenient guise for banning the expression of unpopular views. . . . The State may not, consistently with the First and Fourteenth Amend-

ments, make the simple public display here involved of this single four-letter expletive a criminal offense.

In dissent, Justice Harry A. Blackmun, joined by Justice Hugo Black and Chief Justice Warren E. Burger, insisted that "Cohen's absurd and immature antic . . . was mainly conduct and little speech. . . . Further, the case appears to me to be well within the sphere of *Chaplinsky v. New Hampshire"* (the "fighting words" decision).

A year after *Cohen v. California* a majority of the Court addressed itself to the "fighting words" doctrine and made the definition of that term more specific. In *Gooding v. Wilson,* the Court struck down a Georgia law punishing anyone using "opprobrious words or abusive language, tending to cause a breach of the peace." In his opinion, Justice William J. Brennan, Jr., said the language of that statute was too broad, thereby violating the First Amendment. However, he used the occasion to reaffirm governmental power to punish "fighting words" under carefully and narrowly drawn statutes that did not impinge on constitutionally protected expression. He made it clear that "fighting words" can be defined as *only* those that "have a direct tendency to cause acts of violence by the person to whom, individually, the remark is addressed." That is, it has to be a one-to-one situation, as with Chaplinsky and the city marshal, for this kind of limitation on the First Amendment to stand. A generalized public demonstration, such as that of Cohen and his jacket, cannot be punished under the "fighting words" doctrine.

In recent decades, the most publicized and certainly the most bitterly controversial of all First Amendment cases had to do with whether a demonstration by a band of native Nazis involved "fighting words" that were outside the protection of the First Amendment.

In the spring of 1977 the Chicago-based National Socialist party of America decided to focus its demonstrations on suburban areas with sizable Jewish populations. An initial target was the village of Skokie, on the northern border of Chicago. Of its 70,000 residents, some 40,500 are Jews, and of the latter, 7,000 are survivors of Hitler's Holocaust.

The Nazis intended to hold a demonstration in Skokie on May 1 and July 4, but the village obtained a circuit court injunction preventing it. Because of the First Amendment issues involved, the Illinois affiliate of the American Civil Liberties Union agreed to defend the free speech rights of the Nazis.

As a result of the ACLU's involvement in this case, 15 to 20 percent of its national membership of 250,000 left the organization in furious protest. In the Illinois affiliate, 30 percent of the 8,000 members resigned, leading to serious cutbacks in staff and programs. However, the ACLU felt that its integrity as a civil liberties union would be wrecked if it were to drop the case. Aryeh Neier, the ACLU's executive director, emphasized: "As a Jew, and a refugee from Nazi Germany, I have strong personal reasons for finding Nazis repugnant. Freedom of speech protects my right to denounce Nazis with all the vehemence I think proper. Despite my hatred of their vicious doctrine, I realize that it is in my interests to defend their right to preach it."

After a series of court skirmishes the Illinois Appellate Court ruled in July 1977 that the Nazis could demonstrate or march in Skokie, but they were absolutely forbidden to display or wear the swastika, on the grounds that such display constituted "fighting words." After citing *Chaplinsky v. New Hampshire*, the court defined "fighting words" as "those personally abusive epithets which, when addressed to an ordinary citizen, as a matter of common knowledge, are inherently likely to provoke violent reaction."

Is the swastika speech? Yes, the swastika, as a symbol of both Nazi ideology and such of its results as the Holocaust, is a form of speech. And in this case, said the court, the swastika as symbolic speech *is* "inherently likely to provoke violent reaction." The court added: "The evidence shows precisely that substantial numbers of citizens [of Skokie] are standing ready to strike out physically at whoever may assault their sensibilities with the display of the swastika."

The mayor of Skokie, a Roman Catholic, had testified there was a "terrible feeling of unrest regarding the parading of the swastika . . . a terrible feeling expressed by people [that they] should not have to tolerate this type of demonstration in view of their history as a people." At a meeting in Skokie of eighteen Jewish organizations, a counterdemonstration was planned, in the event the Nazis actually did demonstrate, that would involve twelve thousand to fifteen thousand people. Bloodshed was predicted.

The swastika, the Illinois Appellate Court concluded, falls within the definition of "fighting words" because it "is a personal affront to every member of the Jewish faith, in remembering the nearly consummated genocide of their people committed within memory by those who used the swastika as their symbol. This is especially true for the thousands of Skokie residents who personally survived the Holocaust of the Third Reich."

Filing an appeal, the ACLU contended that in terms of the First Amendment the swastika is fully protected symbolic speech, just as black armbands worn to protest the Vietnam war were protected speech. To allow the state to decide which "symbols" are lawful, and which are not, would dangerously weaken First Amendment freedoms. Who could then tell what the state might suppress the next time controversial symbolic speech is tested?

As for the claim by Skokie officials that they probably would not be able to control the village's fiercely anti-Nazi residents if the National Socialist party were to appear, the ACLU pointed out that it is unconstitutional to ban speech on the basis of a "heckler's veto." If Skokie was so sure that certain hostile groups would be hard to control, the ACLU said, why didn't the village seek an injunction against *those* persons to prohibit *their* unlawful actions? And if extra police power were needed to keep the peace, it must be used to protect speech—even the speech of Nazis.

In Skokie, Los Angeles, Boston, just about everywhere in the nation, debate over the right of Nazis to demonstrate in Skokie grew increasingly bitter. One woman, in New York, offered to speak at synagogues in behalf of the American Civil Liberties Union's First Amendment reasons for providing legal help to the Nazis. As a child, she and her family had barely escaped the Holocaust. Having grown up in Israel, she settled in the United States and had long been active in American Jewish organizations. She was also on the board of directors of the New York Civil Liberties Union.

After a number of journeys to synagogues, she reported, "I have been shouted down, cursed, vilified. They tell me that Nazis have no rights, and I try to tell them the First Amendment has to be for everyone—or it will be for no one. They will not hear this. God, I understand how they feel, but when will they *think* again?"

Other speakers for the ACLU were also shouted down, cursed, vilified—and by no means only by Jewish audiences. The clear majority view among a broad range of groups was that there had to be *some* limits to free speech, and the speech of Nazis was surely beyond those limits.

The debate raged and swirled in newspapers and magazines. Some supporters of the ACLU argued in letters and articles that if demonstrations were to be banned for being likely to provoke violence, what about the historic marches—like the one in Selma, Alabama, led by Martin Luther King in the 1960s? *The Nation* noted, in an editorial, that the Selma demonstration would never have taken place if authorities there had been allowed to ban it on the ground that it would have endangered the peace by provoking the rage of white racists.

This argument did not change the views of the rising number of ACLU members who kept sending in their outraged letters of resignation. Often attached to those letters were their ACLU membership cards—on the back of which is printed the First Amendment. It was grotesque, many of them said, to equate the Nazis with Martin Luther King. As a letter to *The Nation* put it: Martin Luther King's marches furthered human freedom and dignity, and aimed at spreading nonviolence, while the Nazis want to degrade and destroy freedom and dignity, and spread violence."

Others insisted that the Nazis, by being Nazis, had forfeited their own constitutional rights and liberties. Said a *New York Post* reader: "It's very simple really: Those who (by word or deed) seek to undermine and destroy the basic tenets of the Constitution do, at the same time, relinquish its protection for themselves." As a writer to *The Washington Post* put it, "Freedom of expression has no meaning when it defends those who would end this right for others."

Nowhere in the First Amendment does it say that freedom of speech is limited only to ideas and symbols that further freedom, dignity, and nonviolence—or that uphold the very concept of free speech. As Justice Oliver Wendell Holmes put it a half century before the Nazis and Skokie: "If there is any principle of the Constitution that more imperatively calls for attachment than any other it is the principle of free thought—not free thought for those who agree with us but freedom for the thought that we hate." (Even if it is thought dedicated to destroying our freedom.)

Nonetheless, many opponents of the Nazis' right to demonstrate in Skokie kept going back to the argument that the Constitution is not a suicide pact. The goal of the Nazis, it was said, is to gather sufficient numbers to tear down the very Constitution that the ACLU presents as a shield for the Nazis. To be sure, this particular Chicago-based unit is small, but so was another seemingly ludicrous Nazi band in Germany during the Weimar Republic. The more the Nazis are allowed to gain strength in the country, the more the freedoms of the rest of the citizenry—particularly those of Jews and blacks, at first—will be in peril. It is utterly foolish, therefore, to allow total freedom of speech to those committed to destroying the society in which this liberty is cherished.

In answer to this argument, it is worth considering again Justice Holmes's 1925 dissent in *Gitlow v. New*

York. Benjamin Gitlow and colleagues had been convicted of distributing literature proposing "revolutionary mass action" to overthrow the United States government. Although the Supreme Court affirmed the conviction, Holmes, joined by Justice Louis Brandeis, took a view that parallels that of the American Civil Liberties Union in the Skokie case: "If, in the long run, the beliefs expressed in proletarian dictatorship are destined to be accepted by the dominant forces of the community, the only meaning of free speech is that they should be given their chance and have their way."

Holmes's logic, while frightening to many, is inescapable. If speech is to be free, there is always the risk that those who want to destroy free speech may be sufficiently eloquent to use that freedom to end it. But if speech is to be limited in order to prevent that dreadful possibility, then the enemies of free expression have already—at the moment they are silenced by the state—succeeded in having free speech curtailed. Once the concept of limiting expression is established, what is to prevent other hated groups from being added to the censored list? And so, each time the state gags another such group, the enemies of free speech will have moved closer to their goal.

That is precisely what began to happen in Skokie. In May 1977, in order to bar the Nazis by statute, the village passed a set of ordinances regulating certain forms of speech and assembly. The Nazis were not mentioned by name, and so the ordinances applied to *anyone* who wanted to speak, parade, or demonstrate in Skokie.

First it was mandated that no parade or assembly involving more than fifty persons could be held unless the demonstrators obtained a $350,000 insurance policy. Such a policy, covering public liability and property damage, would involve up to nine hundred dollars in fees, depending on the risk. (Should those unable to afford the fee lose their First Amendment rights?) It would also be necessary, of course, to find an underwriter willing to insure such a group, and that might not be at all possible if the group were vastly unpopular. Like the Nazis.

These Skokie ordinances also gave the village council the power to deny a permit for a demonstration if it decided that the proposed assembly *might* create a "breach of the peace" or a "disorder." Also prohibited, under any circumstances, were public demonstrations by members of political parties wearing military-style uniforms. Banned, in addition, were demonstrations that "incite violence, hatred, abuse, or hostility toward a person or group of persons by reason or reference to religious, racial, ethnic, national, or religious affiliation."

So much for Oliver Wendell Holmes's definition of the most basic principle of the Constitution: the protection of all free thought, including thought we hate.

In its wholly understandable hatred of the Nazis, the village of Skokie had forgotten that liberty is indivisible. To shut off speech that it hated, Skokie had set up a system that could suppress many other kinds of speech. Ira Glasser, then executive director of the New York Civil Liberties Union, pointed out that if the Skokie ordinances were allowed by the courts to stand, *"town councils everywhere will then have the discretion to decide which free speech to permit.* That is what is at stake in the Skokie case—not only the rights of those particular marchers in that particular place but the viability of the First Amendment and the rights of the rest of us. These are the same kinds of laws that were used throughout the South to stop civil rights demonstrations, that were used against the

Wobblies in the earlier part of the century, and that were used repeatedly only a few years ago to stop anti-war demonstrations."

And so the ACLU went to court to try to strike down the Skokie ordinances, while throughout the country more of its members resigned.

In January 1978 one of the earlier court fights over the Nazis' First Amendment rights reached the highest tribunal in the state, the Illinois Supreme Court. By a 6 to 1 vote, the court, in *Village of Skokie v. National Socialist Party of America*, decided "reluctantly" that the Nazis do have a constitutional right to display swastikas in Skokie. Quoting from a previous United States Supreme Court decision (*Bachellar v. Maryland*), the Illinois Supreme Court declared: "It is firmly settled that under our Constitution the public expression of ideas may not be prohibited merely because the ideas are themselves offensive to some of their hearers." The swastika is a symbolic expression of such an idea, and since "symbolic expression of thought falls within the free speech clause of the First Amendment," the Nazis have a right to wear the swastika in Skokie.

What of the "fighting-words" doctrine? The village of Skokie, said the court, asks us to "hold that the fighting-words doctrine permits a prior restraint [censorship] on defendants' symbolic speech. [This, after all, was to be a generalized public demonstration, not a one-on-one situation.] In our judgment we are precluded from doing so."

What about the very real possibility of violence if the Nazis, wearing swastikas, were to come to Skokie? "We do not doubt," said the court, "that the sight of this symbol is abhorrent to the Jewish citizens of Skokie, and that the survivors of the Nazi persecutions, tormented by their recollections, may have strong feelings regarding its display. Yet . . . courts have consistently refused to ban speech on the possibility of unlawful conduct by those opposed to the speaker's philosophy. . . . 'It has become patent that a hostile audience is not a basis for restraining otherwise legal First Amendment activity.' " There can be no heckler's veto.

The Illinois court then quoted New York judge Charles Breitel in another case, seventeen years earlier, that had gotten the ACLU into trouble: its defense of Nazi leader George Lincoln Rockwell's right to speak in a New York City park. Breitel had said: "The unpopularity of views, their shocking quality, their obnoxiousness, and even their alarming impact is not enough [to prohibit speech]. Otherwise, the preacher of any strange doctrine could be stopped; the anti-racist himself could be suppressed if he undertakes to speak in 'restricted' areas; and one who asks that public schools be open indiscriminately to all ethnic groups could be lawfully suppressed, if only he chose to speak where persuasion is needed most."

There was another major court battle to be decided: Skokie's set of ordinances aimed at regulating public speech and assembly. In February 1978 Federal District Judge Bernard M. Decker in Chicago struck down the ordinances as unconstitutional.

As to the requirement that demonstrators take out an insurance policy, the court called this a "drastic restriction of the right of free speech and assembly." The insurance is expensive and can be very hard to obtain. Furthermore, this provision of the ordinance allowed the village to exempt certain groups from the insurance requirement. (Already exempted, by the time the case came to court, had been the American Legion and a Skokie

319

property owners association.) "This device," said Judge
Decker, "permits organizations that have the approval of
the village government to avoid the restrictions imposed
on all other groups." Since there are "no principled standards for determining which organizations are exempt,"
village officials can covertly censor groups they don't like.
Indeed, the insurance provision as a whole imposes a
"virtually insuperable obstacle to the free exercise of First
Amendment rights in the village of Skokie."

As for the ordinances forbidding inciting of racial and
religious hatred, these clearly "impose sweeping bans on
the content of speech within Skokie." Yet the Supreme
Court has held (*Police Department of the City of Chicago
v. Moseley*): "Above all else, the First Amendment
means that government has no power to restrict expression because of its message, its ideas, its subject matter,
or its content."

Accordingly, said Judge Decker, the village of Skokie
has "no power to prevent [the National Socialist Party]
from stating [its] political philosophy, including [its]
opinions of black and Jewish people, however obnoxious
and reprehensible that philosophy may be."

Another fundamental First Amendment point made by
Judge Decker was that some of the Skokie ordinances
prohibited certain kinds of groups from speaking and dem-
onstrating on the basis of what the content of their speech
might be. This was censorship in *anticipation* of speech.
Decker quoted from a Supreme Court decision (*South-
eastern Promotions, Ltd. v. Conrad*): "A theory deeply
etched in our law: a free society prefers to punish the
few who abuse rights of speech *after* they break the law
rather than to throttle them and all others beforehand.
It is always difficult to know in advance what an in-

dividual will say, and the line between legitimate and illegitimate speech is often so finely drawn that the risks of freewheeling censorship are formidable."

Judge Decker next came to the Skokie ordinance mandating that "no person shall engage in any march, walk or public demonstration as a member, or on behalf of, any political party while wearing a military-style uniform." The wearing of distinctive clothing, he said, is a symbolic form of expression, and therefore is protected by the First Amendment.

But the village of Skokie had claimed that the wearing of military-style uniforms is "repugnant," both to the "tradition of civilian control of government" and to "standards of morality and decency of the people of the village of Skokie." Judge Decker was not persuaded. After all, "the First Amendment embraces the freedom to advocate even that the government ought to be violently overthrown, let alone that it ought not to be controlled by civilians. Thus the banning of a symbol which is repugnant to a 'tradition' which all Americans are free to reject and openly criticize is clearly unconstitutional.

"The reference to Skokie's standards of decency and morality," Judge Decker continued, "is apparently an attempt to invoke the 'community standards' test applied in obscenity cases (*Miller v. California*). However, to be obscene, speech must in some way be erotically stimulating."

The swastika erotically stimulating?

Judge Decker ended his opinion by saying, "In resolving this case in favor of the plaintiffs [the National Socialist party], the court is acutely aware of the very grave dangers posed by public dissemination of doctrines of racial and religious hatred." However, in terms of the First

Amendment, "it is better to allow those who preach racial hate to expend their venom in rhetoric rather than [for us to] be panicked into embarking on the dangerous course of permitting the government to decide what its citizens may say and hear. . . . The ability of American society to tolerate the advocacy even of the hateful doctrines espoused by the plaintiffs without abandoning its commitment to freedom of speech and assembly is perhaps the best protection we have against the establishment of any Nazi-type regime in this country."

Judge Decker's decision was sustained by the Seventh Circuit Court of Appeals. The opinion there took greatly troubled note of the many survivors of the Holocaust in Skokie, people with indelible memories of family members being thrown into trains on the way to a death camp. One Skokie resident had told of seeing his mother hurled on top of a mass of bodies in a hole in the ground and buried alive.

It would be "grossly insensitive to deny," said the court, "as we do not, that the proposed demonstration would seriously disturb, emotionally and mentally, at least some, and probably many, of the village's residents." But if First Amendment rights "are to remain vital for all, they must protect not only those society deems acceptable, but also those whose ideas it quite justifiably rejects and despises."

The village of Skokie asked the Supreme Court to hear the case, but that tribunal refused, thereby allowing the decision of the lower courts to stand. Two Justices, Byron R. White and Harry A. Blackmun, did want to hear the case. For Blackmun, it was vital that the High Court consider "whether there is no limit whatsoever to the exercise of free speech."

That question, crucial throughout United States history, will come before the Court again and again, for the Constitution is indeed a living document. As we have seen, the First Amendment is never static, never at rest, growing stronger as more people use it, and receding in times of fear of dissenters and other minority voices.

It was Justice Hugo Black who most lyrically expressed the vision of the framers:

> Since the earliest days, philosophers have dreamed of a country where the mind and spirit of man would be free; where there would be no limits to inquiry; where men would be free to explore the unknown and to challenge the most deeply rooted beliefs and principles.
>
> Our First Amendment was a bold effort to adopt this principle—to establish a country with no legal restrictions of any kind upon the subjects people could investigate, discuss, and deny. The Framers knew, better perhaps than we do today, the risks they were taking. They knew that free speech might be the friend of change and revolution. But they also knew that it is always the deadliest enemy of tyranny. With this knowledge they still believed that the ultimate happiness and security of a nation lies in its ability to explore, to change, to grow, and ceaselessly to adapt itself to new knowledge born of inquiry, free from any kind of governmental control over the mind and spirit of man.

Bibliography

BARTH, ALAN. *Prophets with Honor: Great Dissents and Great Dissenters in the Supreme Court.* New York: Alfred A. Knopf, 1974.

BLACK, HUGO. *One Man's Stand for Freedom,* ed. Irving Dilliard. New York: Alfred A. Knopf, 1973.

BRANT, IRVING. *The Bill of Rights.* New York: Bobbs-Merrill, 1965.

CAHN, EDMOND. *The Great Rights.* New York: Macmillan, 1963.

CHAFEE, ZECHARIAH. *Free Speech in the United States.* New York: Atheneum, 1969.

CONLIN, JOSEPH. *Bread and Roses Too: Studies of the Wobblies.* Westport, Connecticut: Greenwood, 1969.

DEVOL, KENNETH S. *Mass Media and the Supreme Court.* (2nd ed.) New York: Hastings House, 1976.

DILLON, MERTON. *Elijah P. Lovejoy: Abolitionist Editor.* Urbana, Illinois: University of Illinois Press, 1964.

325

DORSEN, NORMAN; BENDER, PAUL; and NEUBORNE, BURT. *Political and Civil Rights in the United States.* (4th ed.) Boston: Little, Brown, 1976.

DOUGLAS, WILLIAM O. *The Douglas Opinions,* ed. Vern Countryman. New York: Random House, 1977. Paper: Berkley-Windhover, 1978.

EMERSON, THOMAS. *The System of Freedom of Expression.* New York: Vintage Books, 1970.

EMERY, EDWIN. *The Press and America: An Interpretive History of the Mass Media.* Englewood Cliffs, New Jersey: Prentice-Hall, 1972.

FONER, PHILIP S. *The Industrial Workers of the World, 1905–1917.* New York: International Publishers, 1965.

FRIEDMAN, LEON. *The Wise Minority.* New York: Dial Press, 1971.

FRIENDLY, FRED. *The Good Guys, the Bad Guys and the First Amendment.* New York: Random House, 1976.

GINGER, RAY. *Altgeld's America.* New York: Funk & Wagnalls, 1958.

GORA, JOEL. *The Rights of Reporters.* New York: Discus, Avon Books, 1974.

HAIGHT, ANNE LYON, and GRANNIS, CHANDLER. *Banned Books: 387 B.C. to 1978 A.D.* New York: R.R. Bowker, 1978.

HAIMAN, FRANKLYN. *Freedom of Speech.* Skokie, Illinois: National Textbook Company, 1976.

HAMILTON, ALEXANDER; JAY, JOHN; and MADISON, JAMES. *The Federalist Papers.* New York: Washington Square Press, Pocketbooks, 1971.

HARPER, ROBERT S. *Lincoln and the Press.* New York: McGraw-Hill, 1951.

HARRIS, RICHARD. *Freedom Spent.* Boston: Little, Brown, 1976.

KONVITZ, MILTON. *Bill of Rights Reader.* (4th ed.) Ithaca, New York: Cornell University Press, 1968.

KONVITZ, MILTON. *First Amendment Freedoms.* Ithaca, New York: Cornell University Press, 1963.

LEVIN, MURRAY. *Political Hysteria in America: The Democratic Capacity for Repression.* New York: Basic Books, 1971.

LEVINE, ALAN, and CAREY, EVE. *The Rights of Students.* (Revised ed.) New York: Discus, Avon Books, 1977.

LEVY, LEONARD. *Jefferson and Civil Liberties: The Darker Side.* New York: Quadrangle Books, 1973.

LEVY, LEONARD, and NELSON, HAROLD. *Freedom of the Press. Vol. 1, From Zenger to Jefferson; Vol. 2, From Hamilton to the Warren Court.* New York: Bobbs-Merrill, 1966/1967.

MADISON, JAMES. *Notes of Debates in the Federal Convention of 1787.* New York: W. W. Norton Library, 1969 (by arrangement with Ohio University Press).

MITCHELL, BROADUS, and MITCHELL, LOUISE. *A Biography of the Constitution.* New York: Oxford University Press, 1964.

MOTT, FRANK LUTHER. *American Journalism: 1690–1966.* New York: Macmillan, 1962.

MURRAY, ROBERT K. *Red Scare: A Study in National Hysteria, 1919–1920.* New York: McGraw-Hill, 1964.

PFEFFER, LEO. *God, Caesar, and the Constitution.* Boston: Beacon Press, 1975.

PFEFFER, LEO. *Religious Freedom*. Skokie, Illinois: National Textbook Company, 1977.

PRESTON, WILLIAM. *Aliens and Dissenters*. Cambridge, Massachusetts: Harvard University Press, 1963.

RENSHAW, PATRICK. *The Wobblies*. Garden City, New York: Doubleday, 1967.

RUBIN, DAVID. *The Rights of Teachers*. New York: Discus, Avon Books, 1972.

SCHIMMEL, DAVID, and FISCHER, LOUIS. *The Civil Rights of Students*. New York: Harper & Row, 1975.

SCHWARTZ, BERNARD. *The Great Rights of Mankind: A History of the American Bill of Rights*. New York: Oxford University Press, 1956.

SMITH, JAMES MORTON. *Freedom's Fetters: The Alien and Sedition Laws and American Civil Liberties*. Ithaca, New York: Cornell University Press, 1956.

THOMAS, DONALD. *A Long Time Burning: The History of Literary Censorship in England*. New York: Frederick A. Praeger, 1969.

WESTIN, ALAN, ed. *An Autobiography of the Supreme Court*. New York: Macmillan, 1963.

YOUNG, ALFRED E. *Dissent: Explorations in the History of American Radicalism*. DeKalb, Illinois: Northern Illinois University Press, 1968.

Index